Books by GENEVIEVE FOSTER

GEORGE WASHINGTON'S WORLD

ABRAHAM LINCOLN'S WORLD

AUGUSTUS CAESAR'S WORLD

THE WORLD OF CAPTAIN JOHN SMITH

BIRTHDAYS OF FREEDOM, BOOK I

BIRTHDAYS OF FREEDOM, BOOK II

Initial Biographies

GEORGE WASHINGTON

ABRAHAM LINCOLN

ANDREW JACKSON

THEODORE ROOSEVELT

The WORLD of Captain JOHN SMITH

1580   1631

written and illustrated by

GENEVIEVE FOSTER

CHARLES SCRIBNER'S SONS

New York

The quotations on pages 189, 190, 225, 227, are from the *Works of Samuel de Champlain*, edited by H. P. Biggar, used by special permission of the Champlain Society.

C-2.61 [v]

PRINTED IN THE UNITED STATES OF AMERICA

Library of Congress Catalog Card Number 59-11853

For FRANCES *with happy memories*
of May 1956, when this book was started

CONTENTS

PART I

WHEN QUEEN ELIZABETH RULED IN ENGLAND AND   1
JOHN SMITH WAS A BOY

Telling how Sir Francis Drake returned to England to become a hero after sailing around the world . . . Philip II failed to conquer England with the Spanish Armada . . . Holland declared her independence from Spain . . . Mary Queen of Scots lost her head . . . Catherine de Medici tried to keep peace in France between Protestants and Catholics . . . Sir Walter Raleigh sent the first settlers to the first English colony, Virginia, which was named for the Queen . . . young William Shakespeare went to London to become an actor and a playwright . . . the white plumed Henry of Navarre entered Paris to be King of France . . . Raleigh searched for El Dorado, the fabulous city of gold in South America.

PART II

WHEN AKBAR RULED INDIA AND JOHN SMITH FOUGHT   91
THE TURKS

Telling how the great ruler of India found good in all religions . . . Will Adams, the first Englishman to reach Japan was honored by the Shogun . . . the Jesuit Father Matteo Ricci entered the forbidden city of Peking with presents for the Chinese emperor . . . a new calendar was made in Rome, by order of Pope Gregory. . . .

The famous astronomer Tycho Brahe was driven from Denmark . . . Galileo watched a swinging lamp in Pisa and made his first invention . . . Grand Opera was originated, and a new instrument, the violin, was made . . . Boris Godunov became Tsar of Russia . . .

Francis Bacon began writing . . . a new translation of the Bible was made for King James . . . Guy Fawkes tried to blow up Parliament with gunpowder . . . Santa Fe was founded by the Spanish from Mexico . . . Samuel de Champlain, founder of New France, made his first visit to Canada . . .

PART III

WHEN POWHATAN RULED IN VIRGINIA AND JOHN SMITH IN JAMESTOWN   199

Telling how Jamestown was founded . . . Pocahontas saved the life of John Smith . . . Henry Hudson sailed up the Hudson River on the *Half Moon* . . . French and Indians fought on the shore of the lake named for Champlain . . . the city of Quebec was founded . . . John Rolfe planted tobacco in Virginia, and married Pocahontas . . . Jews from Portugal built a synagogue in Amsterdam . . . the Pilgrims took refuge in Holland . . . the telescope was invented . . . Galileo discovered new stars, was convinced that the earth moved around the sun but was forbidden to say so . . . Michael, the first of the Romanovs, became Tsar of Russia . . . John Smith drew a map of New England . . . Shakespeare died . . . Pocahontas visited England . . . the Pilgrims left Holland for the New World.

PART IV

WHEN THE PILGRIMS LANDED IN NEW ENGLAND AND JOHN SMITH WAS WRITING HISTORY   299

Telling how the Mayflower Compact was written . . . Squanto helped the Plymouth colony . . . the first Thanksgiving was celebrated . . . Thirty Years War began in the German states . . . Hugo Grotius wrote the first book on International Law . . . Peter Paul Rubens went to paint in Paris and sent his pupil Van Dyke to Italy . . . King Charles I took a French bride . . . Cardinal Richelieu came to power in France . . . Russian explorers made their way overland to China . . . the Manchu emperor entered Peking . . . Japan began to close the door against foreigners . . . the Dutch purchased Manhattan Island from the Indians . . . Velásquez became painter to Philip IV of Spain . . . St. Peter's cathedral in Rome was finished . . . Gustav Adolf, King of Sweden, died as a hero in the Thirty Years War . . . Puritans of the Massachusetts Bay Company founded the town of Boston and formed a self-governing commonwealth.

INDEX OF PEOPLE   401
INDEX OF PLACES, EVENTS AND GENERAL TOPICS   404

1580

INTRODUCTION

THIS BOOK is a story of the world. It is a slice of history measured by the lifetime of Captain John Smith, a small, courageous Englishman who was born in the days of Queen Elizabeth I and whose heart, he said, had been forever "set on brave adventure."

From 1580 to 1631 were the years in which he lived, halfway between the time Columbus discovered America and George Washington was born. Those were years of discovery that broadened man's knowledge of the earth and revealed its true place among the stars.

No Englishman had ever sailed around the world before John Smith was born, but that year Sir Francis Drake, gentleman-pirate, completed his famous voyage. Although people no longer doubted that the

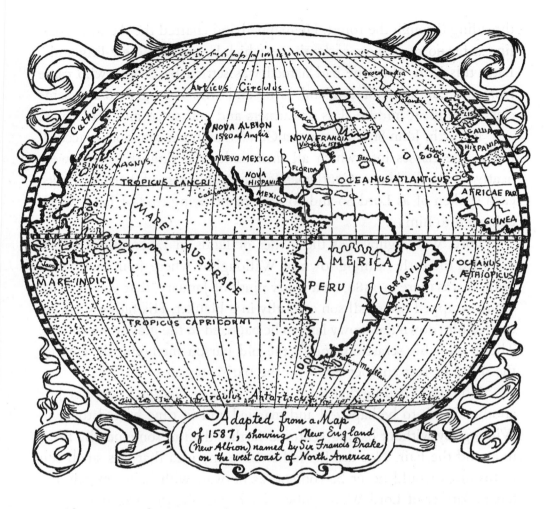

Adapted from a Map of 1587, showing New England (New Albion) named by Sir Francis Drake on the west coast of North America.

world was round, they still believed it to be the center of the universe. The year after John Smith died, Galileo's book supported the Copernican theory that the earth was but another planet revolving around the sun.

In the new world which Columbus had discovered, the Spaniards had colonies as far north as Florida, but in 1580 there was not a single French or English settler in that part of America that was to become the United States and Canada. It was still a land of primeval forests, small Indian villages, and unknown rivers bearing Indian names. John Smith was twenty-seven before the first permanent settlement was founded in Virginia. He helped to establish it. He explored the unknown rivers threading through the forest. He mapped and charted the Atlantic coast line as far north as those rocky shores which he named "New England." Later this land which he had named was settled by people who came from the same part of England as he and who belonged to the same class—the great middle class of farmers and craftsmen and tradesmen.

By birth, John Smith was not a Gentleman but a commoner, according to the classes into which all men under the English crown were neatly divided. Above Gentlemen came Noblemen of various ranks, each spoken of as Lord So-and-So (the name being that of land which belonged to him).

Lord Willoughby was the owner of lands in Lincolnshire which included the little farming town of Willoughby where John Smith was born. It was there in 1580, on a frosty ninth of January, that young Alice Smith wrapped her small son carefully in a blanket. His father Georgie carried him down the snowy lane to be baptized in the gray stone church. There, with his scratching quill, the old parson methodically entered the name of just another Smith in the parish register.

No notion had he that this "John, Sonne of George," was not just another Smith to be baptized and married and in time buried there in Willoughby without having ventured farther than to some nearby town to attend the Fair. Nor did his father have any idea that this small son in his arms would never be content, as he was, with being merely the tenant farmer of Lord Willoughby—for farmer George was not a poor man. He owned cattle, pigs, and several horses, and a good brick house with a fine, solid chimney. He tended his farm, served on the jury, enjoyed bowling on the green on summer evenings, and winter nights slept sound and warm in a tremendous feather bed. Why should not such a comfortable life satisfy his son?

No one could see that within this wee boy wrapped in his blanket was the heart of a knight, forever to be "set on brave adventure." Here was one Smith who would look beyond his village and be filled with a desire to see and know and have a part in the wide exciting world in which he lived. This is a story of that world.

E R

Part I

from 1580:
When Queen Elizabeth
ruled in England &
John Smith was a Boy

PEOPLE *who were Living when*

IVAN *the Terrible,* Tsar of RUSSIA was visited by English explorers in the north east

ELIZABETH I had been Queen of England, since 1558

Sir Francis DRAKE had just completed his famous voyage around the world.

Sir Walter RALEIGH promoted the first English settlement in AMERICA

VIRGINIA was named for the Virgin Queen.

1587 VIRGINIA DARE, the first white child, was born in Virginia.

Potatoes and Tobacco were brought to Europe.

MARY STUART Queen of Scots, was beheaded by order of Queen Elizabeth

& EVENTS *that took Place*

JOHN SMITH *was a small Boy*

The *King of* SPAIN

The ARMADA
sent by Philip to attack
England was destroyed.

PHILIP II
was the richest, most
powerful ruler in Europe.
(died 1598)

The NETHERLANDS led by Holland declared INDEPENDENCE from Spain

IN *F*RANCE *the King was* HENRY III

CATHERINE
de MEDICI

the powerful Queen
Mother died in 1589

her weak son,
the King was
assassinated and

Henry IV
issued the EDICT of NANTES *to foster* Religious Freedom

a BOURBON,
HENRY IV
was crowned
King of France in 1594

between the YEARS 1580~1598

THE QUEEN'S "LITTLE PIRATE"

ONE DAY in late September, 1580, a weather-beaten sailing ship known as the *Golden Hind* was approaching the shores of England and the harbor of Plymouth. On its highest deck, watching the shore line and familiar landmarks coming into view, stood a short, sturdy, barrel-chested man, with a head of crisp curls yellow in the sun, a pointed beard and a great shining pearl dangling from one ear. This was the captain of the vessel, Francis Drake. Returning after a perilous voyage of almost three years, he stood chest out, feet wide apart, in solid satisfaction with himself as the only Englishman who could boast of having weathered the Straits of Magellan and sailed completely around the world.

5

More than that, the hold of the vessel beneath his feet was loaded with Spanish gold—gold enough to make him and the backers of his voyage wealthy for life. It pleasured him to think how he had plundered the rich cities of Chile and Peru and boarded Spanish galleons twice the size of his own ship. No more could those insolent Spaniards feel that the Pacific Ocean was their own private lake and that all the lands bordering it belonged to them. Not since he, Francis Drake, had sailed that ocean from the tip of South America up along the coast of North America to 48° and there claimed land for England in the name of Queen Elizabeth. Ah! what news he brought her of that land (which he had named "New Albion") and what treasure for the Queen!

If . . . if the Queen were still alive! *there* was a possibility to darken his thoughts. No news had reached him while he was away. If she were dead, God forbid, and a king friendly to Spain was in her place, there might be a different ending to his story—a hanging planned for him instead of a welcome. He would soon know.

The bay was full of fishing boats, several coming cautiously toward him. Laying his short brown fingers on the salty rail, Drake leaned over, shouted to the skipper of the nearest smack, and made himself known. The fisherman looked up dumfounded at the name of Drake. This was Drake? Still alive, and his ship still afloat? Over a year ago, one of the ships that had started out with him—the only one of five ever to come back—had brought word of a blinding white storm over an icy sea in which Drake's ship had disappeared. Yet, by all that was good and holy, here he was, saying his own name, and asking after the Queen!

"The Queen," repeated Drake, "is she alive and well?"

"Aye, aye, that she be, hearty as ever," shouted the fisherman, collecting his wits. "But," he added, "the plague is ragin' in Plymouth."

At that news Drake decided to drop anchor where he was and remain aboard for the time being.

The fisherman, turning his boat about, made for the shore, bursting with the marvelous news that the *Golden Hind* was in the harbor. Drake had come home alive! He recalled the first time the town's pop-

6

ular hero had come back with booty from the Spanish Main in '73—on a Sunday—and how everybody had slipped out of church, run down to the wharf and left the parson preaching to nobody. And here he was back again with another shipload of gold! Spreading excitement as he went, the fisherman sped from the dock, past the taverns, through the market, directly to the Mayor, who, alone of all who heard his news, failed to show the proper surprise.

The fact was that the good Mayor of Plymouth had had a secret message from the Queen that Drake was on his way home. The Queen had been told by the Spanish ambassador, who had heard it by way of ships returning from Mexico to Spain. And the Spaniard was furious. That rascally pirate, he declared, who had attacked ships and stolen gold from His Majesty the King of Spain, had to be caught and hanged. To this the Queen openly agreed, but secretly intended that her valuable "little pirate," as she called him, should never get caught. So she had warned the Mayor of Plymouth to watch for him at the harbor to which he was most likely to return.

The Mayor was soon being rowed out over the shining waves, with appropriate words of welcome for the hero. With him went a lady, eager to embrace her adventurous husband and delighted with the beautiful silks and Chinese porcelains he had brought for her collection.

For the Mayor, Drake had several letters, sealed and ready to be sent by special messenger to London, the first and most important being to the Queen. To this, considering the enormous return on her investment, he anticipated an immediate reply. Answers came from the other letters shortly, but not one word from the Queen.

What now? he thought. What was happening at Court? Was there threat of war from the King of Spain? Or was it Lord Burghley? That stuffy old Secretary of the Treasury with his endless caution! Was he demanding that the gold and treasure be returned to Spain? Surely not! Her Majesty had too much at stake for that. . . . Yet for days Drake waited and wondered as his ship lay at anchor behind an island, with the treasure stored in the Castle of Plymouth for safe-keeping.

7

QUEEN ELIZABETH

ELIZABETH, the unpredictable Queen of England, was in high good humor as she stood one morning preening herself like a peacock in front of a full-length mirror. Some bad news had delighted her. The King of Spain had sent troops into Ireland to rouse rebellion in the only spot outside of England that belonged to her. Here was the excuse she needed to use against the Spanish ambassador—excuse enough to get in touch secretly with her "little pirate." She had already sent a letter asking him to come and bring a "sample of his labors." The prospect elated her—more gold, more jewels, more pearls to hang about her neck!

The glittering image in the mirror also excited her, since she saw there only what she wished to see—not an aging woman in a red wig, with skin plastered chalk white, cheeks and eyebrows painted on. What she saw was a woman forever young and beautiful, with gorgeous red hair, perfect height and figure, a brilliant, fascinating creature made even more sparkling and irresistible by the happy turn of events.

Whirling about in her wide stiff skirt, she faced a handsome gentleman, whom she called Robert and who sat idly toying with a chessman awaiting her next move. This was the Earl of Leicester, a middle-aged man, still dark and handsome, but no longer slim as in days long past, when Elizabeth's hair had been genuinely red and his own not yet turned white. In 1558, when she became queen, she had made him her intimate friend and favorite courtier. Both were then twenty-five. Now

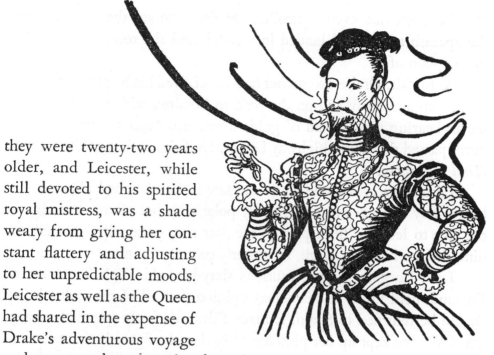

they were twenty-two years older, and Leicester, while still devoted to his spirited royal mistress, was a shade weary from giving her constant flattery and adjusting to her unpredictable moods. Leicester as well as the Queen had shared in the expense of Drake's adventurous voyage and now stood to share handsomely in the profits. They would have seen a "sample" sooner, had Leicester had his way. Why worry about offending the King of Spain? War was inevitable. Why not face the fact?

Elizabeth refused to consider it. The last thing she wanted was war with Spain. She could not afford it. England was a poor, small country compared to Spain. The only other land she had was Ireland, and what good was that? Always in rebellion.

Philip II, King of Spain, was the richest, most powerful monarch in Europe. Elizabeth was afraid of him. She knew that his intentions were to add England to the vast empire over which he ruled. Elizabeth knew Philip well. He had once been married to her half-sister Mary when "Bloody Mary" had been queen. After Mary had died, Philip had planned to secure England by marrying the new queen, Elizabeth, but she had scorned his proposal. Twenty years had passed, but Philip II still had his eye on England. Elizabeth knew it, and she did not intend to antagonize him—not openly, that is. Therefore she had acted properly shocked when the Spanish ambassador had protested against Drake. She had agreed that if he deserved it, Drake should indeed be punished. She had even controlled her desire to see the treasure until the Spanish troops had landed in Ireland, and she too had something to complain of.

As for Mr. Drake. No sooner had he received his belated letter than he was up and away and on the road to London, with a train of pack horses bearing such a load of gold, silver, and precious jewels as had never passed that dusty highway before. Half the ballast of the *Golden Hind* was there.

Elizabeth's eyes shone when she saw it. She laughed aloud in her hearty way and gave him a friendly poke with her elbow, a nudge in the ribs to let the "little pirate" see that she, personally, was all for him, despite her own High Treasurer's contrary opinion.

Lord Burghley, sober, cautious sixty-year-old High Treasurer of England, held firmly to his honest opinion that all of the stolen booty should be returned to Spain. It made Elizabeth fairly spit with annoyance! Yet she kept up her pretense of having the Spanish claim investigated until spring. Then she gave up pretending and sent for Drake to come again from Plymouth, this time openly, by sea and in his famous ship.

Soon the *Golden Hind,* the old weather-beaten vessel that had sailed around the world was in the Thames River, anchored at Deptford, just below London. Crowds coming out from London went wild with joy at the sight of it. Some even proposed to have it hoisted up to the top of St. Paul's Cathedral, to stand in the place of the old steeple broken off in a storm. Everybody wanted to see Francis Drake, the great seaman, the hero of the hour. Crowds trailed him along the streets. Ballads and songs were written in his honor. Through it all he strutted and boasted in a manner quite distasteful to Burghley and certain other members of the court. But his high spirits were so infectious, his self-confidence so contagious, that though the King of Spain demanded his head, the Queen of England decided to honor him by raising his status from that of a commoner to that of a Gentleman—in other words, by making him a knight!

And so, the Queen, glittering with jewels, was carried shoulder-high in her canopied chair to the place where the *Golden Hind* lay rocking gently in the river. Raising her skirt enough to show her ankles, she stepped down and swept in dazzling splendor over the gangplank onto the deck of the famous ship. There a banquet was served, as elaborate and magnificent as those served to her hearty father, Henry VIII. Of this, in her fashion, she partook sparingly. The Queen then rose and took in her hand a golden sword.

The moment had come. The short, sturdy sea captain, in elegant attire, stepped confidently forward and knelt at the Queen's feet, plain Mr. Francis Drake. Touched on the shoulder with the golden sword, he rose Sir Francis Drake, a Knight and a Gentleman. And who had performed the ceremony? The Queen? Ah, no. At the last moment, unpredictable as ever, she had handed the golden sword to the French ambassador. Just in case of trouble with Spain, let France share the blame.

Sir Francis Drake, now shining in the Queen's favor, spent hours with her in the garden that summer, urging her to let him establish a base in the islands off the coast of Spain, swoop down from there on Spanish treasure ships, and so cripple the King of Spain and also fill her own treasury. It was a tempting proposal, but how much of such crippling would Philip II stand before declaring war? That was the question. And Elizabeth did not want war. . . . Certainly not before she had France more definitely on her side—not until the fantastic plan she was pursuing with France that summer had developed further to her satisfaction.

Meanwhile, up in Willoughby, little John Smith, growing more active every month, would soon be starting on his first great adventure, that of learning to walk.

PHILIP II

IN THE MOUNTAINS about thirty miles from Madrid, the capital city of Spain, stood a new man-made mountain of marble and stone known as the Escorial, a combination of palace, church, monastery, and mausoleum. Alone, bent over a heavy carved desk in a gloomy room of this mammoth palace, far removed from the world and its people, sat a slight, narrow-shouldered, sickly pale, gray-haired man dressed entirely in black.

An important document lay before him, which with thin fingers he shoved slowly and deliberately aside. Taking his quill, he dipped it, scraped it neatly on the edge of the inkwell and began methodically checking a column of figures as to the number of flagstones required to finish the monastery courtyard or some other minor calculation that would turn his thoughts from the disturbing document.

This thin man in black was the King of Spain, the royal builder of the Escorial. Philip II was not only the richest, most powerful monarch in Europe. He was also the most painstaking and industrious. Day after day, hour after hour, he sat humped over his heavy carved desk like a busy spider, spinning out long, detailed instructions to gardeners, architects and ship-builders, and forming a web of intrigue with his endless letters and dispatches to spies and ambassadors. Each matter, great or small, he considered patiently, secure in the belief that as God's representative on earth he could do no wrong. Therefore, trusting no one, he laid careful plans to have his royal enemies assassinated as quietly as possible, heretics tortured, stubborn unbelievers wiped out until he had turned all Europe back into one state and one church—that of his own. Then Europe would again be one united Christendom, as it had been for a thousand years until the year 1519, when his father Charles V had been made Holy Roman Emperor by the Germans.

That year something had occurred that he, Philip II, could only regard as a disastrous event, one that had shattered the unity and peace of Christendom. At the first meeting that Charles V had held as Emperor, a German monk had been brought before him for trial. This insubordinate monk, named Martin Luther, had dared to defy the Pope's authority, protesting that the Church of Rome needed to be reformed and to return to the simple teaching of the Bible. This protesting idea, this reading of the Bible, had "spread like the plague" throughout northern Europe. Soon another Protestant reformer arose with much more extreme ideas, a Frenchman by the name of John Calvin, who had been driven out of France but developed his stern doctrine in Geneva, Switzerland. The teachings of both Luther and Calvin had spread into the lowlands along the North Sea known as the Netherlands. This land was the birthplace of Philip's father, Charles V, a land of old and rich and beautiful cities which the Emperor dearly loved.

Philip himself, unlike his father, hated the Netherlands. It was so different from Spain, where he had been brought up. He also hated the people. They were stubborn and disobedient, determined to think for themselves. In Spain, torture had successfully purged the land of Protestants as it had formerly of Jews and Moslems. But try as he might, Philip could not clear them out of the Netherlands or bring the independent creatures to their knees. With Holland in the lead, the traitors had put their rebellious thoughts into writing. The disturbing document lying on his desk was their declaration of independence. He turned to it again.

His thin hand, marked with heavy blue veins, drew the rattling sheet of parchment toward him, and he reread the first sentence:

"Whereas God did not create the people as slaves to their prince to obey his commands whether right or wrong . . ."

Philip stopped. How could ignorant common people expect to judge a prince, whether his commands were right or wrong? A prince was created by God to rule, and they were created to obey without question. Both in religion and in government. The two went hand in hand. If people tried to think for themselves in one thing, they would try to do so in the other. Here in these words was the proof, furnished by these traitors in the Netherlands.

And France and England were helping them. That made Philip's work more difficult; but since it was "God's work," it could not fail. In time he would gain control over both France and England, and in his own way—not by declaring war as his advisers kept urging him to do. A recent letter from his ambassador in England led Philip to believe that the plot to assassinate Elizabeth would soon succeed and bring the desired result. Shoving the troublesome document from the Netherlands once more aside, he reread this encouraging letter.

"Such is the condition of England," wrote the ambassador, "with signs of revolt everywhere, the queen in alarm, the Catholic party numerous, Ireland disturbed and distrust aroused by your Majesty's fleet . . . that if so much as a cat moved the whole fabric would crumble down in three days beyond repair, in which case you could lay down the law for the whole world."

Lay down the law for the whole world. At those last words something like a smile passed over Philip's sad sallow face. "Lay down the law for the whole world!" That was the ambition, the dream of Philip II, the happiness he hoped for.

About the only immediate happiness this king found was in his children, especially his favorite, Isabella, who was fourteen and often helped her father with his letters. He had sent for the children. The door behind him soon opened and there they were—three of them. Isabella, a lovely-looking girl, her younger sister, and their small half-brother Philip. All ran to their father with open arms and returned his greeting with affection. The two girls were the children of Philip's third wife, the French princess Elizabeth, whose brother was now King of France. The small boy's mother was an Austrian princess who had died earlier in that year, 1581, leaving Philip a widower for the fourth time. With his gray hair and beard, the fifty-four-year-old monarch looked more like the grandfather of the little two-year-old boy not yet out of skirts. He came running as fast as he could on his short legs, holding out to his "dear papa" a beautiful ripe peach.

A DECLARATION OF INDEPENDENCE

THE SUMMER of 1581 brought one of the great events of the century—the founding of a new nation, the first one ever built upon a written constitution, the first to include in its constitution the great principle of religious freedom. On July 26, 1581, the Netherlands, with Holland as the leading province, declared their independence from Spain as about two hundred years later the American colonies were to declare their independence from England. They stated much the same reasons, but the tyranny against which they rebelled was far more severe, the fight necessary to make good their declaration much longer and more bitter.

16

The father of his people, the great leader of the Netherlands, was William, Prince of Orange, whose descendants today still occupy the throne of the nation which he helped to found. His more familiar name of William the Silent came to him by accident. In 1559, when he was about twenty-six, he was in France on a mission for Philip II, with three other young noblemen of the court, including a sullen young Spaniard, the Duke of Alva. On a hunting party one day, the French king, Henry II, spoke quite casually to his young guests of a scheme which he had entered into with their king, Philip II, to massacre all the Protestants in their dominions. The King naturally assumed that William of Orange, like the Duke of Alva, was in on the secret and equally willing to go ahead with the ugly business in the Netherlands. This was not so. William knew nothing of it. The Netherlands was his homeland. His own parents were Protestants. He was frozen with horror at the thought. How could any king whose duty was to protect his people contemplate such a crime?

Not one word, however, did he utter to betray his feeling. From his well-timed silence that day came the adjective "silent," which otherwise was most inappropriate for this very frank and friendly young prince.

That day marked a turning point in the life of William of Orange. Up to that time his loyalty to Philip II had been as unquestioning as it had been to Philip's father, the Emperor Charles V, to whom William had been almost like another son. As a boy of twelve he had become a page in the Emporer's household. His own father was of a noble but no longer wealthy family. Their ancestral home was the ancient fortress-castle of Dillenburg, where William had been born. There he had lived a simple, happy life with his younger brothers and sisters, carefully reared by their devoted parents. His mother, an especially remarkable woman, gave her children a true example of good living not to be forgotten.

One day, out of a clear sky, came the astounding news that young William had become the Prince of Orange. The title and the immense fortune that went with it had been left to him by a distant relative! This happy surprise was soon followed by a command invitation from the Emperor Charles V that the new twelve-year-old Prince come to Brussels to the palace, to begin a new and luxurious way of living suited to his new position in the realm. It was all very strange to the boy, especially the first morning, when, instead of jumping out of bed and pulling on his own breeches, he saw courtiers waiting there to dress him, after which he was taken to help lay out the Emperor's wardrobe for the day. But it was not long before it seemed natural. He also changed as a matter of course from the Protestant to the Catholic form of worship, insisted upon by the Emperor. In fact he adapted himself

easily to the court life, and became the typical gay, carefree young nobleman, up to this fateful day in France. That day changed his life.

Upon his return to the Netherlands, William of Orange began to
think deeply and to form the conviction for which he was to sacrifice
all his wealth, his energy, and eventually his life. Every individual, he
believed, had certain rights that must be respected, and among those
was the right to worship God according to his own conscience.

"I cannot approve of princes attempting to rule the conscience of
their subjects," he said later.

He tried in every way to bring Philip II to realize that he was
making a great mistake, but that royal gentleman trusted no opinion
but his own. After four years in the Netherlands, Philip II left the
country, never to return. That was in 1559. The Spanish troops left
behind, following orders, began burning and torturing in the name of
God. The citizens fought back desperately, seizing priests and monks,
breaking images and altars and destroying churches.

The nobles and wealthy burghers at first tried to stay aloof, but
when the whole land was threatened with ruin and no one's life or
property were safe, the nobles, Catholics and Protestants together, went
with a petition to the representative of the King, begging that the persecution cease. The petition sent on to Philip in Spain, was ignored. The
trouble grew worse. Fanatic Protestants increased their senseless destruction of monasteries and churches. A Spanish army of ten thousand
was sent in under the ruthless Duke of Alva. They butchered men,
women, and children and left their bodies lying on the streets or hanging on the trees as a warning to all other so-called heretics. The first
actual battle between Dutch and Spanish troops took place in the spring
of 1568. Six hundred Spanish soldiers were lured into an area of swamp-
land reclaimed from the Zuider Zee and perished in the deep mud. In
the next battle, which the ferocious Alva himself commanded, seven
thousand Dutch troops led by a younger brother of William of Orange
were butchered. It was then that William himself came to the front.
He sold his silver and jewels and mortgaged his estates to raise an army

of twelve thousand men to fight against Alva. At this time he also turned back to the Protestant religion. For twelve years the people fought on as loyal subjects of the King, merely to secure their rights. Philip's stubborn attitude finally drove them to the point of breaking their vows of allegiance and declaring their independence. Here are the words from their declaration which Philip II had been reading:

"Whereas God did not create the people as slaves to their prince to obey his commands whether right or wrong, but rather the prince for the sake of the subjects, to govern them with equity and support them as a father his children or a shepherd his flock, [therefore] when he does not behave thus, but oppresses them, seeking to infringe on their ancient customs and privileges, then he is no longer a prince but a tyrant and the subjects may legally proceed to the choice of another prince for their defense."

"Another prince for their defense. . . ." That raised a question. What prince? The people of Holland had but one answer. Their great leader "Father William" as they called him, should become their prince. William of Orange refused. He would continue to be their Stadtholder, or governor, but he would not be their prince or king. William of Orange looked instead to England and France. He believed that, without the continued help of these strong neighbors, the small new nation could not long hold out against Spain.

Queen Elizabeth was invited but refused to become their sovereign. That left France. William of Orange persuaded the people of the Netherlands to offer the position as their ruler to Francis the Duke of Anjou, a younger brother of the French king. Not that this young French prince had much to recommend him personally. He did not. But, aside from being the brother of the King of France, it was said that he was about to become the husband of the Queen of England. And if that were true, what more fortunate combination could there be for the Netherlands?

THE VIRGIN QUEEN AND HER "FROG PRINCE"

IT WAS TRUE, preposterous but true, that Queen Elizabeth, who had long prided herself on being a virgin, had now come up with the notion of marrying a French prince less than half her age whom she had never seen. She was enchanted with the idea, and even more so with the French ambassador who had come to make the arrangements. So suave was he—so gallant—so handsome—and what a way he had of making love! It was irresistible!

"Like another rose" he made her feel as they walked together through the paths of the garden in the summertime. That same summer in the same garden, on days that she could spare from the fascinating Frenchman, Queen Elizabeth listened to the plans of Sir Francis Drake for attacking Spain, plans which she was determined should not be undertaken before the successful outcome of this alliance with France.

The French ambassador, whose lovemaking was all in the line of duty, was far more eager to be replaced by the prospective bridegroom than the Queen was to accept to change. He kept urging her persistently, yet delicately, to send for Francis, knowing how many other suitors this unpredictable creature had flirted with and refused to marry. He also knew that the Privy Council wanted no Frenchman or Catholic sharing the throne of England.

Charmingly persistent, as ever, the Frenchman finally persuaded the Queen to sign a passport for Francis, who was then at his new post in Holland, to travel incognito to England. Even then the French ambassador felt his worries far from ended. One look at the prince might stop Elizabeth. The poor fellow was so pathetically unprepossessing. Hardly taller than a dwarf, he bobbed along as he walked, his eyes popping. His face was scarred with smallpox pits and he had a queer-shaped blob of a nose. The Frenchman could but shrug his shoulders and hope for the best. To his amazement all went well, far exceeding his fondest hopes. Elizabeth actually seemed to like the boy, playfully calling him her "Frog Prince." Francis, bedazzled by her wit and brilliance, left after his secret visit of two days with dreams of ruling England whirling in his head. The French ambassador had still to get Elizabeth to announce the date of the wedding. The Queen hesitated, not without her suspicions. One day she turned upon him with a shrewd glint in her bright eyes.

"I hear," she remarked, "that it has been said in France that the Prince would do well to marry the old creature. Then he could send for a poison that would make him a widower in five or six months, after which he could marry her cousin Mary Queen of Scots and be sovereign over both Scotland and England. What say you to that?"

The ambassador pooh-poohed the rumor as incredible. And Elizabeth, loath to end these charming negotiations, invited the Prince Francis to return in the late fall of that year 1581.

The French ambassador, on the alert, watched for the first opportunity to have the marriage announced. One morning he came upon the Queen and her Francis walking in the gallery with a number of courtiers, including Lord Leicester. Then and there he forced her to admit their betrothal, exchange rings, and seal the happy bargain with a kiss. This was too much for Elizabeth. This was going too far! What could she do? She was in a trap! The poor boy refused to be discarded. "Madame," he wailed, "I would rather be cut in pieces than not marry you and be laughed at by the whole world."

Poor fellow! Elizabeth liked him, but she did not want to marry him any more than she had ever wanted to marry anyone. And the Privy Council gladly came to the rescue. They forcefully insisted that the disappointed bridegroom should depart. A group of Councillors, among them Lord Leicester and a newcomer, Sir Walter Raleigh, were appointed to escort poor discarded Francis back to Holland. The Queen rode by his side as far as Canterbury. There she took leave of him tenderly, urging him to write to her often as if she were indeed his wife.

MARY STUART

I̅T WAS WINTER. Cold fog hung about the gardens and walls of a "very strong, very fayre, very stately" English country house in Yorkshire. In one of its richly furnished rooms, a woman in a red velvet gown sat sewing at a tapestry frame, outlined against the tall leaded window. Her slim white hand holding the needle rose and fell continually, pulling a long thread in and out. At her feet in the soft folds of her gown lay a small silky-eared spaniel, his flat brown nose pointed toward the fire on the hearth.

It would have been difficult to tell the woman's age. She was not young, but there was a softness about her, a certain radiant charm that was ageless. For this was Mary Stuart, who had been Queen of Scotland, who had been also queen of France, and who was still living like a queen in this luxurious home, but was in fact a prisoner. For thirteen years she had been held in England as a prisoner by her cousin, Queen Elizabeth.

23

At the thought of that "dear cousin" of hers whom she had never seen, hate darkened Mary's face. She stabbed the needle into the tapestry, tugged madly at the thread, threw up her arms, then rose and thrust the whole thing from her. It seemed that she had been sewing forever, that this miserable day—this deadly monotonous life—would never end! She pressed her hot cheek against the window frame and stood peering out into the fog, waiting, waiting, waiting as always for the message that might make her a queen again, that would certainly set her free. Never would she accept freedom from Elizabeth—not at the humiliating price of renouncing her claim to the English throne which she had inherited from her father, James V of Scotland.

James V, Mary's father, had died in 1542 a few days after she was born. A few years later, her French mother, remaining in Scotland as regent, had sent the small winsome girl home to France to be near her uncle the Duke of Guise and be educated with the royal children. When she was sixteen Mary had married the oldest prince, Francis II—and after the death of his royal father, they had been King and Queen for one glorious year, with all of their problems handled by Mary's uncle, the Duke of Guise. Then came the death of the boy King, quickly followed by word that Mary's mother was also dead and she must return to be Queen of Scotland. It was heart-breaking to leave the beautiful, gay, beloved France that was home to her, for the grim, poverty-stricken land of Highlands and Lowlands. Everything seemed as strange and primitive as the wild skirling of bagpipes which Mary heard for the first time playing a welcome to her on the outskirts of Edinburgh.

Actually there was no real welcome for Mary in Scotland. The Protestant lairds and nobles of the strict Scottish Kirk did not favor a Catholic queen. Nor did it please them to have her choose as chief adviser an Italian musician, Rizzio. Added to that, Mary soon fell madly in love with her handsome but soft-headed Stuart cousin, Lord Darnley, secretly married him, and gave the Scots a Catholic King—that is, temporarily. She did not give her new husband the royal title for life, which so infuriated the fellow that he joined other disgruntled nobles and murdered the queen's chief adviser, Rizzio. Four months later, Mary, with her love for her husband turned to loathing, gave birth to their son—another James Stuart—a future King of Scotland, a male heir to the throne of England. It was then June, 1566. A few months after the birth of his son, Darnley was murdered. Lord Bothwell, a broad-chested soldier, devoted to Mary, was accused of the murder but acquitted in a mock trial, and Mary, blindly infatuated with the man, ran off and married him. The Scots, glad of any excuse to be rid of her and quite ready to believe the worst, forced the Queen to abdicate and imprisoned her in the castle of Lochleven. Loyal friends helped her escape and cross the border into England, where she was made a prisoner by the Queen.

Here she was, thirteen years later, still a prisoner, but waiting, as she stood looking out into the fog, to hear that the plot to assassinate Elizabeth had succeeded, leaving the throne for her. There was also a scheme afoot by which her French cousin, Henry, the Duke of Guise, was to invade England, aided by Philip II. Weeks had passed, however, with no reply to all her many letters to both—no word from either France or Spain.

The only recent news that reached her had been the breakup of the ridiculous affair between Elizabeth and Francis, Mary's former brother-in-law, the youngest of the royal children with whom she had been brought up. She thought of his pretty brother Henry III, who was now King, of their mother Catherine de' Medici, who herself had taught the girls their lessons, of lovely Elizabeth who had married Philip II, of naughty little Marguerite who would never sit still. Mary smiled as the thoughts of those full, happy days filled for a moment the empty present. Turning slowly from the window, she seated herself again at the needlepoint, which also recalled those faraway days in France and her first thimble. Selecting another bright thread, she began sewing again, while the little brown spaniel resumed his favorite place in the folds of her velvet gown.

Royal Relatives

THE FIRST OF THE TUDORS: HENRY VII

THE STUARTS

SON

DAUGHTER

4 Anne of Cleves

5 Catherine Howard

3

6 Catherine Parr

HENRY VIII

Jane Seymour

2 WIFE 1

Anne Boleyn

Catherine of ARAGON (SPAIN)

MARRIED

MARGARET TUDOR

JAMES IV STUART of SCOTLAND

ALSO MARRIED

ARCHIBALD DOUGLAS

EDWARD VI

MARY
wife of Philip II

MATTHEW STUART

MARGARET DOUGLAS

JAMES V

MARIE de GUISE from France

Elizabeth

HENRY STUART Lord Darnley

Mary
QUEEN of SCOTS

Francis II of France

James I
OF ENGLAND

JAMES VI
OF SCOTLAND

THE THREE HENRYS
AND THE QUEEN MOTHER OF FRANCE

FRANCE was at peace in 1582. But before long, one of the three
young Frenchmen known as the "Three Henrys" would add another to the seven horrible wars of religion that had raged through

27

France in the past twenty years. Wars between Catholics and Huguenots, as the Protestant followers of Calvin in France were called.
These wars were political as well as religious—part of a very compli-
cated struggle for power between the King and the nobles of France.

Henry, Duke of Guise, tall, blond, thirty-two years old, was head
of the Catholic party. Henry, King of Navarre, dark and dynamic,
twenty-nine years old, was head of the Huguenots, and between them
stood the frivolous Henry III, King of France, thirty-one years old,
unbalanced, and too easily influenced by foolish advisers to be a good
King. He was the despair of his mother, Catherine de' Medici, the
queen mother of France, who for the past twenty years had been the
most important person in the land, its greatest politician. No one knew
better than she how easily any one of the three young Henrys could
upset the peace which she had established with utmost difficulty.

Grateful for peace, however, while it lasted, she emerged from
the doorway of the Louvre one morning into the bright April sunshine
of Paris. Drawing a deep breath, she stood there a moment looking
toward the new palace of the Tuileries she was building, and the gardens beyond. . . . A tremendously stout woman dressed all in black,
she wore a widow's cap and veil, on top of which she had perched a
small black woolen hat. The huge shadow cast by her ample figure in
the sun moved with her as she proceeded down the broad stone steps
to a sedan chair, where men in bright livery stood waiting. Seated inside
on the velvet cushion, she straightened one leg in which she felt twinges
of sciatica (thinking herself lucky at sixty-three not to feel it more)
and asked the bearers to carry her beyond the city walls into the green
fields where she could collect her thoughts. Her voice was deep and
musical as she spoke, and there was not a wrinkle on her smooth white
forehead as she looked out upon the beautiful morning. All about her
pink chestnuts were in blossom; the Seine was sparkling as they crossed
the bridge. On the island to her left rose the twin spires of Nôtre Dame
Cathedral, built three hundred years ago at the end of the Crusades.

There was no thought, then, that those so-called Christians of

France would ever be murdering one another in the name of God. In those years there was but one Church in Europe, Rome was its center, and the Pope was the absolute ruler of Christendom. The division in the church had come much later, within her own lifetime, and Popes who were members of her family had seen the break begin. It was Pope Leo X, her great-uncle, who had excommunicated Martin Luther. Another relative, Clement VII, had been Pope when Henry VIII declared himself head of the Church of England and divorced his first wife to marry Queen Elizabeth's mother.

That was in 1533, a year that Queen Mother Catherine well remembered, for she too had been married that year. Pope Clement himself had brought her to France. There she soon found herself resented as a foreigner, spoken of as "that Italian woman" and scorned by the French when she became queen, because she was not of royal blood.

That had not prevented her from loving France and its people. She trained herself to endure silently what she could not alter, and so to control her feelings that some said she had no feeling at all.

Far worse things had been said of her after her husband, Henry II, died, and she stood behind her young sons, determined, as each became king, that neither Catholics nor Huguenots should get control of the high places in the government. There in the dangerous middle ground she had been attacked from both sides, blamed and cursed and reviled by both Catholics and Protestants. To this day people think of her as evil. She was at least conniving, playing both sides, interested chiefly in her own security.

The Queen Mother, riding along in her sedan chair that spring morning, was not thinking of that. She had no time for self-pity. Her pity was for France, and all her thoughts centered on the problem of making Frenchmen of both religions live together in peace. In spite of being told that it was no more possible than "asking cats and rats to live together," she clung to the principle that both should be protected by the King.

It was twenty years ago, when the three Henrys were still little boys, that Catherine had issued the first royal edict forbidding religious persecution. This had satisfied neither Huguenots nor Catholics, and soon war had broken out. Henry of Navarre's father was killed in war, and the father of Henry of Guise was assassinated. Peace came, but again war broke out, again and again for the second, third, and fourth times as the years passed and the three young Henrys grew from boys into men.

Handsome young Henry of Navarre had taken part in the fourth war. He was then seventeen years old and it had seemed to Mother Catherine that in the interests of peace it would be well to have the popular young Huguenot as a son-in-law. It was a difficult marriage to arrange, opposed by both Catholics and Huguenots, but the Queen Mother in her persuasive way finally succeeded. In 1572, her youngest daughter Marguerite married Henry of Navarre, though the ceremony had to be performed on the steps of Nôtre Dame, since, as a Huguenot, he could not be married inside the Cathedral. Paris was filled with wedding guests, and four days later, on the night of St. Bartholomew, a hideous wholesale massacre of Huguenots occurred all over the city. For this, as was to be expected, Catherine was blamed. Touched off by this awful massacre war raged again. After peace was declared, Catherine saw the death of her second son, Charles. Henry III, then twenty-three, had taken his brother's place as King of France, that foolish frivolous Henry, who loved to attend masquerades decked out in rouge and pearls and ribbons and laces. Again the peace, which the Queen Mother worked so hard to establish, did not last long. More wars followed.

In 1578, when it looked as though trouble might break out again, Catherine had put on her small black wool hat atop her widow's veil and set forth on a long journey through the provinces, to try to prevent the outbreak. She was gone three years, travelling in all kinds of weather over all kinds of roads, sometimes walking, sometimes riding on a "little mule" which, as she wrote in a letter to a friend, must have been a laughable sight for one so stout as she. From town to town she went,

30

from city to city, settling disputes, smoothing out difficulties and returning with the joyful feeling that she had accomplished her purpose. For
the time being there was peace. But how long would it last?

Small wonder that the Queen Mother, who knew the situation so
well, should be concerned, as she rode forth in that spring morning of
1582, lest any one of the three young Henrys upset the delicate balance
of peace and start another war.

There was also danger from Spain, of which Catherine was well
aware. She knew that Philip II wanted France torn apart and weakened
by war. She knew he was sending aid to the Duke of Guise and the
Catholic League, so that through them he might get control of France
and make it part of his empire. Catherine needed help against this former
son-in-law of hers. She needed the help of England as England also
needed the help of France. For that reason she had promoted the
marriage of her youngest son Francis and Queen Elizabeth. Although,
knowing Elizabeth, she was not astonished to have the marriage fall
through, she was regretful.

Her thoughts turned to Francis, Duke of Anjou, and the place he
now occupied in the Netherlands. Would he ever be King of France,
she wondered. She had not seen his face when she had consulted the
astrologer. She had been shown the future kings of France passing one
by one across the surface of a dark mirror, but his face had not been
there. After Henry III had followed the dark, exciting face of Henry
of Navarre! If anything happened to Francis, Henry of Navarre was
next in line. And he was a Huguenot.

God forbid that she should live to see the war that would tear
France apart, before he could make good his claim to the throne and
become Henry IV. She closed her eyes as if to shut out the dreadful
future.

"God be pitiful to me!" she prayed. "I have lost so many. Allow
me to depart soon . . . as befits my age."

31

YOUNG WALTER RALEIGH AND VIRGINIA

THE YOUNG CAPTAIN, Walter Raleigh, came into London, very cocky, very handsome, very ambitious to capture the attention of the Queen and make a place for himself at court. It was said that one day when her Majesty, coming to a "plashy place," hesitated to go on, Raleigh swept off his new plush cloak and spread it on the ground for her to walk upon. Whether this actually happened or not, it might have. It would have been like the young Raleigh. He had a dashing way about him. Even though it might have been his only cloak, as it probably was at that low tide in his fortunes, he would have

32

felt it worth the gamble. One way or another, he did attract the attention of Queen Elizabeth, became one of her favorites, and was knighted.

Young Raleigh had arrived in London just after Christmas, 1581. He came from Ireland, where he had been fighting for a year and a half, dashing about the countryside in pursuit of the Irish rebels who were being helped by the Spanish. He returned with an idea of a better and cheaper way to rule the land than keeping soldiers there. That was to win over the chiefs of the various Irish tribes and let them keep their countrymen in order. Lord Burghley, the High Treasurer, was naturally interested in economy, and Raleigh was given an audience with the Queen, who had a miserly eagerness to save pennies.

The Queen sized him up shrewdly and saw that here was a useful young fellow as well as a very handsome one. Not so young as he seemed—he was twenty-nine—and with considerable experience as a soldier. He had gone with a company of English volunteers to help the Huguenots in France. He had fought in the Netherlands against Spain in a company of English volunteers organized by his half-brother, Sir Humphrey Gilbert. He had also raided Spanish ships with Gilbert on the Atlantic. Sir Humphrey Gilbert . . . Elizabeth knew him well. In 1578 he had received a commission from her to make an expedition in search of a new route to India, and failed. Since the days of Columbus Europeans had continued to search both northeast and northwest for such a route and had failed. John Cabot, who had discovered the continent of North America, had tried in the days of Elizabeth's grandfather Henry VII to find an eastward passage through the icy waters north of Siberia. Two other men had later tried and failed. A third had reached Archangel and from there made a trip through the unknown land of the Russians to the town called Moscow. From this Muscovy he brought back to Elizabeth a letter from its Tsar, Ivan the Terrible, and also a sample of the rich furs that were to be had by traders. So the Muscovy Company, an association of English merchants, had been formed for trading with these strange people, the Russians.

Sir Martin Frobisher, friend of Sir Francis Drake, had sailed northwest three times trying to reach India, but had gone little farther than the southern tip of Greenland.

Then Sir Humphrey Gilbert had tried and failed. But he wanted permission to try again, was that it? asked the Queen. Raleigh said it was, and begged her gracious permission to accompany his brother. The Queen said no, most emphatically. Sir Humphrey might go, though she personally considered him "no great hap as a sailor," but go alone. She would not have "her Water," as she called him, gallivanting off to strange parts of the world, risking his life among man-eating lions, ferocious unicorns, and red savages.

So in 1583, Raleigh was not with Sir Humphrey Gilbert when he set forth on a last great exploration, one on which he lost his life. Only one ship returned. The survivors reported that they had reached New-foundland, but had seen no lions, no unicorns, no savages. Nor had they found any good place for a settlement.

A settlement, an English settlement in the new world! That was the dream that Walter Raleigh was urging upon the Queen. Spain, he told her, should not be allowed full sway in America. England should become an empire like Spain. Elizabeth was not interested. England was enough for her to manage. Besides, she added, this first attempt to settle had plainly been a mistake.

That was true, quite true, said Raleigh. And the mistake had come in not knowing where to plant the colony. Next time he would send out an exploring party first. Beginning just north of the Spanish colony in Florida, they would go up along the coast until they found a likely place for a settlement.

Won over by his enthusiasm, the Queen reluctantly consented, but again she would not let the young man leave her side. He was so engaging, that sweet "Water" of hers, so witty, so intellectual, so entertaining. He wrote such delightful poetry.

So in 1584, Raleigh again was not with the explorers who sailed for America. They were gone all summer.

In September they were back, bringing with them two Indian boys,

34

one more friendly than the other. The friendly one said his name was Manteo.

Manteo lived on an island not far from a larger island, called ROANOKE. The explorers reported they had gone ashore there, fully armed, but found the red-skinned people friendly. They were met by a chief named Granganimeo, a brother of the great Indian king of that region. He "made signs of joy and welcome," they said, "first striking his own head and breast and then ours, smiling and trying to show that we were all brothers made of the same flesh."

Granganimeo wore a broad plate of gold or copper about his head, like a crown. A day or two later, when the English began to trade with the natives, the one thing that he most desired was a shiny tin dish, which "he hung around his neck declaring with signs that this would shield him against enemie's arrows.

"His wife was very beautiful, small in stature and shy. She wore a long cloak of leather [and] earrings of pearls big as peas hung down to her waist."

The white men were entertained in the Indian village. They feasted on shad and a curious root called POTATO, and they said:

"We found the people most gentle and faithfull, voide of guile and treason, such as live after the manner of the Golden Age—a more loving people there cannot be found in the world. The soile is most plentiful sweet, fruitful, and wholesome in all the world. Ourselves proved the soil, and put some of our pease in the ground and in tenne days they were fourteen inches high."

Raleigh was delighted. The Queen was delighted. It was agreed upon that this wonderful virgin country should be named for the Virgin Queen. It should be called VIRGINIA!

Right away, Raleigh, the enthusiastic promoter of empire for England, set to work on plans for "planting" the first colony in Virginia, spending huge sums of his own money to equip the expedition that would leave for Roanoke the following spring.

35

NO GOLD—BUT TOBACCO

EARLY IN APRIL of 1585, Raleigh had a fleet of seven ships at anchor in Plymouth harbor ready to sail. The colonists were on board, 103 of them, all men. Manteo and the other Indian boy, after a winter in London, were on their way home.

Mr. Ralph Lane was to be the governor of the colony.

Sir Richard Grenville, Walter Raleigh's cousin, an admiral in the navy, was in command of the fleet. They sailed on the ninth of April and after a more or less eventful voyage landed in Virginia on the island of Roanoke. Every man who set foot on shore, from cabin boy to admiral, was hoping and expecting to find gold, quantities of gold such as the Spaniards had found in the New World.

Grenville was not to remain in Virginia with the settlers. But before sailing back to England, he could not resist making one short excursion back into the forests in search of a gold mine. On the way he lost a small silver drinking cup which caught the eye of an Indian and was stolen by him. In revenge, Grenville burned an entire Indian village to the ground. So, having committed the first outrage against the natives, the brave admiral departed. He promised to return in the early spring, bringing more provisions and supplies.

The voyage home was profitable, for on the way he attacked and captured a Spanish ship loaded with gold. And on the way back the following April, with his shipload of supplies, he wasted so much time hunting for more Spanish ships that he did not reach Roanoke Island until August. Then it was too late. There was no need for the supplies. There was no one to use them.

The settlers, as Grenville learned later, had been rescued by Sir Francis Drake. Back in England, and thankful to be there, they told a pitiful story of how they had suffered during the winter, when the island which was so balmy in summer became windswept and desolate. Governor Lane shuddered at the thought, and declared, "Nothing but the discovery of a gold mine or a passage to the South Sea will ever make our countrymen settle in Virginia."

He told how they had failed to find gold, and how they had been deceived by an old Indian chief. After they had taken him prisoner for the purpose of helping them, he had described the way to a rich mine that did not exist. They set out and kept going on and on, until they had only one pint of corn per man and two mastiff dogs that could be boiled with sassafras leaves and eaten on their way back. They found then that they had been deceived by the old Indian, merely because he resented being made a prisoner.

Then there was Chief Wingina, who pretended to be their friend, but for some reason apparently had no faith in the good intentions of the white man. While they were searching for the gold mine, Wingina urged his people to cut them off from their base of supplies on the island, hoping to destroy them. On their safe return, Lane said he sent word to Wingina to come there for a meeting. The Chief appeared with seven or eight braves.

"Thereupon," said Lane, "I gave the word agreed upon (which was Christ our victory) and we twenty-five men began to fire. Wingina fell to the ground . . . as if dead . . . then suddenly got up and fled . . . running so fast we could not catch him. An Irish boy in my company shot him in the back with my petronel. Another followed him into the woods. I had given up hope of seeing him (the boy) alive when he returned carrying Wingina's head."

It was then the first of June, long after Grenville should have been there with the much-needed provisions. Another week passed and he had not come, and they were practically starving when at last they sighted a fleet of ships—the ships of Sir Francis Drake. Drake had been plundering the Spanish cities of Santo Domingo and St. Augustine. Leaving Florida, he had stopped by to see how the settlers in Virginia were making out. Seeing their plight, he had said he could spare a month's provisions, but the ship carrying the provisions to shore capsized. That was the last straw. The desperate, hungry men abandoned the settlement and clambered aboard the ships of Sir Francis Drake. He took them back to England.

"They raced to the shore as if a mighty army were at their heels," said one of the men; which was true, he added soberly. "God stretched out his hand against them because of the cruelties and outrages they had committed against the natives."

This was the sad tale, the dismal outcome of Sir Walter Raleigh's great dream, the first failure at founding a settlement in the new world. He was disappointed, yes—but discouraged? Never. He set to work immediately on plans for another group of settlers to be sent out the following spring.

Meanwhile he was fascinated by something that Lane and Drake had brought home to him. A weed that grew wild in Virginia, and the implement or pipe that they had seen the Indians use in smoking it. Tobacco. Raleigh might have heard of it. A Spanish physician had sent it from Mexico to Philip II, believing it to have miraculous healing powers. Seeing it in Portugal, a French ambassador, Nicot, had sent seeds to Catherine de' Medici—and from his name came the word NICOTINE. Governor Ralph Lane, however, was the first person to smoke it in England, and Sir Walter Raleigh took it up and made pipe-smoking popular among the Elizabethan courtiers. It is said that one of Raleigh's servants, when he first saw him smoking, thought he was on fire and threw a bucket of water over him.

No one suspected that this weed would one day be used as money in Virginia, or be in any way a substitute for the gold which the settlers for years to come would still be searching for.

38

LITTLE JOHN SMITH

LITTLE JOHN SMITH was now six years old, but he did not look it, he was so small and short for his age. His blond head hardly came above the opening in the fireplace, and he had to climb on a bench to hand his mother the pewter plates from the top shelf. They were used for company. For everyday meals they used wooden trenches and spoons. His father carved them in the winter, making lots of chips, but these didn't show much. They just fell into the rushes on the floor. It didn't matter, only sometimes baby Alice picked up the curls of wood and put them in her mouth and choked. Once in a while his mother swept out all the dirty rushes and gave the house a good cleaning. She hung out the blankets from the best bed and the second-best bed and then folded them away in a big chest for the summer. Then John and his father brought in fresh rushes for the floor. Francis helped too, Francis, John's brother, who was five.

If Francis's last name had been Drake instead of Smith, he would have had the same name as the great hero Sir Francis Drake. Everybody in Willoughby knew about *him*. John's father and the other men talked about him, standing around after church, and they wagered that he could capture any Spanish ship, no matter how big it was. He had sailed clear around the world, this Francis Drake had. If you went down to London, you could see the ship he sailed in. . . . John wished he could see it. He wished he lived in London town where the big ships came in.

He wished that ships came into Louth. His father said he could go there to grammar school when he was big enough. Louth was a big town, not like London, maybe, but bigger than Alford, where he went to school now. Alford was four miles up the highway. Boys who went there had to be at St. Wilfrid's Church at six o'clock in the morning in summer and seven in the winter or they would be late for the opening psalm and prayer, and that was almost as bad as saying a swear word. The younger boys like Francis had a horn book with the letters on it, A B C and all the rest. John had had a horn book first, then an A B C book with real pages in it, and now he had a Primer. He carried it to school in his satchel with his penknife and his writing quills and a small cloth to wipe his pen and a bigger cloth to keep his nose clean.

You had to sit still a long time in school. Sometimes he thought he'd even rather be hoeing corn or pulling weeds or chasing pigs out of the new fields. Chasing pigs was the most fun there was on a farm. He didn't believe he wanted to be a farmer when he grew up. He'd lots rather be a sailor, like Sir Francis Drake.

What if he went to London someday and saw Sir Francis Drake and met him! And what if the great admiral said, "Come on, John, aboard my ship, help me polish up my sword and my helmet. We're going off to fight the Spaniards . . ." Oh, John could fairly hear him say it. The lines in his primer turned to waves on the ocean; he could feel the wind in his face . . .

"What-ifs" often seemed to John that way—as real as if they had truly happened. Maybe they always would.

TO AND FROM HOLLAND

SILENCE and the sadness of death lay upon the town of Delft and spread throughout the Netherlands; black despair travelled along the canals and streets of the cities. Out across the windmill-dotted countryside went the word that the great leader was dead.

William of Orange had been assassinated!

It was July 10, 1584. Four years earlier, Philip II had offered a large reward to anyone who would "take him from this world as a public enemy" and "chief disturber of the whole of Christendom." When news of the deed was reported to him, Philip II merely remarked, "Better late than never." In June, Francis, the Duke of Anjou, had died of typhoid fever, which ended Holland's close connection with France. That left only Elizabeth to be assassinated before he, Philip, would have matters well in hand.

Queen Elizabeth, shocked by the assassination of Prince William and the death of Anjou, and fearful now for the safety of England, resolved to help the Netherlands fight Spain openly and officially, instead of secretly as heretofore. It was a daring step to take, but in self-preservation how could she do otherwise? She sent word to the States-General at The Hague, the capital of Holland. Deputies came at once to England to arrange the life-saving alliance. Queen Elizabeth met them at Greenwich. On bended knees they begged her to become their sovereign. This she refused. But the treaty should go forward. The ambassadors should meet with the members of her Privy Council at the palace.

One of the members of the Council at this time was a Mr. William Davison, a most loyal and capable servant of the Queen. His life and his undeserved misfortune are important in this story chiefly because of their effect upon the life of young William Brewster. This personable young man had come to be secretary to Mr. Davison that fall, well recommended for this first position at court as a graduate of Cambridge University and a member of the gentry. Years later he would be known as Elder Brewster, one of the Pilgrim Fathers who founded New England, after living many years in Holland. That was to be in 1620, far in the future. . . . In this fall of 1584, young William Brewster, seventeen years old, stood near Mr. Davison in the castle at Greenwich, taking notes on the treaty being arranged between England and the Netherlands.

According to the treaty, Queen Elizabeth was to furnish Holland with five thousand soldiers and one thousand horses. In return, as security, the two fortified Dutch towns of Flushing and Brill were to be turned over to England, under an English governor. Mr. Davison went to Holland to take charge of affairs until the governor should arrive. With him went his secretary, William Brewster. On his first night in Holland, young William slept with the gold keys to the city of Flushing under his pillow, and was relieved indeed to hand them over to the governor, Sir Philip Sidney, upon his arrival.

Lord Leicester was General-in-Chief of all the forces. A tremendous ovation marked the arrival of this famous favorite of the Queen. Landing in all his usual magnificence at Flushing, he was greeted with fluttering banners, ringing bells, and the roar of cannon. The way from Flushing to Amsterdam and on to The Hague was illuminated with torches and fireworks.

As a climax, the Earl of Leicester was offered the absolute sovereignty of the Netherlands, which Queen Elizabeth herself had refused. In a ceremony of almost royal pomp and splendor, he accepted the responsibility and the honor.

Mr. Davison translated all the negotiations into English for Leicester, who wrote the Queen that Mr. Davison had "great credit here among all persons of any account." His parting gift from the Netherlands was a handsome gold chain, which he handed young William to wear until they reached London. As they were delayed by storms on the Channel, Davison went directly to report to the Queen. He found her in a towering rage.

"I will not endure it!" she screamed, pacing back and forth. "No man shall exceed the authority I give him."

What right had Lord Leicester to accept the sovereignty of the Netherlands, without asking her permission? He had reported to Lord Burghley, had he? Indeed! And why not to her? She was the ruler of this land!

Mr. Davison was at a loss for words. Lord Burghley also. "In very truth," someone wrote to Leicester, "all your friends are at their wits' end what to say in your behalf." It was the end of March before Her Majesty had had time to cool off and Walter Raleigh was able to write Leicester, "The Queen is, thanks be to God, well pacified and you are again her 'sweet Robyn.'"

The Earl of Leicester remained in Holland a year, helping the Dutch to defend their country against Spain. Then he was summoned home to help settle the fate of Mary Stuart, whose life more and more endangered that of the Queen. A recent plot originating in Spain to assassinate Elizabeth and make Mary queen had been thwarted just in time, and the perpetrators given their just deserts. But what to do about Mary Stuart was a problem. Burghley and many members of the Privy Council said she should be brought to trial. How could she be? There was no evidence in her own handwriting that she had favored the assassination. Besides, she was a royal person. Could a royal person be tried?

Mr. Davison was involved in this difficult decision. The unfortunate part he had to play was to ruin the life of this capable, conscientious man and alter the well-started career of his young secretary, William Brewster.

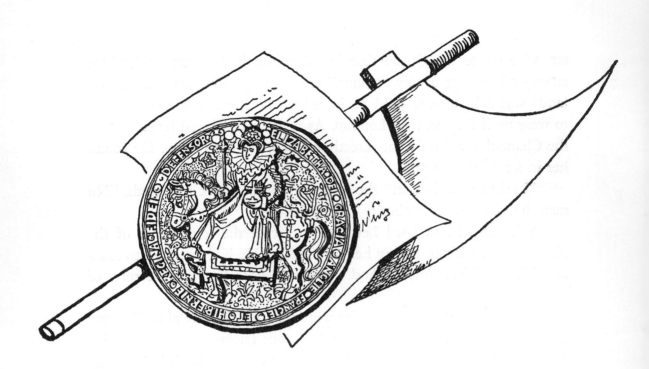

MARY STUART AND THE ''HONEST'' MAN

IT WAS A SUMMER MORNING—the tenth day of July, 1586, to be exact. Bright summer sun streamed through the castle window into the writing room where Mary Stuart and her two secretaries, both Frenchmen, were decoding and reading letters that had been smuggled in that morning. One letter had sent such a flush of vivid color to Mary's cheeks that she looked even more beautiful to the two men than usual. Like all who fell under the spell of Mary Stuart's charm, they longed to protect her. The exciting letter had come from a man named Babington who planned to rescue her. She would have answered it at once had not both of her secretaries begged her not to do so.

"Madame, we beg of you," said both men, speaking in French, "do not become involved in this so-dangerous affair."

For some time after the last plot against Elizabeth had been discovered, the castle had been so strictly guarded that any communication with the outside world had been impossible. At last, praise be, a man had been found who could be trusted to carry messages in and out.

Mary called him her "honest" man. He was the drayman who delivered a barrel of beer to the household once a week. In the bung of the barrel was a hollow cork containing a letter which Mary's butler removed after having placed a letter in the cork of the empty barrel going out. It was as simple as that!

A second reading of Babington's letter still made Mary's heart beat so fast that she could almost hear it. At last these endless years were coming to an end. Soon she would be free . . . soon she would be housed in the royal palace, on the throne of Elizabeth! For what did he say, this Babington? She read these words aloud:

"Myself with ten gentlemen, and a hundred followers will undertake the delivery of your royal person from the hands of your enemies. There be six noble gentlemen, all my private friends who for the zeal they bear the Catholic cause and your Majesty's service will undertake the tragical execution." What loyalty! What devotion! She could do no less than write a reply. She turned to her secretaries. . . .

"But Madame," they repeated, "do not consent to this affair in writing. We beg you, we implore you to have caution."

Caution. Caution! Mary had no use for such a word as caution. Regardless of their warning, Mary Stuart commanded the secretaries to help her compose a reply. For three days she kept them writing, turning it into a secret code. In it were these words:

"The forces being in readiness . . . it shall be time to set the six gentlemen to work, taking order that upon accomplishment of their design I may be suddenly transported out of this place."

The day was July 17, when Mary, full of hope, handed the letter to the butler. The butler placed it in the hollow cork of the beer barrel and the "honest" man carried it away.

A few hours later a copy of the decoded letter was in the hands of Walsingham, head of the secret service for Queen Elizabeth, a most efficient man. Mary Stuart had fallen into his trap. The "honest" man had been hired by Walsingham for the very purpose of securing a letter that would prove Mary guilty of consenting to the murder of Elizabeth.

45

Each letter that went in or out of the castle was first decoded and read before being sent upon its way. Walsingham now had all the facts he needed and proceeded to act upon them.

On August 4 the first arrest was made. Soon young Babington and a friend who had fled in terror to the woods were caught and led back in chains through the streets of London to the Tower. There was a great rejoicing. The Queen had been saved! Bells clanged and rang in all the churches from St. Paul's to Charing Cross. Bonfires blazed along the river. Long queues of shouting, hilarious people grew more and more hilarious as they wound their way up and down Cheapside, in and out of narrow alleys, in and out of taverns. In foaming tankards of ale they toasted their good Queen Bess, who was as English as they were, God bless her. Grandchild of a plain merchant, wasn't she? And proud of it, wasn't she? Bless her good soul! God bless the Queen!

Meanwhile, Mary, unaware of what had happened, was still full of hope and excitement. On August 9, her eyes shining, she rode off (under guard, of course) in a handsome hunting costume for a stag hunt, accompanied by her two secretaries, her chamberlain, and her physician. They had cantered through the gates of the park and were approaching the castle where the hunt was to begin, when she saw there a troop of mounted soldiers. One came forward, bowed, raised his plumed hat and told her bluntly that she was under arrest.

Mary stared at him wide-eyed, speechless. Then the cruel truth hit home. This was all part of a plot—this hunting trip—part of a terrible plot to destroy her! Even now they must be searching her rooms for evidence to use against her.

A few days later found her in Fotheringay Castle, which was no pleasant country house, but truly a fortress. She had no doubt what her fate was to be. She could yet save herself on terms offered by Elizabeth, but she would not accept the terms. Admit that she was guilty, that she had taken part in the conspiracy? Ask humbly for Elizabeth's gracious pardon? Never. She would die as a queen. And let Elizabeth suffer for having shed the blood of a queen, if she were willing to do so!

46

Elizabeth was in a bad spot. She did not want to do away with Mary. Yet what would happen to England if she were allowed to live? What if another such conspiracy should be successful? Then surely England would be plunged into a bloody war. Yet what would the world say if one queen allowed another queen to be brought before a jury and tried like an ordinary mortal? Yet this is what Lord Burghley, Walsingham, and other councilors told her was necessary for the peace of the land. Queen Elizabeth, therefore, reluctantly appointed a jury of distinguished gentlemen to try Mary Stuart, Queen of Scots.

Elizabeth herself was not present at the trial. To represent her, an empty throne under the royal canopy and the coat of arms of England had been placed at the end of the hall of Fotheringay Castle. Mary glanced at the empty throne and spoke of it as her own rightful place as she swept in, head held high, and was escorted to a lower seat.

The questioning began, with false answers given by Mary, until, faced with her own letters, she had to admit the truth. She was found guilty of approving plans to injure the royal person of the Queen.

Parliament had decreed that the sentence for such a crime was death, but the Queen herself had to sign the death warrant. This she hesitated to do, until she had driven herself and her councilors almost frantic by her indecision. Finally on the first of February, 1587, Mr. Davison received a message from Her Majesty to come at once and bring the death warrant for her signature. He brought it with a number of other papers which she signed quickly, one after the other. At last it was done—signed! But it still had to be sealed.

"Take it to Lord Burghley, to have the Great Seal put on," Elizabeth told Mr. Davison, seeming greatly relieved, laughing and talking brightly of this and that before dismissing him.

He was at the door when she suddenly called him back sharply.

"Is there no other way to do this? Couldn't someone be found to do it there in the castle—quietly?" Mr. Davison had nothing to suggest but the legal carrying out of justice, and as there was no change made in the orders he proceeded to carry them out.

Mary Stuart listened with no show of emotion to the death sentence. Making the sign of the cross, she said simply:

"In the name of God, these tidings are welcome. I bless and pray Him that the end of all my bitter sufferings is at hand."

She planned her costume with utmost care for this last act of her life, that it might be beautiful.

The morning came, February 8, 1587. The hall of Fotheringay Castle was filled with noble spectators, facing the scaffold which had been built for the occasion. A side door opened. Mary entered wearing a long gown of black velvet patterned in gold and holding an ivory crucifix. She mounted the scaffold and the sentence was carried out.

Two days later, when the information reached Queen Elizabeth, she was astonished, furious, and horrified. Mary Stuart was dead? Put to death without her knowledge? Without her direct command? She stamped the floor in rage; she sobbed; she wrung her hands, she screamed at her councillors. She stormed at Lord Burghley, who said he had affixed the Great Seal when her Majesty's order had been conveyed to him by Davison.

"Davison!" she shouted. Never had she told him to take the death warrant and have the Great Seal affixed. Davison was the guilty man. She had him brought before the high court, whose members, echoing the Queen's words to save themselves, proclaimed that Davison was to blame. Davison had had no witnesses. It would not have changed the verdict if he had. If the Queen was to be innocent of the death of Mary Stuart, somebody had to be declared guilty.

Davison was fined £10,000, which was far more than he was able to pay, so he was thrown into prison for debt.

William Brewster remained with Mr. Davison for some time, doing many faithful services, hoping against hope that the storm would pass over and he would be pardoned. It was a false hope.

At last the young man left London, and went north to his old home in Suffolk County—to the village of Scrooby.

James VI

8 years old and
as a young man.

JAMES

JAMES Stuart, King of Scotland, twenty-year-old son of Mary Stuart, blubbered and sobbed when he heard that his mother had been condemned to death. Not that he cared, but he was embarrassed.

He didn't know what to do. If he didn't try to prevent it, what would the other kings of Europe think of him? Yet if he did, Elizabeth might not name him her successor—he might never be king of England. It was indeed a dilemma.

He sat in his palace in Edinburgh, a poor sickly figure twisting his spindly legs this way and that, snuffling, wiping his nose on the sleeve of his dark green jacket, wishing he didn't have to worry about this woman who cared no more for him than he did for her. From a wee lad he had been taught to hate and distrust his mother as a "bludy woman and a poysining witch." So far as he could remember, he had never seen her. Nor had he seen his father, Lord Darnley, who had been murdered soon after his son's birth. The house in which he was staying had been blown up with gunpowder and his body found lying in the garden. His mother had had a hand in the plot, so James had been told. One day, dressed in mourning with a long black veil, she had come to see him, bringing an apple. He had shrieked and screamed at the stranger all in black, and clung to his lady nurse. And that was their last meeting. When he was just thirteen months old, the puny baby had been crowned James VI, King of Scotland. Dressed in cloth of gold embroidered by his mother, he had been carried in his nurse's arms to the grim gray kirk in Edinburgh for the coronation ceremony. The aged Presbyterian preacher, John Knox, in a long fur-trimmed gown, came leaning on a stick, to preach the coronation sermon.

From then on, the boy king growing up in the castle was constantly under someone's eyes, for he was constantly in danger. Friends of his mother might murder him, he was told. She had escaped from Scotland, fled to England, but the Catholic nobles wanted to restore her to the throne. One day his uncle Mornay, who ruled for him, had been murdered. Five days later his "guidsire" (that grandfather whose hand he had held when he had first met the Parliament) lay stiff and dead. The next morning two men came and fastened iron bars across the window of the boy's room, bars that threw horrible shadows over his bed at night and frightened him so that he could not even scream.

Every morning a tutor had come to give Jamie his lessons. His head was so big for his small, weak neck that he could hardly hold it up, sometimes he looked as though he might not be bright enough to learn anything. But on the contrary, he could memorize long lessons in Greek, Latin, geography, astronomy, history, and philosophy, and his mind became literally crowded with facts. About the only exercise he had was hunting, for while his rickety legs did not hold him up well enough to walk unaided, he could ride a horse.

At seventeen James had really begun to govern Scotland. And he had had great hopes of governing England one day, until this miserable business of his mother's trial and death had come up to embarrass him. He had been careful what he wrote to his "Cousin Elizabeth" about the trial, but now that his mother had been actually beheaded, he feared it would look bad not to show some indignation. He did so. He declared that the deed must be avenged, and added that no messengers from England must cross the border into Scotland. His own messengers would receive all necessary letters at the border. Two letters soon came from England. One was from Walsingham, expressing his opinion that James VI would be the next king of England. This made it very easy for James to believe the words in the other letter, which came to him from Queen Elizabeth, declaring her innocence, saying she "had never thought to put the queen your mother to death."

"Ye purge youre self of ane unhappy fact," James was happy to reply, and hoped further "her honourable conduct would become known to the world."

That done, he gave thought to the years he might wait to be king of England. How many years of waiting might that be? Fifteen, sixteen? It could be. Elizabeth, now fifty-eight, might well live to the full age of threescore years and ten. . . . However, with a bonny bit o' good fortune for him she might not. There was always a chance that agents of the King of Spain might cut her life short. It was also now known for a fact that Philip II was building a great fleet of ships, making ready to attack England and invade the country. . . .

"LORD ROANOKE" AND VIRGINIA DARE

SPRING WAS HERE AGAIN. The spring of 1587. The enthusiastic Raleigh had again completed plans for founding a colony in Virginia. On May 8, settlers and crews were aboard the ships in Plymouth Harbor ready to sail. There were seventeen women, with bags and bundles, and nine children, hanging to their mothers' skirts or tearing around getting into mischief.

The Governor of the colony, this time, was to be John White, a modest, sensitive man and a talented artist. He had been to Virginia on the previous attempt at settlement. While Lane and Drake had brought back tobacco, John White had brought back his maps and drawings of the Indians, the finest ones to reach Europe.

Governor White's daughter Eleanor and her husband, Annanias Dare, were also going. They were expecting a baby before the end of the summer, but not until August. By that time, they thought, they would surely have a little house of their own built on the beautiful island of Roanoke. What should they call the baby, this first girl or boy to be born in the new land? There was so much to look forward to during the long voyage, as they gazed out over the waves, up at the swelling sails, back at the white lines of foam. Then finally came the birds, the seaweed—the first sight of land. And they were there—or almost there! This was Cape Hatteras. Roanoke was five miles north.

John White himself later wrote the story, always speaking of himself, not as "I," but as "the Governor."

"The two and twentieth day of July we came safely to Cape Hatteras, where our ship and pinnace anchored. The Governor went aboard the pinnace [a small boat with a single sail], accompanied by forty of his best men, intending to pass up to Roanoke. He hoped to find fifteen Englishmen whom Sir Richard Grenville had left there the year before. At sunset we went ashore on the island in the place where the men were left. But we found none of them, nor any sign that they had been there, saving only that we found the bones of one of them, whom the savages had slain long before. . . . We found the fort razed but all the houses standing unhurt, saving that the lower rooms of them and of the fort also were overgrown with melons of different sorts and deer were in the rooms feeding on those melons. . . . The order was given that every man should be employed in remodelling those houses which we found standing and in making more cottages."

On July 28, Howe, one of the men, was killed by savages hidden in the high reeds. They espied him wading in the water, trying to catch crabs. They wounded him with sixteen arrow shots. Then they killed him with their wooden swords, and escaped to the mainland. These Indians belonged to the tribe of the chief Wingina, who had been killed by white men the year before. This the settlers learned from Manteo's people on the island of Croatan. Twenty men and their friend Manteo sailed from Roanoke to the nearby island where Manteo's people lived, "to renew our old friendship," said Governor White. "When we landed on the island, they ran away. Manteo called to them. As soon

53

as they heard their own language they returned, throwing away their bows and arrows. We asked the Croatans to tell Wingina's men, that if they would accept our friendship, we would forget all unfriendly happenings of the past. The chiefs promised the Croatans to come to (meet) us within seven days, but when they did not appear we decided to find them and take revenge. To guide us we took Manteo. The next day we landed near our enemies' dwelling place so early that it was still dark. We saw flames of their fire, and the savages sitting around it. . . . We attacked at once, taking the miserable souls by surprise. Now we realized our mistake. These savages were our friends from Croatan! They had come to gather fruits and grain (that our enemies had left). Manteo was grieved by our mistake, but he blamed the savages. If the chiefs had kept their promise the fight would not have taken place. On August 13, our friend Manteo was christened by command of Sir Walter Raleigh. He received the name Lord Roanoke in recognition of his faithful service."

On the following Sunday, a small daughter, born to Eleanor and Annanias on the eighteenth day of the month, was also christened, and "because," wrote her grandfather, "this child was the first Christian born in Virginia, she was named *Virginia Dare.*"

The Governor, now a grandfather, looking about the little settlement, must have felt that it was really taking root.

"By this time," he said, "our shipmasters were newly calking and trimming their vessels for their return to England." The settlers also prepared their letters and gifts to send home. There were plenty of supplies to last until the ship returned the following spring, but then more would be needed. Governor White was unanimously chosen to go back to England and collect them. The Governor stated that he "had no desire to return to England, not wishing to be accused of abandoning the colony, but finally they put their request in writing and he agreed to their demand."

They did not know, as they waved goodbye to him from the shore, that it was goodbye forever.

THE SPANISH ARMADA

ENGLAND was in a terrific state of suspense and panic. She was frantically preparing for what would prove to be one of the greatest events in English history, the defeat of the Spanish Armada—the tremendous fleet of ships that Philip II was building to conquer England. When Governor John White arrived he could not make his voice heard. The needs of little far-off Roanoke were as nothing compared to the needs of England. Not a single ship was allowed to leave an English harbor. Every one was needed to guard the land and fight off the attack. Terrible tales went round, of torture wheels and thumbscrews that the Spaniards were bringing to be used upon the English. All adults who did not obey Spanish orders upon being tortured were to be put to death. Seven thousand nurses were being brought over to take care of the motherless babies. As fear and suspense grew with such horrible rumors, everyone rallied to defend the country. Merchants offered their vessels, and the number increased until there were 197 of various kinds and nearly 16,000 seamen.

The army was mobilized at Tilbury, where the Spanish were expected to land. The Queen did not want war, she hated war, but now that war was here, she faced up to it with courage. She appeared at Tilbury, on horseback, dressed in armor, intending to remain there day and night as long as the soldiers did.

"I know," she told them, "I have the body of a weak and feeble woman, but I have the heart and stomach of a king. And I think foul scorn that Spain or any other prince of Europe should dare invade the borders of my realm."

On either side of her, both wearing heavy armor, rode Lord Leicester and his stepson, the handsome young Earl of Essex, who was now crowding out Sir Walter Raleigh and all other contenders for the place Leicester had so long held as the Queen's favorite.

The ships of the navy were anchored in Plymouth harbor, commanded by Admiral Lord Howard. Under him were Hawkins, Frobisher, and Drake, whose daring had already filled the Spaniards with unholy horror. Drake had a magic mirror, they said, in which he could see enemy ships beyond the horizon. By a few black-magic words he could change the way the wind blew. His most recent exploit had been to set fire to all the Spanish transport ships in the harbor of Cadiz. If he had had his way he would also have destroyed all the warships in the harbor of Lisbon. For some strange reason Queen Elizabeth would not allow him to continue this singlehanded war against Spain. So the Spanish Armada was on its way, or would be as soon as spring came again. The order had gone out to ports along the east coast that bonfires were to be lighted to spread the word as soon as any Spanish ships were sighted.

Philip II was a patient man. For thirty years he had been tormented by the English. They had captured his treasure ships, raided his colonies in the New World, helped the Netherlands rebel against him. And he had done nothing about it. He drove his advisers almost mad. They could not seem to get it through his head that he would never regain the Netherlands, never be safe in the New World, until England was conquered. Finally he saw the light. Then his impatience to start, without enough preparation, was equally maddening. He would take no word of advice, not even from his oldest and most able commander, the Marquis of Santa Cruz, who was to command the Armada. Santa Cruz pointed out that, for one thing, they needed to secure safe ports along the North Sea before they started out. Philip II would not listen. He knew better. The Armada must sail in April, he said, April, 1588. He had worked out all the dates and details. The Marquis of Santa Cruz did not live to carry them out. He died in February.

The Duke of Medina Sidonia, a wealthy nobleman, was then chosen by Philip II to replace his great admiral. Medina Sidonia was no coward, for he had saved Cadiz from Drake. But, he wrote the King, it actually made him seasick to go on board a ship. He was sure to fail. Philip II replied calmly that he could not fail in this cause of God, and sent him his orders. Sidonia was simply to sail up the English Channel and clear out the English ships, so that the Duke of Parma, who was gathering troops in the Spanish Netherlands, could transport them across the Channel and invade England.

Now the Duke of Medina Sidonia had no choice but to obey his King. He joined the fleet at the port of Lisbon, where he found matters in horrible shape. Spoiled food and bad water had given the crews dysentery. Fish and meat were rotten, the biscuits were crawling with worms.

The Duke did the best he could to improve conditions, to repair the ships and to get more food and ammunition. And when at the end of May the new day for sailing came, he gave the order to sail. At sunrise the gun was fired and the flags unfurled. Trumpets were sounded, prayers were said, and the vessels set forth.

A terrible storm arose, and the damaged ships were driven back into port. Medina Sidonia made an unsuccessful attempt to persuade Philip to give up the expedition. It was not until July that the ships actually sailed out into the ocean. A week later they sighted the English coast. Very soon they saw columns of smoke rising at intervals, then beacons flaring, evidently spreading the news that they had been sighted from the shore. . . .

At Plymouth on the afternoon of Friday, the nineteenth, day of July, 1588, the English sea captains were engaged in a game of bowling on the green, just to pass the time away. Drake, Frobisher, Hawkins, and Lord Howard. They had not been able to get permission from the Queen to sail out and attack the Spanish fleet before it got started, so there they were, with their ships still anchored in the harbor.

Suddenly a small boat scudded in from the sea, a sailor rushed ashore with the news that the first ships of the Armada had been sighted off the Lizard Point. There was no time to lose.

Drake picked up his ball, so the story goes, saying, "We've plenty of time to finish the game and beat the Spaniards, too."

However, there was a strong wind blowing in from the sea, and it would take quick work and skillful maneuvering all night to get the vessels out of the harbor, if they were not to be caught "like rats in a trap." All through the night could be heard the creak of rigging, the sounds of voices shouting orders, the splash of water, the flap of sails in the wind as the vessels one by one warped out of Plymouth harbor. They were all small, fast sailing ships, and by Saturday afternoon fifty-four of them were almost out to the Eddystone Rocks. It was about dawn on Sunday morning when the English captains first caught sight of the Spanish fleet. Old-fashioned clumsy ships they were, towering deck upon deck above the water. The huge ships were then sailing slowly up the Channel in a curved formation—a crescent, seven miles long.

As soon as they were within range, the English began firing on them, darting here and there like terriers at the heels of a mastiff, but never coming near enough for the Spaniards to throw out their grappling hooks. The Spaniards tried to return the fire, but their guns were so high that the cannon balls passed over the decks of the low English ships and did almost no damage.

All day the English under Drake and Howard kept up their low firing into the Spanish hulls, scoring some hits on the flagship of the rear squadron. By evening the unfortunate Medina Sidonia was forced to abandon two of his best ships, one of which had been blown up by gunpowder stored on deck, one crippled by a collision. Day after day the Spanish fleet sailed on up the Channel with the English following. Medina Sidonia sent frantic letters to Parma, in the Netherlands, asking for small ships and cannonballs.

Parma was regretful, but he was not a naval commander, he was a general. He had only flat-bottomed barges for transporting his soldiers, either to fight on shipboard in a sea battle, or to take them across to invade England after the sea victory was won. As a matter of fact he did not even have his barges ready in time to join the Armada.

Sunday came again. It was one dreadful week since the Armada had sighted the English shore. The Spanish ships were anchored near the harbor of Calais, on the French coast. The day wore on, ominously quiet. Just after dark the Spanish saw unusual lights moving among the English ships. At midnight eight dark objects came floating toward them and burst into flame. They were fireships, flaring in the wind! Medina Sidonia ordered pinnaces to make a screen and to grapple with and tow the fireships away. However they came in such close formation that this was not possible, and only two fireships seem to have been beached. In panic, the captains of the fleet cut their anchor cables and let their ships loose. What a disaster!

The next morning found the Spanish ships scattered. Some managed to return to formation, but these were left to fight what it was plain to see must be a losing battle. This lasted from nine in the morning to six at night. The Spaniards fought desperately and with great courage. But the English gunfire was devastating and by the day's end many Spanish ships were badly hurt.

Medina Sidonia felt he must save as much of the fleet as he could. The Spaniards would not surrender, but their ammunition was gone. It was decided to sail north around Scotland, out into the Atlantic and from there home.

The English began the next day in high spirits, certain that in a few hours they would have a complete victory. But, suddenly, at a moment's notice, the wind changed and a terrific storm blew up, in which the Spanish ships sank or were scattered, and the English had all they could do to save their own.

That was enough, said the Queen. God sent the wind and scattered their ships. They would pursue the Spaniards no further. Drake would have allowed no Spanish ships to escape, but royal orders had to be obeyed. The campaign was over.

Many Spanish ships sailing for home by way of the Atlantic were dashed to pieces on the rocky coasts of western Ireland. Several thousand sailors were drowned or killed by soldiers. Only 65 of the 137 ships that started ever got back to Spain, and fewer than half of the 24,000 men. At home, the Spaniards were horrified at the disaster. Some blamed Medina Sidonia. Others blamed Parma. All clamored for vengeance, except the King.

Philip II, alone, received the news with perfect calm, had no word of blame for anyone. He accepted the defeat as God's will. He was now a sick man, pale and wan and suffering constant pain.

With this defeat of the Spanish Armada the power of Spain was broken and the supremacy of England began. It was a turning point in English history, the high spot in the reign of Queen Elizabeth. In November the Queen decreed that thanksgiving services should be held in every church in England in gratitude for "the common safety of them all, accomplished by special favor of God."

The streets of London were draped with swags of blue cloth, the color of the sea, as Queen Elizabeth went in state to St. Paul's Cathedral to offer thanks. Crowds lined the streets to see her pass in a gilded coach. There she was! She was wearing a purple gown. Her red hair sparkled with jewels. This was their queen! God bless her, their good Queen Bess! And these were her people she looked out upon—her good English people! Who could wish for more on that glorious day than to be their queen—the queen of England?

WAR OF THE THREE HENRYS

THE YEAR of the Spanish Armada saw the French people involved in another of their wars of religion, known as the War of the Three Henrys. As the year began there was a lull in the fighting. Henry of Navarre, the small, dark, lively leader of the Huguenots, had retired temporarily to his castle in southern France.

Henry III, the weak and pretty king, had made a sort of halfway peace with Henry of Guise, head of the Catholic League.

Tall, blond, handsome Henry of Guise, who now carried a distinguished scar across one cheek, had become so popular and so powerful that, to keep the peace, he had been forbidden by the King to enter Paris. Scornful of the King, pretending not to understand the order, Henry of Guise marched into the city with his troops and swaggered boldly into the palace of the Louvre. Henry III was so furious that he would have had the bold visitor assassinated that day before he left (as friends advised him to do), had not the Queen Mother Catherine detected and thwarted the purpose of her son.

So Henry of Guise stalked as boldly out of the Louvre as he had stalked in, and three days later he had roused the whole city in rebellion. He had the Louvre surrounded and besieged. He had the streets barricaded to cut off the various companies of royal troops from one another and from the King. Henry III barely managed to escape. Leaving through a gate in the Tuileries, he fled across the Seine and took refuge in the castle of Chartres, twenty miles away.

The Queen Mother remained in Paris. Next morning, though so ill and crippled that she could barely reach her chair, Catherine insisted upon being carried through the barricaded streets to see Henry of Guise. At each barricade she had to persuade the soldiers to make an opening, which they did, "standing aside with heads uncovered" to let her pass through. And she persuaded Henry of Guise to accompany her to Chartres to confer with the king.

It was a one-sided conference, at which the bold duke dictated humiliating terms. He forced the king: (1) to appoint him head of all the armed forces in the country; (2) to reject Henry of Navarre as heir to the throne; (3) to summon the Estates-General to nominate another heir who was a Catholic.

As the delegates from all over France gathered in the highroofed assembly hall at the palace of Blois where the meeting was held, the King saw well enough that they were all his enemies, all allied with Guise, and that he was to be further humiliated. He could see no way out of the shameful predicament but to have the powerful, insolent Guise assassinated.

"Assassinate ME! He would not dare do it!" scoffed the Duke when warned of this possible danger from the King.

Henry III was careful this time to keep his rash plan hidden from his mother, which was not so difficult as Catherine was now confined to her bed. Her apartment was on the first floor of the palace. A narrow secret stairway hidden in the wall connected it with the King's apartments on the floor above. Early on a December morning Henry had eight armed men stationed in the anteroom of his bedchamber. Shortly before nine, in the nearby council chamber, the various nobles who had been summoned for a meeting were waiting for the King to enter. It

62

was a cold, wet morning and the Duke of Guise, newly arrived and wearing a splendid coat of gray satin, was standing by the fire, when the royal secretary approached him with word that the King wished to see him privately. Guise stepped into the antechamber and the waiting soldiers did their work. Stabbed again and again, he staggered on into the King's chamber and fell at the foot of the royal bed.

Taking one look at him, the wildly excited King clattered down the secret stairway, burst into his mother's apartment, crying, "He is dead! I have killed him. Now, I am truly King of France!"

Catherine shook her head slowly. "France is ruined," she said. "You cannot sew the pieces together." She was spared the rest of her weak son's tragic story, for a few days later Catherine de' Medici's prayer was answered—her life ended.

Henry III was now completely alone. Where should he go? What should he do next? He had very little choice. A few members of the Parlement of Paris still loyal to him had assembled at Tours. So he went to Tours. And from there he weakly appealed for help to his Huguenot brother-in-law, Henry of Navarre—the heir to the throne whose rights he had so recently rejected.

Henry of Navarre was more than ready to respond, for the sake of France. Even then his chief lieutenant was drafting an appeal to the three parties in the kingdom to end their differences and unite.

It was arranged that the two Henrys should meet at the château of Tours, which stood on an island in the Loire River. There on an April day, the King, in elegant attire, surrounded by his nobles and a guard of soldiers, waited in the park while Henry of Navarre stepped into a boat and crossed the river, quite alone, as heedless of danger as he was of his appearance. The courtiers saw him come walking briskly toward them in his dusty boots, a crimson cloak flung over his torn and shabby doublet and a large white plume which he always wore on the battlefield waving in his helmet. His skin was ruddy and wind-burned, his black eyes sparkling as he swept off the white-plumed hat and fell on one knee before the King. He rose, was embraced, and arm in arm the two Henrys entered the château. Soon a proclamation was issued by the King, again naming Henry of Navarre as his successor to the throne.

Paris was now being held by a brother of the murdered Henry of Guise and his Catholic army. Navarre urged Henry III to march on Paris with their combined forces and try to recapture the capital. By July 30 they had reached St. Cloud on the outskirts of the city. Leaving the King there, Navarre was marching farther along the Seine, when word reached him to turn back—Henry III had been assassinated.

The deed, he found, had been committed by a fanatical monk who had been hired for the purpose by a sister of the murdered Henry of Guise. Having been given a magic potion which he was told would make him invisible, the gullible monk had set out for the royal camp with a knife hidden in his wide sleeve, arriving at midnight. Early next morning he showed a forged letter to the guard and was admitted to the King, who had not yet finishing dressing. As the King took the letter, the monk stabbed him in the abdomen. The King screamed, the guards rushed in. At first the King's wound was not believed fatal, but by night Henry grew worse, confessed his sins, and begged the nobles to obey Henry of Navarre as the next king.

It may be supposed that the nobles offered no protest, gathered around the King's death bed, but a day later Henry of Navarre overheard them mumbling that they "would rather die a thousand deaths than accept a Huguenot for their King." One of them told him point-blank that unless he turned Catholic, they would turn against him. And for the most part the royalist troops, who were Catholics, soon deserted Henry of Navarre. He had only his small army of Huguenots left, numbering not more than seven thousand men. Against him were twenty-five thousand troops of the Catholic League, commanded by the brother of Guise, and also six thusand troops coming in from Spain. Though the new King would have help from England, the odds were heavy against him, and five years of fighting lay ahead, from 1589 to 1594, before he would be able to enter Paris.

THE LOST COLONY

OVER A YEAR had passed since the Spanish Armada had been defeated. Governor John White was still in London. No relief ship had been sent to his little colony in Virginia, and Raleigh's fortunes were at such a low ebb that he could not finance another venture. A company of English merchants had been formed by John White to take over Raleigh's rights, but the new company ran into so many difficulties that still another year passed by before three ships were ready to sail, and it was almost four years from the day that Governor White had bid farewell to the colony of settlers that he again caught sight of Roanoke island.

What did he think? Did he really expect to find them alive? Was the hope to be shattered that he had held so long?

To his great joy, from where the ship was anchored he could see a column of smoke. Early next morning he rowed to shore with a few sailors, but found that it was only a brush fire, not made by men.

The next day they saw another fire on the island and rowed toward it, and when they came opposite, sounded a trumpet call and played familiar English songs, but got no answer. "At daybreak we landed," said the Governor, "and found the grass and some rotten trees burning. We proceeded to walk along the shore, until we came to the place where I had left our colony. As we went on shore up the sandy bank we saw a tree on the brow of the cliff curiously carved with the clear Roman letters CRO. We knew at once what these indicated. Before I left we had agreed upon a secret token. They were to write or carve on trees or doorposts the name of the place where they had settled. And they should carve a cross over the letters or name if they had trouble. We discovered that their dwellings had been torn down and that a strong enclosure with a high palisade of huge trees, had been built. One of the trees at the right side of the entrance had had the bark stripped off and five feet above the ground in clear capital letters was carved CROATAN without a cross or sign of distress. We entered the palisade where we found some iron bars, iron cannon shot and other heavy things, overgrown with grass and weeds. Some of the sailors reported a spot where several chests had been hidden, but dug up again and opened. Three of them were my own and these lay open. My things were spoiled, my books torn from their covers, the frames of my pictures and maps were rotted and broken by rain and my armor was almost eaten through with rust. Though it grieved me much to see my goods spoiled yet on the other hand I was deeply joyful for the certain token of their safe arrival at Croatan where the savages of the island were our friends and where Manteo was born.

"The next morning the captain and I agreed to go to the place at Croatan where we thought to find the planters . . . We kept on our course for two days . . . Then foul weather set in . . . So we were forced to run before the wind on the exact course for England. On Saturday, the 24th of October, we came in safely, God be thanked, to an anchorage in Plymouth . . ." No one ever knew what happened to the settlers.

At home Governor John White sent the account of his voyage to "his very good friend, the worshipful Richard Hakluyt," a student of geography, who had admired the drawings of Indians and scenes in the New World which John White had made. These were illustrations for a book on Virginia, which appeared in Latin, French, English, and German. Many years later John White's drawings were to be of great interest and help to John Smith, who in 1591 when Governor White wrote his account of the Lost Colony, was only eleven years old.

JOHN SMITH, SCHOOLBOY

JOHN SMITH, twelve years old, sat at his desk in the Free Grammar School in Louth, his hair brushed and neat, his face clean, his feet together on the floor. His Latin Grammar was open to the proper page, but his eyes were not on it. They were watching a branch of leaves waving outside the window, his mind was centuries away.

He was at the court of King Arthur. Surrounded by knights in shining armor, knights who were naturally brave and loyal and temperate and just, without ever having to memorize moral verses from a schoolbook. He was there with Tom-a-Lincoln, whose story he had been reading and was never to forget. Tom had lived right here in Lincolnshire and had grown up tending sheep on these very hills and pastures, but he was really the son of King Arthur, though he didn't know it. He had been laid at a shepherd's door with a purse of gold as soon as he was born, but never knew this until the shepherd was dying. Even then Tom did not know who his real father was, until after he had gone to King Arthur's court and become a knight, and come back from faraway countries as a hero. Then as the great King Arthur lay dying he told Tom-a-Lincoln who he really was! John sighed.

If only he had lived in those wonderful days! If only he could have been a knight, instead of just a plain old farmer. Why, just because he was the oldest son, did he have to follow in his father's footsteps? Why must he be a farmer? There certainly must be something he could do that was brave and exciting.

Looking out of the school window through the trees, John could see the church steeple where the weathercock had been blown off in the same storm that wrecked the Spanish Armada. There! That was something he'd like to do—fight those Spaniards if they ever tried to conquer England again. But for that he'd have to be in the navy—or somehow get aboard a ship. Sometimes he was almost ready to sell his satchel and books and everything he had, steal away, and go to sea.

He could walk to Lynn. It was only about sixty-five miles or so, if you went by way of Boston. And Lynn was a big seaport. Yet he didn't feel comfortable going straight against his father's wishes. A boy should respect his father's feelings, and if he went to sea as a common sailor his father would feel disgraced. But how else could he get started? He was not a king's son, nor a relative of the Queen, nor the son of Lord Willoughby or of any other lord or gentleman. Nobody would single him out!

In time John Smith's father himself had a suggestion to make. How would John like to be a merchant? Master Thomas Sendall of Lynn, whom he knew, was the greatest merchant in those parts, shipping wool and other products to the Continent. He had a warehouse down by the wharf, where ships came in from the Atlantic, the Mediterranean, and even the Indian Ocean. What would John say to becoming an apprentice to this great merchant of Lynn? When he was fifteen, he would be old enough, and his father would be willing to sign the papers, if John agreed. John certainly did agree. It looked far better to him than being a farmer. To be where ships came in from the Atlantic, the Mediterranean, and even the Indian Ocean! Who could tell what might happen there? It could well be that Master Sendall might send him to sea!

SIR WALTER RALEIGH was now out of favor with the Queen and had retired to an estate which he had in Ireland, to wait until he saw some way to get back into the Queen's good graces.

"Nobody is with the Queen now but my Lord Essex," it was being said in London. After the death of Lord Leicester, Raleigh and Essex had been bitter rivals for the Queen's favor and about to fight a duel, when Raleigh, losing out, left London for Ireland.

Here in Ireland he occupied his time remodeling his castle, experimenting with potatoes and tobacco, and reading and writing poetry. Besides his old favorites Homer and Virgil, he relished a new long poem being written by a neighbor, an Englishman who lived not too far away at Kilcolman Castle in the County of Cork.

Edmund Spenser was the poet's name and his poem was called *The Faerie Queen*. It was an allegory laid in the days of King Arthur, in which Queen Elizabeth was represented as Gloriana, the "Queen of Faerie Land." On the first page was this dedication.

To the most high mightie and magnificent

Empresse

renowned for pietie, vertue and all gratious government

ELIZABETH

to live with the eternitie of her fame.

Three parts were already completed, and the enthusiastic Raleigh urged Spenser to come with him to London. He would introduce him to the Queen and the Queen would certainly have the poem published.

Spenser fell in with Raleigh's plan for going to London, but first he said he must write an introduction telling his readers what his poem was about in case they might not understand the allegory. This he put into form of a letter to "the right Noble and Valorous Sir Walter Raleigh, Knight."

That done, Spenser still had to write complimentary verses introducing his poem to a long list of influential people, from "That excellent Lord, the Earl of Essex," on down, including all the gracious and beautiful Ladies in the Court.

All preparations finally completed, the poet Spenser and the promoter Raleigh set forth for London with the poem. Their visit was well timed. Raleigh's rival, Lord Essex, was banished in disgrace. He had married, and the Queen was furious. No favorite of hers had the right to marry without her permission!

Queen Elizabeth was ready indeed to turn her sweet smiles upon Sir Walter, the still faithful bachelor, and to bestow her gracious favor also upon Edmund Spenser. She granted the poet a yearly pension of fifty pounds, which was no great amount, but it almost gave Lord Burghley a heart attack to spend even that much money for a poem.

The first parts of the "Faerie Queen" were published in 1590 and its author proclaimed the foremost poet of the day. Spenser returned to Ireland but Sir Walter Raleigh, delighted to be at court again, stayed on enjoying the society of the Queen, until the summer of 1592. Then Lord Essex got back into her favor and Raleigh was banished in disgrace. He, alas, had also fallen in love. What made the crime even worse, his beloved was a Maid of Honor to the Queen, and so was also allowed no love affairs without Her Majesty's permission.

"Off to the Tower with them!" was the royal decree.

So Sir Walter Raleigh and Elizabeth Throckmorton were married in the Tower of London and spent their honeymoon in separate cells. Both were released in a few weeks, but Lady Raleigh was never forgiven and Sir Walter never allowed to return to court.

ON A LATE APRIL DAY in 1593, a young man who had just celebrated his twenty-ninth birthday was passing through St. Paul's Churchyard in London toward the sign of the White Greyhound, a stationer's shop where his first book of poems was being offered for sale. His name was William Shakespeare. By profession he was an actor. He was also a playwright, but since plays were written only for actors to use and not printed to be read, they did not count as literature.

This poem was, as he called it, the "first heir of his invention." He was pleased that the printer and publisher Richard Field, a friend from his home town, had made it into a fine-looking little book. The name stood out sharply on the title page, which was used to advertise it, and the page showed up well among the other notices stuck on various posts along the streets.

He sincerely hoped that the young Earl of Southampton, to whom he had dedicated the poem, would enjoy it. His Lordship was only nineteen years old, just the right age to appreciate the old familiar story of Venus and Adonis, put into verse. That was the poem—*Venus and Adonis*—the story of the love-sick goddess who wooed the young hunter but with all of her wiles failed to win the "rosy-cheeked" lad, since it was "hunting he loved and love he laughed to scorn." If the young Lord was pleased with the poem, he would pass it about among his friends at court. That should make it popular and profitable, which was important for a young writer who needed to earn his living.

Noblemen who wrote verses, as most of them did, could afford to be less commercial. They passed their poems around among their friends at court in their own handwriting. It was more elegant and exclusive than having them printed.

Young university graduates, however, from Cambridge and Oxford, whose writing was also a means of livelihood, were definitely eager to see their works in print. The home of Sir Walter Raleigh was a favorite meeting place for one group of these young men from the universities. Among them all, the most brilliant, in Will Shakespeare's estimation, the one he most admired, was Christopher Marlowe.

Marlowe was a graduate of Cambridge with a master's degree, and he was a genius. His play *Tamburlaine the Great,* was truly original, the first English play to be written in blank verse. Shakespeare had been so impressed by its style when he saw it produced, that he adapted the style for his own play *Henry VI.*

This play was the first one in which Shakespeare used characters from English history. The audiences had liked it immensely. It proved so popular, in fact, that it roused the jealousy of a sharp-tongued university writer by the name of Greene, who fairly frothed at the mouth when he found that an actor had written it. Greene also wrote plays, and successful ones, but he had no respect for "ignorant" actors, who merely repeated "the words that playwrights put in their mouths to say, having no thoughts of their own."

"Actors," he said, "are like the crow in Aesop's fables, who decked himself out in other birds' feathers."

What irritated Greene still more was that actors made more money than he did. And when he saw an "upstart crow" of an actor set himself up as a playwright, his pent-up wrath exploded into words. Pouncing on a line in the play of *Henry VI,* in which the Duke of York rails against a wicked queen, saying:

"O tiger's heart wrapped in a woman's hide!" Greene read it: "O tiger's heart wrapped in a player's hide!" Seizing his pen, he wrote, "There is an upstart crow, who, with his tiger's heart wrapped in a player's hide supposes he is as well able to bombast out blank verse as the best of you, and being an absolute Johnny-do-everything, is in his own conceit the only SHAKE-Scene in the country." He then went on to beg Christopher Marlowe and the other poets to take warning from

72

his own poverty-stricken state, and not waste their time writing plays.

Shakespeare naturally did not enjoy reading these words, and said as much to the editor who had published them. But he spoke in such a courteous and reasonable way that the editor published an apology.

The irritable Green died shortly after the tirade. Imagine what he would have said had he lived to see the "upstart crow" further invade his field and become the author of a published poem that became so popular as did *Venus and Adonis*. Every year for nine years the poem was reprinted, and undergraduates at Cambridge, it was said, slept with copies of it under their pillows.

The author, who was never idle, immediately wrote and dedicated another poem to his wealthy young sponsor. It was fortunate that this poem too was profitable, for as an actor, William Shakespeare was out of a job. The theatres in London, all three of them, were then closed because of the plague. As soon as the theatres reopened he would be acting again and writing plays. For first and always, William Shakespeare was an actor and a playwright.

Queen Elizabeth loved the theatre; so did the court. All of the English people were glad to pay their hard-earned pennies to see a good show full of blood and thunder and excitement. Except the Puritans, who said that all theatres should be destroyed. They were temples of sin. Actors were "fiends, hell hounds and vipers" sent by Satan to lure people to eternal damnation, with their glitter and tinsel. When the plague came and the theatres had to be closed they called it punishment from God for allowing such vile places to exist, even though they had to be built outside the city walls, and there were only three. The THEATRE and the CURTAIN were a mile out on Shoreditch Road, and the ROSE across London bridge in Southwark.

The plague became so severe that soon a thousand people were dying every week. Soiled bedding and rags were heaped up in the alleys, infested with black rats which carried the disease, though no one suspected it. One man, however, who had visited a clean German city, did venture the opinion that if slums were torn down, and filthy alleys

73

cleaned up, there might be no more plagues. This struck the City Council as far-fetched as well as impractical, but they knew that large gatherings of people caused the plague to spread. And so the theatres were closed in September, 1592, not to be reopened for two years.

That left the theatre companies stranded. Many actors formed traveling groups, filled a wagon full of costumes and properties and toured the outlying towns and provinces, where they put on their plays in the courtyards of the inns or in the local Guild Halls. One company, known as the Queen's Men, went to Stratford-on-Avon. This was a town northwest of the city, about seventy-five miles away, where Shakespeare had been born and had lived until he came to London.

There little Will Shakespeare had seen his first play. In the year 1568, when he was four years old, the first touring company ever to visit Stratford put on a play in the Guild Hall. His father was then High Bailiff (or mayor), and wore a scarlet robe trimmed with black fur at Council meetings, at church, and for all such special occasions as the theatre. Mr. Shakespeare and his Council saw the play first to make sure that it was "godly and learned as well as mirthful," and since it met with their approval, they paid the actors and the people came in

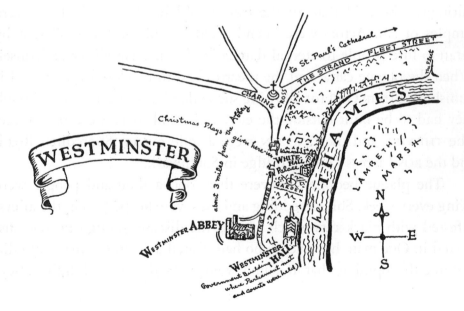

free. The hall was crowded. As High Bailiff, Mr. Shakespeare in his scarlet robe occupied the front bench. Standing between his father's knees, a small boy of four had a perfect place to see and hear.

The year that Will was twelve, two companies came. The leading actor in one of the companies was James Burbage, who took his part so well that it was hard to believe he was not actually the character he was playing. What a great difference there was in the way actors spoke their lines! Some sounded the way people really talked and others sounded false. Part of that was of course the fault of the men who wrote the speeches. Sometimes it was easy for Will to see where a little change would make it sound just right. . . .

Every summer more and more companies came from London. In 1587 five of them played in Stratford. James Burbage's son Richard,

who took leading parts that year, seemed to Shakespeare an even better actor than his father. He was only twenty. (Shakespeare was twenty-three.) Yet Richard Burbage was an established actor with a good income. Actors, he said, were well paid in London, where the theatres were always crowded with people. There were three theatres there and an opportunity to be an apprentice to one of the older actors and learn the ins and outs of the acting profession like that of any other trade. London was the place to begin.

And so before very long William Shakespeare left Stratford-on-Avon and went down to London. And when he went he left behind not only his father and mother, brothers and sisters, but also his own wife Anne and their three children, Susanna, who was about five, and the twins Hamnet and Judith, who were two years younger.

Anne Shakespeare, who had been Anne Hathaway before she was married, was eight years older than her husband and had been brought up as a Puritan. Perhaps she refused to go to London with him, feeling that it was not respectable to be the wife of an actor. Perhaps she preferred to bring up her children in Stratford, where they could go to the same good free school that their father had attended.

Whatever the reason, Shakespeare, unlike most of the actors, who had their wives and children with them, lived in hired lodgings which he found in Shoreditch, within walking distance of the THEATRE and the CURTAIN. There he worked with Richard Burbage and his brother Cuthbert, who became his best friends. In acting and directing he progressed rapidly, and he had written three plays, *Two Gentlemen of Verona, The Comedy of Errors,* and *Henry VI,* before the plague closed the theatres and he turned to writing *Venus and Adonis.* Perhaps he paid a visit to his home town of Stratford during that time. No one knows. But when the plague was over and the theatres reopened, Shakespeare was back in London ready to step on the stage again, and had another play ready for rehearsal. It was called *Love's Labours' Lost,* a comedy in which he called the leading character the King of Navarre and the other characters also had names taken from news reports coming in from France.

THE WHITE-PLUMED HENRY

QUEEN ELIZABETH, the court, and all of England watched with extreme interest what was happening in France. The failure to conquer England with his Armada had not discouraged Philip II from trying to gain control of France. Piles of gold and thousands of soldiers were being sent in to help the Catholic League, and Philip had high hopes of making his daughter Isabella Queen of France.

All of England's sympathy lay naturally with Henry of Navarre, the Huguenot, the rightful heir to the throne, and Queen Elizabeth had begun sending soldiers to help him as soon as possible after Henry III was assassinated. That was the summer of 1589. At that time Henry of Navarre had had such a small army left that he had had to abandon the attempt to capture Paris. He went north on the seacoast to Dieppe,

77

where the English troop ships were due to arrive. There almost at once, with his back to the sea, Henry had to battle the forces of the League, commanded by the brother of Guise. In spite of their overpowering numbers, Henry managed his troops so skilfully in a triangular valley beneath the castle of Arques that he won the battle.

The white plume was still flying bravely in his helmet when the English fleet came at last, with four thousand soldiers aboard, commanded by the Earl of Essex. There was wining and dining aboard the flagship in the harbor. Toasts were drunk and guns fired in salute to Queen Elizabeth and Henry IV, champions of the Protestant cause. From then on Protestants in the Netherlands and Germany also were praying for Henry of Navarre in his fight to be recognized.

All winter Henry spent in Maine and Normandy, riding and fighting continually, never being able to lodge his army for even one night without "having in some sort to fight for its shelter." But as he went, town after town was captured, and four-fifths of the bishops recognized and accepted him.

The spring of 1590 brought his most famous victory—the battle of Ivry, near Mantes, where he was faced by the combined armies of the League and Spain, reinforced by hired German soldiers. It was on a cold, windy morning following a night of rain. After a few hours' sleep, Henry jumped up from a pile of straw in a barn, wide awake, refreshed, outwardly gay, inwardly calm, as always.

"My comrades," he said, "God is with us. We face His enemies and ours. If you miss your banners in the battle, rally to my white plume. You will find it always in the path of victory and honor."

He gave the order, the artillery opened fire on the enemy, and the battle began. The German soldiers, caught by the fire, retreated so fast that they broke the ranks of cavalry behind them, and all men and horses scattered in wild confusion in the blinding smoke. Through an opening in the smoke, Henry suddenly saw what had happened. He spurred his horse and dashed forward. His soldiers followed, their eyes on his white plume. In less than an hour after it began the battle was over, the army of the League had been defeated and the victory won.

That was a happy night for Henry IV. That night he slept in most luxurious comfort at the château of his good friend the future Duke of Sully on the banks of the Seine. Next morning, up bright and early as usual, he went hunting with horse and hounds in the woods between the castle and his headquarters at Mantes.

From there he began another siege of Paris. In this second siege he cut supplies from the city and tried to force the people to surrender from starvation. After two months, the people had devoured all the food, eaten cats, dogs, and even rats, and were grinding the bones of the dead into flour. Henry could stand it no longer . . . He sent word that all those who wished to leave the city might do so, without harm.

Queen Elizabeth was utterly disgusted, and sent him a letter saying, "I am astonished. You are too tardy in doing yourself good. If so many had not left the city, by your permission, starvation would have forced Paris to yield."

Henry knew that, but he did not want Paris at such a price. "I love my city of Paris," he explained. "I am like the mother in the Book of Solomon. I should almost rather not have Paris at all than have her ruined and laid waste with so many persons dead."

The next concession that Henry IV made to save all of France from further suffering so antagonized and offended Queen Elizabeth that her letters to him were filled with sarcasm and irony.

In 1593, Henry of Navarre, the Huguenot, renounced the Protestant form of Christianity, and was received by the Cardinal of Broughes into the "Catholic Apostolic and Roman religion."

For some time members of the Estates-General and of the League who had turned against Spain had been urging him to accept the religion held by the majority of the nation, and so gain their support. It seemed the wise thing to do. Especially since he knew that as king he could then assure to the Huguenots their freedom of worship. Even his good friend Sully, a staunch Huguenot thought it advisable. To another who reproached him, Henry said he saw no other way out.

"And perhaps after all the differences between the two religions are created largely by the mutual antagonism of those who preach them. Some day by my own authority I will try to overcome it."

The coronation of Henry, King of Navarre, first of the Bourbon family, the last family of kings to rule over France, took place in the grand old cathedral at Chartres in February, 1594.

A month later Henry IV, in full armor, crossed the bridge of St. Michel and entered Paris, walked to the cathedral of Notre Dame and there gave thanks for the deliverance of the city. Bells rang in all the churches and crowds gathered, curious to see the man who they had been told for years was a ruthless fiend and a devil. They were relieved and delighted as they saw him walk to the Louvre, carrying his white plumed helmet. Though his hair was gray, his step, his look, his

Paris!

actions were those of a man young in body and spirit. Nothing escaped
him. He saw one soldier steal two loaves of bread and made him give
them back to the baker. He paid the debt of another soldier who had
been seized by a bailiff. He had sheets printed giving his free pardon
to all except the assassins of Henry III. He dined at the Louvre at a
long table heaped with meat and fruits and wine, leaving the doors
flung open for the entertainment of the people who enjoyed seeing
royalty at the table.

Next afternoon he watched from a window over the gate of St.
Denis while the Spanish troops marched solemnly out of the city. As
they saluted him, not too willingly, he waved and called:

"Commend me to your master King Philip, gentlemen, but come
back here no more."

Henry IV was the first and greatest of the Bourbon kings. Assisted
by the Duke of Sully, his chief minister, he devoted all his energies to
restoring agriculture and trade, and repairing the damages done to
France in almost forty years of war.

Never forgetting the cause of those wars, Henry IV issued and
signed the Edict of Nantes on April 13, 1598. This was an act of justice which guaranteed to Huguenots freedom of worship and the same
civil rights as Catholics in schools, parliaments, and courts. It was to
be one hundred years before the great principle of religious freedom
was to be recognized in England.

El Greco

EL GRECO AND PHILIP II

THIS KNEELING FIGURE of the lonely King of Spain is from "The Dream of Philip II," a large canvas by the great painter of Spain known as EL GRECO, meaning "the Greek." For he was a son of Spain only by adoption. When he arrived in the old city of Toledo in his late thirties, about 1576, he came carrying a long roll of canvas. A strange-looking man he was, in a long sable-lined coat, with a strange intent look in his eyes as if he saw through human forms to the spirit lying within. To those who asked he gave his name as Domenico Theotocopuli. Stumbling over the last name, they called him Domenico the Greek, and then simply EL GRECO.

To those who asked why he had come to Toledo and from whence, he told them he had come from Rome, because Rome, once the holy

city, had grown worldly and dissipated, and Toledo was the home of the spirit. Here he could live and breathe and paint. Then he unrolled his paintings and the good Dons of Toledo gazed in amazement, shocked by the strange, wraith-like figures floating in space, unlike any they had seen before, puzzled and yet moved by them. They gave him an order to make an altar painting for the church, but when it was finished they were so terrified by the scene that they refused to pay him for the painting. They were ordered to do so by the judge after a famous trial which spread the name of the painter throughout all of Spain. It reached the ears of Philip II, who ordered a painting for the church of the Escorial, fifteen feet high and ten feet wide. Philip took one look at it, shuddered, refused to have it hung, and commanded the artist to hide it away as a shameful thing. The saints were too large and too white. They stood on nothing. All the martyrs were naked. It was a monstrosity!

The artist accepted the verdict of the king with the self-assurance of one who knew his own worth and in addition never was lacking well-paid commissions for portraits and paintings.

The "Dream of Philip II" shows the King kneeling beside his father, Charles V, and gazing into a cloudy heaven filled with angels, while behind him the wide-open jaws of a monster from Hell are filled with miserable sinners.

In 1598, the dreams which Philip II had cherished of conquering England and ruling over France, of laying down law to the whole world, had crumbled away to nothing. And he had not long to live. . . .

Sick and stooped and old, he could occasionally be seen shuffling slowly along the endless corridors of the Escorial leaning on the arm of a chunky boy of fifteen, his son Philip, talking to him, asking him questions about government. The boy took so little interest as to be the despair of his father, who wished it were possible to leave the throne to his lovely, capable daughter Isabella.

As weeks passed and he could no longer sit at his desk, or shuffle along the corridors, he spent hours in the window of his chamber looking down upon the altar of the church, watching the priest conducting the mass and listening to the chanting of the monks.

Under the altar was a chamber containing the coffins of the dead, where he would soon lie. He worked out careful details for his burial service, the size of the coffin, the height of the bier, which must not be so high that smoke from the candles would blacken the ceiling. . . .

Many days and nights were spent in agony before the end came. Three days were spent in making a confession of his whole life. He said he had never knowingly harmed a human being for his own gains. The Archbishop of Toledo stood by his bedside when the king said, "Now, give it me, the time has come." A consecrated candle in one hand, a crucifix in the other, he breathed his last and was gone.

Then the bells rang, carrying the word from village to village across the length and breadth of Spain . . . across the mountains to France, across the Channel to England. Ships carried it across the oceans to South America, and Mexico, and to the islands in the far Pacific that had been named for him, the Philippines. To all the great empire of Spain, which he had patiently and painstakingly sought to rule to the best of his ability, went the word that Philip II was dead. Philip III was king.

It was in the year 1598 that Philip II died, on September 12. Almost exactly six months before that, Henry IV had established the great principle of religious freedom, against which Philip II had fought so blindly and fanatically—the principle so deeply valued and widely accepted in all free nations today.

84

JOHN SMITH, WOULD-BE KNIGHT

ONE FINE DAY John Smith, clad in armor and helmet, mounted on a spirited steed, rode clattering over the drawbridge of a castle, across the courtyard on into the tiltyard. There, whirling his horse about, he faced his jousting opponent, also in armor. The two went galloping toward each other, long lances extended. It looked like a tournament in the days of King Arthur, of which little John had so often dreamed. But this was no dream—no creation of John Smith's imagination. He was twenty years old and actually there at Tattersall Castle, being trained in riding and fencing by a most excellent master, an Italian gentleman who was rider to the Earl of Lincoln.

Tattersall was the earl's castle, twenty-five miles from Willoughby, and the greatest castle in Lincolnshire. Though not extremely old, it had been built like those of the Middle Ages, when each served as the fortress of a feudal lord. It had moats, drawbridges, towers and turrets, and in the cellar was a low-vaulted guardroom. There when his lessons were over John Smith sat with the guards about the open fire listening to their tales. Many had traveled far. Some had fought in battles against the "terrible Turks"—their part growing more hair-raising and valorous with every telling. In comparison John Smith's own adventures seemed exceedingly tame.

John had done his best as an apprentice to the merchant of Lynn for a year after his father had signed the papers. Then he could stand the humdrum business no longer, so he ran away. His good father was then no longer alive to know or care what he did. As for his mother, she had married again, left Willoughby, and forgotten about him, or so it seemed. John had his share in his father's estate and hoped that his guardians would let him have enough money to travel abroad. In this they had disappointed him. However, Peregrine, the younger son of Lord Willoughby, was then going to France, and arrangements were made for John to join the party, which included a tutor, two servants, and two horses. They crossed the Channel, met Peregrine's older brother Robert in Orleans, and from there they all went on to Paris. Exactly what John was supposed to do didn't seem clear to any of them, and after six weeks, "his service seeming needless," the young gentlemen gave him enough money to return to England.

The money was nearly gone by the time he reached the seacoast, so John decided to go into the Netherlands and enlist as a soldier in the war against Spain. After many months, during which he picked up ideas he was to make good use of later, the young soldier had earned enough money to continue his journey home. He went by the roundabout way of Scotland, having with him a letter from a chance acquaintance he had met in Paris, introducing him to important people at the court of King James. In Scotland, John found the people most kind, but he saw that he had neither money nor means to become a courtier. So, lacking other plans, he had returned to Willoughby, where everybody naturally was curious to see him, hear about where he had been, where he was going next, whether he was going to settle down sensibly now and run the farm. On and on they went till John could stand it no longer. He had read about knights retreating from the world and living like hermits for a while, and wondered why. Now he knew, and decided to do the same. There were two books that he had been wanting to read—books about war, one by an old Roman emperor, Marcus Aurelius, another by an Italian named Machiavelli, who had lived about a hundred years ago. With the two books in his saddle-bag, John got on his horse, rode out into the countryside, and built himself a shelter of boughs beside a brook. There he lived, reading his books, exercising his horse and feasting on venison—until his solitude was broken in upon.

To retreat as a hermit might have been common for a knight in the days of King Arthur, but it seemed strange to the sensible towns-folk of Willoughby. Well-meaning friends and relatives put their heads together. They persuaded the Italian gentleman who was rider to the Earl of Lincoln, to invite John Smith to become his pupil and stay with him at Tattersall. This had proved most agreeable to John, so long as he kept learning something new. The trouble was, he learned too quickly. He could soon handle his horse and weapons and wanted to put what he had learned to some good use.

Every night then, as he sat in the guardroom listening to tall tales of valor, he grew more and more uneasy to be up and off like a true Christian knight, on the trail of some evil dragon that needed to be slain. From all accounts, the Sultan of Turkey answered the description, snapping his jaws and threatening to swallow up another chunk of eastern Europe. John decided to set forth for Hungary, join the army of Rudolph, the German Emperor, and flourish his new sword against the Sultan Mohammed, and his "terrible Turks." The year 1600 saw him on his way.

EL DORADO—CITY OF GOLD

E L DORADO! Guiana! South America! That's the place for gold!"
exclaimed Sir Walter Raleigh. He called to his wife, Elizabeth,
to listen to what he had been reading from an old book about
the magical city of gold for which the Spaniards had long searched.

Lady Raleigh looked up from her sewing. "That's a fable, isn't
it? You don't believe such a city actually exists, as . . ."

"El Dorado? Certainly," the excited reader said, "and whatever
prince shall possess it, shall be lord of more gold, cities and people
than either the King of Spain or the Grand Turk."

It was a Spaniard, Martinez, who had called the Indian city of
Manoa "El Dorado," or city "of gold." He was led there blindfolded
by the Indians. Inside the city they uncovered his eyes. All was gold.
In the palace of the Emperor, there were life-size figures of beasts,
birds, trees; everything in his country copied in gold. At festivals, the
Indians covered themselves with gold dust until they were shining

88

from head to foot. Martinez had brought out as much gold as he could carry—rather he had been given that much—but he was robbed of it by border tribes along the Orinoco River, so that when he got to Puerto Rico he had only a few gourds filled with gold beads. These he gave to the friar who heard his confession on his deathbed. Many others had searched for the city in the jungle, but none had found it. They had not gone far enough, Raleigh believed, or they had gone the wrong way. There was every reason to believe that such a city might exist. Had not Cortez found gold in Mexico and Pizarro in Peru? Why then should not someone find gold in Guiana, and why should not he, Walter Raleigh, be that fortunate someone? Soon he was sending out explorers to look over the region and question the natives. They brought back word that the Spanish governor of Trinidad was going to try again to find El Dorado. That put Raleigh on his toes. Obtaining permission from Queen Elizabeth, who no longer cared where he went, Raleigh was off in the spring of 1595 to seek, find, and claim the fabulous city and the country of Guiana for England.

He consulted the Spanish governor of the island of Trinidad, who discouraged him from trying to go up the Orinoco River into Guiana. The Indians were hostile. They shot poisoned arrows that made their victims turn black and burst open. The Indians were hostile, thought Raleigh, because the Spaniards were cruel. He would tell them all white men were not Spaniards. He would show them a picture of their new Queen Elizabeth, who would protect them from the Spaniards.

With 160 men, Raleigh went four hundred miles up the Orinoco River into the Indian country. Most of the way the thick, poisonous jungle came to the edge of the narrow streams, and they had to use their swords to chop their way through. The steamy air was sickening. There was a maze of streams, in which they would have been lost without an old Indian guide. He kept telling them of a village just around the next bend. Coming upon it at last, they found an Indian king 110 years old. Where was Guiana? they asked him. All around them, he said. And where was El Dorado, the city of gold? they asked.

"Far off," answered the old one, "where the sun sleeps."

By that time the rains were beginning, the river was rising. On the return voyage Raleigh had planned to stop in Virginia and search for the lost colony, but they were running short of supplies, the winds were unfavorable, and so they sailed directly back to England.

Alas. The glowing report which Raleigh had to make about Guiana, the new land he had discovered and claimed for his Queen, roused little interest. If there was a city of gold, said the sceptics, why did he not bring home a sample to prove it? The Queen and her ministers found it of less importance than many other matters.

"I beseech you," Raleigh wrote to the new Prime Minister, "to move her Majesty so that she shall not lose that country of Guiana which I have discovered for her and hope to conquer without her cost."

Raleigh sent out two more expeditions in 1596, while he wrote a book—*The Discovery of the Large, Rich and Beautiful Empire of Guiana.* It was reprinted in German, Dutch, and Latin and caused a great sensation, for in it were described cannibals and people who lived in trees, warlike women who lived on the Amazon river, and a "nation of headless people whose eyes were in their shoulders and their mouths in the middle of their breasts" (a description Shakespeare later used in *Othello*).

"Though it may be thought a fable," Raleigh added, "I am resolved that it is true."

Many of his readers were also resolved that the whole strange and marvelous story of El Dorado and Guiana might very well be true. Just as many scoffed and laughed.

Let them laugh. People had laughed at Marco Polo three hundred years ago when he brought back fabulous tales of the Great Khan of China. Later these proved to be true.

How could any one who had never left home know what others saw who crossed the oceans, and traveled to far places? Or what strange things, beautiful lands, wonderful people were to be seen and discovered all around the world?

90

Part II

from 1600:

When Akbar
ruled in India &
John Smith fought the Turks

PEOPLE who were Living when

In INDIA

AKBAR
was visited by English merchants with greetings from QUEEN ELIZABETH

WILL ADAMS
first Englishman to enter JAPAN was honored by the SHOGUN

MATTEO RICCI
Jesuit missionary reached the Emperor of CHINA

RUSSIA

In 1600 the EAST INDIA TRADING COMPANY was formed

TSAR BORIS GODUNOV
turned peasants into serfs to be sold with the land.

TEA
was introduced in Europe by 1610

EL GRECO
was the great painter of SPAIN

& EVENTS that took Place

John Smith was a Soldier

A new English translation of the **BIBLE** was ordered by the King.

NEW FRANCE

NEW SPAIN

1604 CHAMPLAIN helped form the first French settlement in America.

OÑATE founded the Spanish settlement to be called **SANTA FE**

1603 JAMES I
became King of England

In ITALY

MARIA de **MEDICI** married **HENRY IV** and became the Queen of France

The first **VIOLIN** was made and the first **GRAND OPERA** performed.

The great plays of **SHAKESPEARE** were being written and played

between the YEARS 1600-1607

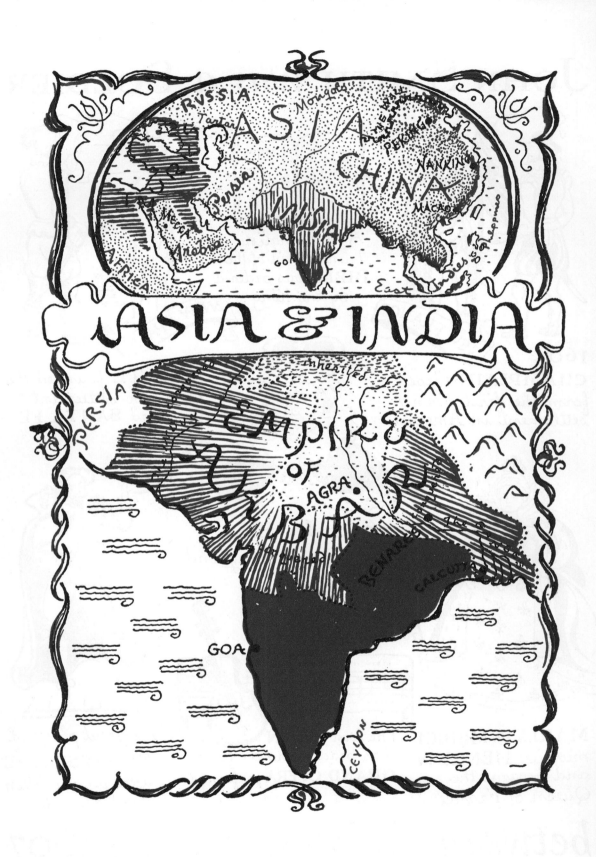

AKBAR OF INDIA

I N THE YEAR 1600, the mighty Akbar was ruling in India. He was the
Great Mogul, the ruthless conqueror of northern India, but so good
and just a ruler that the conquered people called him the "Guardian
of Mankind." Akbar's fame had spread throughout Europe. His very
name, coupled with that of the fabulous land over which he ruled, con-
jured up visions of emeralds and rubies, of jewel-bespangled elephants and most delectable spices in the minds of less fortunate rulers
such as Queen Elizabeth.

In the year 1600 Queen Elizabeth chartered a trading company, the English East India Company, and also sent her first ambassador to India—bearing a letter of introduction to the mighty Akbar.

Akbar was not a young man. He was fifty-eight and had been ruling more than forty years, two years longer than Elizabeth. But he was still so full of vitality in mind and body that he could leave anyone exhausted who tried to follow him through a day.

Seventeen years before, when he had received his first letter from the Queen of England, introducing three travelers, Akbar's favorite sport had been to ride fighting elephants in the ring and control the mighty, snorting, plunging beasts. He loved hunting. A tiger hunt usually preceded a war of conquest or a battle to quell an insurrection. He was a tireless fighter, forever conquering and adding more and more of India to his empire. Fighting, hunting, conferring with his ministers by day, he would recite Persian poetry by night, listen to music, or discuss religion and things of the spirit, with which he was also passionately concerned. After a mere two or three hours of sleep, he would be wide awake, ready for another day.

Queen Elizabeth addressed her letter to "the most invincible and most mightie prince Lord Zeladim Echebar," using her peculiar way of spelling his full name which was

JALÀLU-D-DÍN   MUHAMMED AKBAR,

meaning "Splendour of Religion"—the religion of Mohammed—and Akbar—"very great." The year of his birth, 1542, was, to him, the year nine hundred and fifty-one—meaning nine hundred and fifty-one years from the flight or Hegira of the Prophet Mohammed from the city of Mecca, holy city of the Moslems.

Two years before Elizabeth had come to the throne of England, young Akbar, then fourteen, had inherited the comparatively small kingdom in northern India which was all that was left of the territory conquered by his father's father, Babur, founder of the Mongol (or

Moghul) dynasty in India. The capital city was Agra. Babur was descended from Ghengis Khan, the greatest Mongol conqueror of all time.

Akbar's mother was Persian, and Persian was the language which he spoke. So Akbar, as a Moslem of Mongol, Turkish, and Persian blood, was completely foreign to the Hindu people of India. Yet he did not wish them to regard him as a foreigner. He determined to see that their rights and religion be protected by the law. He righted the first wrong that came to his attention. Hunting tigers west of Agra, near a holy place visited by Hindu pilgrims, he learned that each pilgrim was obliged to pay a tax. A tax for worshipping God? Would God be pleased with such a law as that? he said. Surely not. Let it be done away with. A king must be as he is called, "the Shadow of God."

So exhilarated then by having done what was right, he said to his companions, "Come on, let's *walk* back to Agra!" It was thirty-six miles; only three managed to make it.

Eager that his son and heir should be truly of India by brith, as he was not, Akbar took as his first wife the Hindu princess of Jaipur. Seven years later, although he had other Indian wives and many concubines, and there had been several children who died, he still had no son. About twenty-three miles west of Agra, in a tiny village of Sikri, there was living at this time a holy man who had made the Moslem pilgrimage to Mecca twenty-two times. Akbar appealed to him, and there in the village nine months later the King's first son was born. They named him Salim, and to glorify the lucky place of his birth, Akbar turned the village into a beautiful city, filled with magnificent palaces, mosques, temples, schools, baths, gardens, and public buildings. He called it Fathpur Sikri, "wonderful" Sikri. Some of the beautiful, though deserted, buildings are still there to be seen and admired by travelers to India today. And a mile east of Agra stands one of the world's most beautiful buildings, the Taj Mahal, built by the son of Salim, the grandson of Akbar.

A House of Worship, one of the buildings which Akbar built, he deliberately destroyed when he saw that it did not answer its purpose.

He had long been confused by the violent differences of opinion between the followers of Mohammed. So he built this house as a meeting place where Moslem scholars might discuss their differences and come to some agreement. Akbar himself presided, eager to know where the Truth lay, to better understand the will of God. He became utterly disgusted as the arguments degenerated into meaningless words, and began to search for truth in other religions.

About a year after the House of Worship was built, Akbar's interest in the Christian religion was aroused. Amazing news came from Bengal of the absolute honesty of two Christian priests in dealing with the imperial government. Upon inquiry, he learned that the best-educated Christian missionaries were at the Portuguese settlement of Goa.

His invitation to appear at his court seemed almost unbelievable to the Jesuit fathers, who had been trying in vain for many years to introduce the gospel of Christ into the Mongol empire. Three monks were appointed to go. It was a long, wearisome journey to Fathpur Sikri, but the moment they arrived, exhausted, the impatient Akbar, who did not know what "tired" meant, sent for the three monks and kept them answering questions until two in the morning. They had brought him a beautiful Bible, printed in four languages. As a sign of respect Akbar removed his turban, kissed the Bible, and placed it upon his head. He desired to know its teaching regarding the will of God. How did it differ from that of the Koran? Why not have a series of debates between the Moslem scholars and the Christians on this subject? When the debaters seemed to be too much concerned with nonessentials, it was proposed that the Truth be tested by fire. A Moslem holding the Koran and a Christian holding the Bible should enter the fire and the one who came out unhurt would be the teacher of the Truth. Akbar rather liked the idea, but one of the Jesuits objected. He refused to see any good in the teaching of Mohammed, whom he called "an infernal monster."

"Our ears hear nothing but that hideous name of Mahomet," he reported to Goa, "and we dare not speak out the truth about him."

What they had said was enough to show Akbar that the intolerance of these Christians equalled that of the Moslems. However, he built a chapel for them, had his artists copy pictures for them of Christ and the Virgin, and invited them to instruct his second son in the teachings of Jesus. He continued his search.

There was another religion which seemed to him to hold much that was beautiful and true. It was a Persian religion, derived from the teaching of the prophet Zoroaster, who lived in Persia about 600 B.C. Though it had died out in Persia, there was a group of Parsees (or Persians) in India who kept the religion alive. Akbar had learned of them during a bloody war, when he captured their city of Gugarat. Upon his return to the capital, he sent for a Parsee teacher to come to Fathpur Sikri. The Parsee spoke of God as Ahura Mazda, god of Goodness and Light, whose symbol was the Sun, which they worshipped by keeping sacred fire forever burning on their altars. Akbar had a sacred fire lighted and prostrated himself daily in prayer before the symbol of God. In the evening when lamps and candles were lighted in the palace, he insisted that the court rise in respect, saying:

"To light a candle is to commemorate the rising of the Sun."

Among the Hindus there was a sect known as the Jains, whose teaching Akbar also investigated, inviting a *guru,* or teacher, to come to court. Every living thing contains a Jiva, or soul, said the *guru.* Even the life of the smallest insect is sacred. He persuaded Akbar to release all his caged birds. Akbar even gave up his favorite sport of hunting.

Tauhid Ilahi

In all the beliefs he had investigated Akbar had found good, but still he was not satisfied. He cherished the dream of one religion that would combine the best in all of them.

He proclaimed such a religion, calling it TAUHID ILAHI, or "Divine Monotheism," the worship of the one God recognized by all men as their creator. It was short-lived. It had no real roots. It died when Akbar died. His death came at Agra in 1605. He had spent his life searching to know the Truth, trying to the best of his ability to know and follow the will of God. No one can do more.

The oldest sacred book used in the world today is the *Rig Veda* of India, written in Sanskrit about 1000 B.C. Akbar had this translated into Persian, so that he could hear it read. He had never taken the trouble to learn to read himself, but he loved and collected books and had a phenomenal memory. The writers of this ancient *Rig Veda* showed an eagerness to know about the Creator of the Universe not unlike his own. OM was the word they used for him. Later the Hindus spoke of Brahma as the Great Self within all things, saying that those who find him within themselves, "to them belongs eternal happiness, eternal peace."

The Ramayana

The *Ramayana,* the most famous poem of India, was also translated for Akbar into Persian. This is a long epic poem written about 500 A.D. by the poet Valmiki. It tells the life story of a hero prince, Rama, who was so pure and just that he might truly be called the "Shadow of God." While Akbar was having the poem translated into Persian, it was being rewritten by another poet, in Hindi, the language widely spoken by the Indian people along the Ganges River. And it was not merely translated word for word, it was so enriched in meaning and beauty by the poet TULSIDAS, that his version of the *Ramayana* became and still is the most revered and widely read poem of India.

Tulsi Das was born and lived in Benares on the Ganges River, where he saw the Hindu pilgrims coming to wash away their sins in the sacred water. Tulsi Das, who had always loved the old story of Rama, came to believe that in him Brahma (or God) had actually come to earth in human form to set an example of a pure and righteous life. Those who read of Rama's deeds, who held his image in their hearts, might be purified of sin as were those who bathed in sacred waters.

In the poem a hermit in the forest speaks to Rama, saying:

"They, Oh Rama, in whom there is no lust, anger, passion, pride, envy or violence—they, Oh Rama, who are careful to say what is both loving and true—in their hearts, Oh Rama, there indeed is your home!"

The influence of the *Ramayana* for good had been so lasting that the poet Tulsi Das has been called the greatest man of his age in India, though he lived so quietly that Akbar never heard of him.

MR. PILOT IN JAPAN

FAR TO THE EAST, a third of the way around the world from the island kingdom of England off the coast of Europe, lies another island kingdom off the coast of Asia—JAPAN, empire of the Rising Sun. Until the year 1600 no Englishman had ever visited this faraway island empire; none had ever sailed into its blue green waters, nor seen the snow-white peak of sacred Fujiyama.

The first Europeans to visit Japan had been the Portuguese, who had come about 1540, first as traders, then as Jesuit missionaries. It was soon after Columbus discovered America that the adventurous Portuguese had first sent trading ships around the end of Africa to India and on to the islands of the East. The wonderful goods which the Portuguese traders brought back, especially the spices—ginger, cloves, and pepper—were then carried to the cities of northern Europe by the Dutch. But after their rebellion against Spain, all Dutch ships were barred from Portuguese harbors. Then the Dutch, independent and en-

terprising as they were, set out themselves for the lands of the spices. They would have preferred a northern route, where they would be safe from attack by the Portuguese. Since no such new route had been found, they dared the well-known way around the Cape of Good Hope at the tip of Africa, and so reached the Spice Islands, the Malay Peninsula, and Java. They returned two years later with such valuable cargo that the next spring (the spring of 1598) twenty-two ships sailed forth from Holland for the Indies. All took the old route, except five. These five sailed west across the Atlantic Ocean and passed through the Straits of Magellan into the Pacific Ocean. On board one of the five Dutch ships, the *Liefde* (Charity), was an Englishman, an expert navigator who had been hired as the Pilot-Major of the vessel. His name was Will Adams.

This man, Will Adams, had been at sea since he was twelve years old, but of all the voyages he had ever made, this was by far the worst. The weather was bad crossing the Atlantic, the passage through the Straits was a drawn-out agony of bitter cold and hunger; while off the coast of Chile a "wondrous storm of wind" completely scattered the fleet. The Captain had been killed by hostile Indians, the crew were sick and dying, when Will Adams took command of the *Liefde* and the small battered vessel pushed its lone way across the Pacific. After a seemingly endless voyage, during which they headed north to avoid

103

Spanish ships coming from the Philippines, the Dutch ship dropped anchor on an April day in 1600, off the Japanese island of Kyushu. And Will Adams was there, the first Englishman to visit Japan. Traveling the long way around the world from the coast of Europe, he had reached the far-off islands of the Rising Sun.

Soon the shore of Kyushu, where the *Liefde* had anchored, was lined with peasants, and the water was dotted with sampans filled with fishermen in flat straw hats, squinting up at the deck of the strange-looking ship, pointing and chattering in their queer tongue. Very soon a Portuguese priest was found to act as interpreter, and though the Dutch had no love for the Portuguese, the sailors, uncertain of their fate, were glad enough to see a European face among these strange people.

It was not long before a messenger arrived from Osaka, the military headquarters of the kingdom, with the request that the two honorable foreigners come there to be interviewed by the great military leader, Iyeyasu, who was actually the ruler of the land and was soon to receive from the Emperor the official title of Shogun. The emperor, or Mikado, was a mere figurehead. The actual ruler of Japan was this military and political leader, Tokugawa Iyeyasu. His request was a command. Will Adams, with a Dutch offcer and the Jesuit priest as interpreter, journeyed to Osaka, partly by sea in a Japanese boat, and partly on horseback, attended by a bodyguard. They were treated as guests but guarded as prisoners.

The city of Osaka appeared to Will Adams to be as large as London, and its river reminded him of the Thames. The castle in which the great Iyeyasu lived was a powerful fortress rising from the water's edge, two and a half miles around, with ramparts of tremendous stones and a keep topped by a golden dolphin. Passing through gate after gate in the outer and inner walls, the prisoner-guests were ushered at last into the Hall of Audience. A screen was silently folded back. Seated before him Will Adams saw the all-powerful Shogun of Japan. A rather plump man, Iyeyasu was dressed in a dark brocaded silk robe. He had a moon-shaped face and eyes that were scarcely more than shining dark slits. His appearance gave no hint of his superior intelligence and character. Yet this man's word could mean life or death to the foreigners.

The Portuguese monk, taking advantage of the fact that the newcomers could not understand what he was saying, hastened to inform the Shogun that these Europeans were pirates and heretics. As he spoke, however, Iyeyasu observed the strangers through his narrow bright eyes, and drew his own conclusions. His round face shone with interest and curiosity when Will Adams took from his pocket a compass—something Iyeyasu had never seen before. At his bidding, Adams returned later to show him the ship's instruments, the cross-staff and the astrolabe, and try to explain the science of navigation. Iyeyasu was tremendously interested, especially in a rough map Adams had drawn to show where Japan was in relation to England and how they had come. By the time he was finally dismissed and allowed to return to the ship, the sailors, who had long believed him dead, had "weeping eyes" at the sight of him. All set to work to clean and repair the vessel for the return trip to Europe. They were waiting for permission to depart, when instead they received word to sail at once to Yedo Bay on the island of Honshu.

There they found Iyeyasu in a small fishing village called Yedo, turning it into a new capital city for Japan, to be known as Tokyo. Rising among the fishermen's huts was an old and not too elegant castle where Iyeyasu was installed, while thousands of workmen were leveling the hills, digging a wide moat, and piling up ramparts for a more elegant castle (where the imperial palace stands today).

Separated from the other sailors, Adams was escorted to lodgings in the home of a Japanese knight, or Samurai, whose daughter Bikuni San, gliding softly about in a flowery kimino, bowed and smiled a greeting and welcome to this taller, fairer man from another world.

On his first visit to the Shogun, Will Adams learned that Iyeyasu wished to buy the *Liefde* and also have "Mr. Pilot" stay on to design and build more ships, and help him increase Japan's trade with other countries. As he spoke, Will Adams realized that he was not a free man. He would never be given permission to return to England!

The thought was shocking at first, but the soft, sweet presence of Bikuni San made forgetting easy. The beguiling ways and shy artful glances of his host's younger daughter proved irresistible. Plain Will Adams, however, could not offer himself as the son-in-law to Bikuni's father. That gentleman was a nobleman—a Samurai, or "two-sworded man," one whose pride and privilege it was to carry not only a heavy battle sword, but also a small dirk with which, if necessary, to commit harikari (honorable suicide). At his next meeting with the Shogun, Adams proposed a bargain. He would design and build the ships for Iyeyasu, if Iyeyasu would grant him the two swords of a Samurai.

The swords were soon delivered by special messenger from the palace to AnJin Sama, or "Mr. Pilot" and Will Adams the Englishman became a Japanese Samurai. He was given an estate yielding ten thousand *koku* of rice and ninety farmers to till the rice fields, and his faithful and loving wife Bikuni San gave him a son, Joseph, and a daughter, Susannah. By that time, the Dutch had come to Japan in greater numbers and established a trading post on the island of Kyushu.

Meanwhile, in England, to compete with the Dutch, who raised the price of spices too high and almost tripled the price of pepper, London merchants decided to form their own company, send out their own ships, and bring back their own spices.

Eleven years later, Will Adams saw the first English spice ship appropriately named the *Clove,* arrive in Japan. The captain was to establish an English trading post in Japan, and Will Adams introduced him to the Shogun. Both suggested that Yedo was the ideal place for the trading post. Unfortunately the captain was a haughty gentleman who scorned to take the advice of Will Adams, whom he considered but a common sailor "only fit to be the master of a junk." So instead of establishing his trading post at Yedo, under the protection of the Shogun, he stubbornly insisted upon going to Kyushu, where the rival traders from Holland were already established. The sickly English trading post lasted only ten years.

ENTRANCE TO CHINA

T HE YEAR 1600, on the calendar of the great and ancient empire of China, was the twenty-seventh year in the reign of the Ming Emperor Shen Tsung, "Son of Heaven." On his red dragon throne in the purple city of Peking, Shen Tsung believed, as had all emperors before him, that this Middle Flowery kingdom was "All-that-is-under-Heaven." All wisdom and knowledge were contained in the words of the master teacher Confucius.

In the moon of summer rain, it had been announced to Shen Tsung that two foreigners from lands beyond the sea were approaching with tribute and gifts. This was not unusual. Barbarians from beyond the Great Wall had always brought tribute and useless gifts to the Son of Heaven. But these gifts, as listed, aroused the Emperor's curiosity. A map of the earth, a new chart of the heavens, a mysterious "time machine with wheels marking and sounding the hours."

Summer passed and the gifts did not appear. As Shen Tsung lounged in his Palace of Cloudless Heaven, surrounded by soft-spoken concubines and by eunuchs, the ministers who ran the empire were hopeful that the Son of Heaven had been lulled into forgetfulness. They were far from pleased when one day he asked about these foreigners and their gifts. Where were they? Let them be found and brought to him at once! Word therefore had been sent to the city of Tientsin, where the two foreigners had been arrested and thrown into prison.

In January, 1601, the last month of the Chinese year, Shen Tsung was told that the foreign gentlemen had reached Peking and were approaching the palace area, known as the Forbidden City.

From a distance the two Europeans dressed in Chinese costume did not look like foreigners. The older of the two was speaking fluently in Chinese to the eunuch who was acting as their guide. This journey to Peking was the climax of his life and work as a Jesuit missionary. He had lived in China nearly twenty years. All through those years, his dream had been to bring the teaching of Christianity to the heart of the empire. And now he was here. Father MATTEO RICCI—or as the Chinese called him, LI-MA-TOU. Soon he and his companion, a younger Jesuit, were following their guide across the vast courtyard toward a bright red palace with curving roofs of yellow tile. A flight of marble steps guarded by stone lions led to the Hall of Audience and the dragon throne.

In addition to the gifts which they were bringing, Father Matteo had a number of books on mathematics concealed in his baggage, though it was not entirely safe to have them. The proud Imperial Board of Mathematicians might suspect him of interfering in their sacred duty of computing the yearly calendar. Yet the books would be needed if his services were called upon. Though in his modest fashion Father Matteo disclaimed any great knowledge on the subject, it was his reputation as a scientist that had brought him thus far. Long ago in Rome his fellow-students had described Matteo as a mathematician. That was why the young monk had been wanted for work in China by the head of the Portuguese mission. Matteo Ricci was not Portuguese himself, but Italian. He had been sent to study law at the College in Rome founded by the Spaniard, Loyola, who originated the Jesuit order. His fondest hope was to work in the Far East, preferably China. He was fascinated by the thought of the ancient land to which Marco Polo had traveled three hundred years before and which since then had been practically unknown to Europeans.

It was in 1582 that he had landed at Macao, a small, rocky island which the Portuguese traders were allowed to rent from the Chinese as a base for their business operations. There they had a town of about seven hundred and a Jesuit mission. So far the priests had not ventured onto the mainland, and the traders were prevented from doing so by the Chinese officials, all of whom, regardless of their rank, the Portuguese called by their own name, "Mandarin."

The first Jesuit mission on the mainland was at Chao Ching, the capital of Kwantung Province. There the Viceroy, won over by the promise of a "time machine," had allowed them to build a mission just outside the city walls. As the monks worked, the ignorant, curious towns-folk watched peacefully from a safe distance until roused by a rumor that these "foreign devils" who worshipped a strange god were building their pagoda to storm the city. Then they began throwing stones.

The Viceroy, however, continued to favor Matteo Ricci and his fellow Jesuits. He recognized them as scholars, which made them worthy of highest honor in China. Gradually other Mandarins and gentlemen came to talk with the learned foreigners, charmed by their courtesy and by the fact that they did not try to force their beliefs or opinions upon their visitors.

(Confucius)

Matteo Ricci had too great respect for the ancient culture of China to think of doing so, for he had read and studied the wisdom of their great sages. Yet, since they knew so much about history, literature, poetry, and government, he was surprised to find how much less they knew about any of the sciences—geography, astronomy, or mathematics. The Chinese had many curious ideas. They thought that the sun hid at night behind a mountain on the edge of the earth; that when the moon could not be seen, it was because it had gone too far away from the sun and turned pale with fright; that volcanoes blew out sparks that caused the stars.

道

A map of the world which Matteo had hanging on his wall attracted the Viceroy, but also puzzled him. Why was the world round, when it should be flat and square? And why was the Middle Kingdom on the edge, when it was the center of the world? Matteo explained as well as he could, and then pleased the Viceroy by copying the map for him, using Chinese characters and placing China in the center. Though he considered himself far from an authority on such subjects, Matteo did his best to explain what he had learned in Rome, making charts, globes, and brass rings to illustrate his words. These novelties caused his fame to spread from province to province.

In May, 1595, after thirteen years in China, he was able to travel north with a friendly Mandarin as far as Nanking. There, a little over a year later, he handled a crisis in a way that further won the confidence of scholars and Mandarins.

The Imperial Board of Mathematicians in Peking, which was about four hundred miles north of Nanking, had sent out warning of an eclipse of the sun, telling when it would occur and how long it would last. At the proper moment all the Mandarins in Nanking had assembled and were banging on their bronze instruments to help the sun and moon through the trying ordeal, when suddenly it was over—much sooner than predicted. How did that happen, they asked in amazement. Matteo Ricci explained that an eclipse can be greater in one place than another. "They were contented," he said, "because my words did not contradict those of the Imperial Board of Mathematicians."

Father Matteo had then translated the geometry of Euclid into Chinese. This was one of the books hidden in his baggage as he entered Peking that January day in 1601.

The red dragon throne was empty as he and his companion, escorted by the eunuch, entered the Hall of Audience. They were not surprised. Foreigners must not look upon the face of the Son of Heaven. They kowtowed, touching their foreheads to the floor six times, then presented their gifts to the empty throne.

Shen Tsung, after seeing the gifts, was so curious to see the foreigners that he commanded the court painter to make portraits of the famous Li-Ma-Tou and his companion. The painter was persuaded by ministers of the Imperial Board of Rites to make them as ugly as possible. The ministers were jealous and hostile because, according to etiquette, they and not a eunuch should introduce all foreigners. Three times they tried to have Li-Ma-Tou seized and deported, but with no success. The Jesuit fathers had won the emperor's favor with their magical gifts and were allowed to remain in Peking. The small clock that chimed the hours was the gift that most fascinated Shen Tsung. He could not bear to part with it when the Empress Mother asked to see it. Yet a son's duty to parent forbade his refusing, so he had the bell disconnected, which made it no longer a thing of wonder, and she sent it back. Later it became dirty and stopped, and Ricci got word by breathless messenger to come at once and fix it.

The Jesuits were then established in a home in Peking, with four servants to care for them. Visitors soon began to arrive, eager to talk on many subjects with the learned foreigners. Father Ricci, always patient, gracious, and courteous, gradually began to explain to them the truths of the Christian faith, taking pains to point out similarities in the teachings of Confucius. For instance the "Golden Rule":

"Do not do unto others what you would not have them do unto you;" those are the words of Confucius. Christ said, "Whatsoever ye would that men should do to you do ye even so to them."

"We have not come to deny the words of your great Master Teacher, but to tell you of additional proof that God whom you call Tien has given to the world of his mercy and loving kindness."

Matteo was to live and work nine years in Peking. Before his death, which came quite suddenly in 1610, a number of the imperial family were Christians, and there was a chapel within the walls of the Forbidden City.

"I leave you facing an open door," were the last words to his followers spoken by this man whose understanding and courage had so gently opened a door that was never to be entirely closed. For the next two hundred years, although Christian missionaries were to be severely persecuted at times, they were never completely banished from the empire as they were to be in Japan.

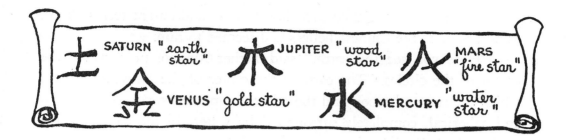

土 SATURN "*earth star*" 木 JUPITER "*wood star*" 火 MARS "*fire star*"
金 VENUS "*gold star*" 水 MERCURY "*water star*"

SUN, MOON, AND STARS

THIS IS A CHART of the Universe as drawn by the Greek geographer Ptolemy about the year 200. Since it was still being used in Europe, Matteo Ricci copied it for use in teaching the Chinese.

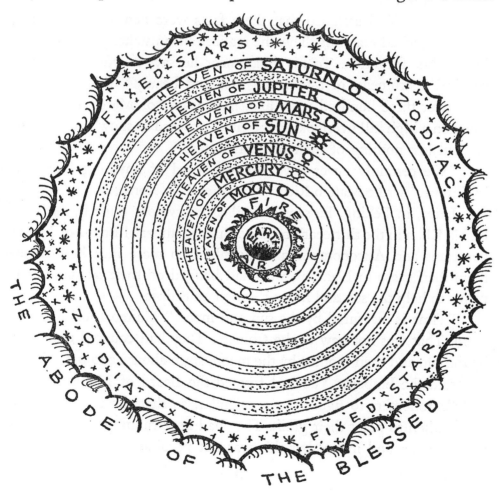

Therefore what Matteo Ricci had learned and taught seems almost as odd to us as the Chinese beliefs had seemed to him.

"Here you see the earth," said Father Matteo, pointing to the center of the circles. "The earth is the center of the Universe around which the sun and moon and the other five planets revolve. It is solid and spherical, completely surrounded by water. In the center of the earth is the hell of the damned. Surrounding it are ten circular heavens or orbs, outside of which is the home of God and the blessed ones. The orbs are of a clear solid crystal substance in which the stars stand fixed. The planets move in circles. Time is measured by the movement of the sun and moon. In fact the sun by revolving around the earth produces night and day."

Matteo Ricci assumed that these facts were new to the Chinese, until he reached Nanking. Then he realized his mistake. They had been known but forgotten. To his amazement he saw in Nanking "astronomical instruments of astonishing size and beauty" which had been built over three hundred years ago, in the days of Marco Polo. They stood on a high hill overlooking the city, "exposed to snow and rain and yet had lost nothing of their original luster."

"We certainly never have seen or heard of anything like them in Europe," wrote Matteo Ricci to his friends in Rome.

Later, in Peking, he saw a similar observatory built by order of Kubla Khan in the thirteenth century. But the Imperial Board of Mathematicians and Astronomers in Peking had no more idea how to use them than those in Nanking who had banged on their bronze instruments to help the sun and moon through an eclipse.

"Time is measured by the sun and moon," Matteo Ricci had told them. That was not new to the Chinese. They had counted their days by the sun and their months by the moon, since about 2000 B.C. Then it was said the Emperor Yao had formed the Board of Mathematicians and Astronomers to figure out a calendar, so that the farmers might know when to plant their grain. They had kept running into difficulty with the sun and moon, but this was not peculiar to the Chinese. It happened to all people who ever tried to make a calendar, because the number of days from one new moon to another will not divide into the number of days in a year according to the sun, without having days left over. A calendar that is not properly adjusted keeps getting worse and worse. The Chinese calendar was a mess.

Until the year 1582, the year Matteo Ricci had come out to China, the calendar used in Europe was ten days out of order. And no wonder. It had not been corrected since 45 B.C., when it had been made by Julius Caesar. At long last, in 1582 it was decided by the astronomers in Rome to abolish the old Julian calendar and figure out a new one.

This "New Style" calendar was established by Pope Gregory, and so known as the Gregorian. This new calendar, the one which we use today, was made by Matteo Ricci's old teacher of mathematics in Rome, a German monk by the name of Clavius.

Today in Vatican City in the Tower of the Winds may still be seen the Calendar Room, where Clavius and his fellow astronomers set up a simple experiment to convince the Pope why the reform was necessary. On the floor they drew a white line from north to south corresponding to the longitude of Rome. In the south wall they made a small hole through which the sun's rays fell upon the line. As Pope Gregory watched it from day to day, and week to week, he saw that the sun struck the line at different points and at different angles. From this as a start, he gradually came to understand how the calendar could get out of order, which was what the astronomers were trying to explain.

To keep the new calendar perpetually in order, Clavius worked out a clever system of leap years in which one day was added every four years. Italy, Spain, Portugal, and France accepted the new calendar at once, and the next year Switzerland and the Netherlands, where the population was divided between Catholics and Protestants, accepted it. But it was not adopted for another two hundred years by England and her colonies—not until 1752. China adopted this calendar in 1911, Russia in 1918.

A STAR GAZER, TYCHO BRAHE, AND HIS DOG

THERE was no observatory in Rome. The scientific center of the world was a small island off the coast of Denmark. There, in 1576, Frederick II, the king of Denmark, had built an elaborate observatory called Uraniborg (Castle of the Heavens).

There, night after night for the next twenty years, sat one of the great observers of all time gazing at the stars. His name was Tycho Brahe. He had no telescope. He had only his eyes. Tycho Brahe could see no more than the seven planets which the early Babylonians had seen and named. Yet he observed what he could see more accurately, and left a fund of exact measurements and information for others to use.

His ideas were extremely odd. About comets he wrote: "They are formed by human sins and wickedness rising from the earth, which forms into a kind of gas, and is ignited by the wrath of God. This poisonous stuff falls down again on people's heads and causes all kinds of mischief, such as pestilence, sudden death, bad weather . . . and Frenchmen."

An irritable man was he! With a hot temper and a sharp tongue. And only half a nose. The other half got sliced off in a duel. He stuck on a false piece made of gold or silver which served him very well.

Both he and the observatory were so famous that there were scores of visitors. Those who were truly interested in astronomy he was glad to talk to, but he was crusty with mere sightseers, and young Christian, the King's son, who really annoyed him got a piece of his mind.

James VI, the studious young King of Scotland, was one of his most interested visitors. The visit to the observatory, the whole trip to Denmark, was a major event in the life of James—the first and only time he was ever outside of England or Scotland. This was his wedding trip. The year was 1589. His bride was the Princess Anna, whose twelve-year-old brother Christian IV had been made king the year before when their father died. James the king of Scotland was twenty-three, Anna the Danish princess was fifteen, and, strange to say, they had been married in Norway—by accident.

The first wedding ceremony had taken place properly in Copenhagen, with a Scottish nobleman acting as proxy for the king. Then the bride, her mother Queen Sophie, and attendants had embarked for Scotland. James, who had spent his life entirely among men and books, was in a nervous dither, waiting for her to arrive in Edinburgh for the second ceremony. He kept pulling the miniature out of his doublet and looking at it. The face with its thin pointed nose and small mouth had not seemed overly bonnie until now, when he knew she was his. Early in September all Edinburgh was bright with plaids and flags flying against its gray walls. Highlanders stood ready with their bagpipes to greet the new Queen, but she did not arrive as expected. No one knew why until a week later, when word came of a storm at sea in which all of the Danish fleet had disappeared. James was fairly beside himself. Not until October did he learn that Anna "his only love" was safe, but stranded in Norway.

James, roused to action, most unusual for him, vowed he would go himself to fetch her. No matter how stormy the winter sea was, he would go. The crossing was not too bad, and after five days the royal party landed in a small harbor on the Norwegian coast. Two weeks later they had ridden over the icy, almost roadless, Norwegian countryside, through fishing villages, pine forests, and along deep fjords, until at last they reached the old walled city of Oslo. Tired and dirty, the impatient bridegroom, without stopping to shave or even wash, rode into the castle, found his Anna, and kissed her on her small mouth, even before the second wedding. This was performed in the church in Oslo, using the French language—the only one they both understood.

James was now ready to return with his "only love" to Scotland, but Queen Mother Sophie would not hear of it. He must first pay a visit to Denmark to meet Anna's brother Christian IV and the rest of her family. So the royal party packed up, and off they went through a "frosty wilderness" to the border of Sweden. There they were met by a brother of the Swedish King, who with four hundred horsemen escorted them to Helsingfors, where they took ship for Denmark. At Elsinore they were welcomed by the young King Christian, and all the rest of Anna's brothers and sisters down to handsome little Prince John, who was only six. The welcoming guns "thundered for half an hour," and the wonderful new castle of Kronburg (which Shakespeare was later to use in *Hamlet*) was bright with lights and filled with a delectable aroma. Rich pastries, meats, and wines were ready for the cold, hungry travelers. How warm and cheerful it all was compared to the cold gray castle in Edinburgh! James stayed on until spring.

It was in March that he made the visit to Uraniborg and spent seven hours with the celebrated Tycho Brahe. He noticed that the astronomer loved dogs, which gave him an idea.

Upon his return to Scotland, James sent Tycho Brahe a dog—an English mastiff. The dog indirectly drove Tycho Brahe from his Castle of the Heavens and from Denmark. One day the Danish Chancellor kicked the dog out of his way. Tycho Brahe exploded.

"You lout, you bully!" he cried, and gave the Chancellor such a violent tongue-lashing that Mr. Chancellor made up his mind to ruin the astronomer. Christian IV was also glad to get even with the gruff old man who always made him feel like a stupid lout. So the King and Chancellor put their heads together and gradually withdrew the money that the astronomer needed. Then they appointed a committee to pass on Tycho Brahe's work. The committee obligingly declared it to be full of errors and "damaging to the religion of the Danish people." The Danish people, thus aroused, so attacked the famous old astronomer that he gathered up his records and notes and fled from Copenhagen, and from Denmark.

In June, 1599, he reached the city of Prague, where he found a patron and a friend, the German Emperor Rudolph II, who gave him a castle and an observatory. There he lived and worked the last two years of his life. And there, fortunately for both of them, the old Dane met a young German, also an astronomer, by the name of Johann Kepler, who had been appointed Principal Mathematician to the Emperor Rudolph. Kepler was a frail, sickly man who worked with a feverish intensity, driven by his imagination. As Tycho Brahe was dying, Kepler sat beside him and promised to publish the mass of observations and tables of measurements which represented Brahe's life work.

"Dedicate them to our prince, the Emperor Rudolph," said Tycho. "Call them the Rudolphine Tables."

Later, in looking over the tables, Kepler saw that the timing of the planet Mars that Tycho Brahe had recorded would be wrong by eight minutes if Mars traveled in a CIRCLE. What about an oval path, he thought—an ellipse? He tried one oval after another, figuring carefully, and finally hit upon the ellipse that exactly fitted the recorded time! And so out of Tycho Brahe's observations and Johann Kepler's imagination, came the first discovery that was to erase the old circles drawn by Ptolemy: *planets move in ellipses, not in circles!*

Long before he left his Castle of the Heavens, Tycho Brahe had discovered a new star in the constellation of Cassiopeia which was later said to foretell the birth of Gustav Adolf, a prince of Sweden who was to be known as "The Star of the North."

The BALTIC·SEA:

GUSTAV ADOLF—STAR OF THE NORTH

IN 1599, on one of those long summer days in Sweden, five-year-old
Gustav Adolf was striding along through the meadow near the
castle of Nyköping, well ahead of his father Duke Charles and a
younger companion. He was whipping off the heads of the tall grasses
as he went, with his sword made of a strong stick. He started toward
a clump of bushes when the younger man shouted.

"Watch out! Don't go in. There are snakes!" That was silly. Why
should he be afraid of snakes? thought Gustav Adolf.

"I'll kill them with my stick!" he called back, and then he heard
his father chuckle and say, "You didn't think you could frighten little
Viking, did you? He'll take care of things, that one, have no fear."

His father had no fear of things either, Gustav knew, but just
then he heard Duke Charles say he did fear something—that he might
not be crowned King of Sweden for some time to come. That was queer
talk. If his father was not King of Sweden, who was? His father was
ruler of Sweden, and if he was the ruler how could it be that he
wasn't King? That was too puzzling for a boy to think about, especially
as he now saw a big hawk circling the sky. Behind it was a cloud that

looked like a huge white horse with a flying mane—like those horses Valkyries rode carrying the souls of Viking warriors to Valhalla! Some day he wanted just such a big white horse!

Briefly, the puzzling situation in Sweden was this: Duke Charles' brother Johan had been king of Sweden until he died in 1592, seven years ago. He left a son twenty-four years old, who by that time was living in Poland as King Sigismund III, having inherited the throne from his grandfather on his mother's side. This he could do because he had been brought up as a Catholic, and Poland was a Catholic country. But Sweden was a Lutheran Protestant country. And when his father Johan died and Sigismund came back to be crowned King of Sweden the Swedish people did not want him because he was a Catholic. Also, when he went back to Poland he acted as if Sweden were no longer free but belonged to Poland, and the Riksdag and Rad (the Swedish Parliament and Council) were of no account. So Duke Charles had stepped into the empty place of the absent king and acted as ruler. And the Riksdag trusted him and let him govern the country. This he did for about three years until King Sigismund raised an army in Poland and came to Sweden to fight with his uncle and drive him out. Instead,

Sigismund himself was defeated and deposed by the Riksdag and went back to Poland. Then Sweden had *no* king. That was what Gustav Adolf did not understand, even though he did know that his father had won a war against the King of Poland.

Next spring, after he had had his sixth birthday in December, Gustav heard that his father was going to war again. Only this time it was not to be in Sweden, but in Estland, at the other end of the Baltic Sea, and the whole family were going with him. That meant that he was to have his first long ride on a ship. The harbor from which they sailed was full of ships, but not one could he see with a painted dragon's head such as the Vikings had. There was a fine ship, though, with a lot of guns that would make a big booming if they all went off at once—a warship, his father said.

The ship they sailed on did not have so many guns, but it had huge sails that filled with wind after they started. His mother felt queer in her stomach and his sister couldn't eat, but he and his father liked it when the ship rolled and the water splashed high on the sides. This was the Baltic Sea. Lots of land around it belonged to Sweden, the part called Finland and the place called Estland where they were going to stay in a castle while his father went off to fight against the Poles. And also the Russians. Karl Filip, his baby brother, was born there the next spring, and when fall came again they all started home to Sweden.

On leaving Estland, Duke Charles and his family had such a narrow escape from being shipwrecked that before they reached Sweden it was rumored that the "king," as they were beginning to call him, had been drowned. When happily he arrived with his family, after making the journey by sleds around the Gulf of Bothnia, the Riksdag members in their relief were quite ready to declare him King Charles IX of Sweden, though he was not actually crowned until two years later.

King Charles IX now looked at his son and heir, eight-year-old Gustav, who was so skillful in many sports that he was equal to a twelve-year-old, and decided that his formal education for the task of ruling Sweden should begin. The boy as yet spoke only Swedish and

German, the language of his mother, Queen Kristina. Now he must learn Latin, the language in which all business relations between nations of Europe was carried on. A most intelligent young man named Johan Skytte was engaged as his tutor, and soon Gustav was reading and speaking Latin. As the years went by he learned to speak French, Dutch, and Italian, understood English and Spanish and some Polish, Russian, and Greek, and knew a great deal about history.

One other young man who also joined the King's court at Stockholm at this time was the new Chamberlain, Axel Oxenstierna, who was to be the lifelong friend and wise counselor of Gustav Adolf. The only fault he found with the brilliant young prince was that he was too impetuous, not cautious enough in the face of danger.

Gustav was also learning to write with a quill, and one day the eight-year-old might have been seen carefully forming the letters of his name on his first state document. It was a letter written for him to send to a six-year-old German prince, who was Count Palatine (named Frederick). If the astrologer consulted by Queen Kristina at her son's birth had predicted that he was to lose his life in a Thirty Years' War in which Frederick was to lose the first battle, he would have read the stars correctly.

From the time Gustav was ten, King Charles had him attend the meetings of the Rad to listen and become "accustomed to affairs." At fifteen he was trusted by his father with hearing and remedying minor grievances of the people.

"Be gracious," his father told him. "Punish evil; trust all men fairly; be no respecter of persons before the law; invade no man's just privileges, and before all things, fear God. Keep the will of God ever before your eyes."

The father knew that the boy he had trained so carefully would be worthy of his trust. During an illness, when certain of his ministers expressed grave concern over the state of the nation in case of his death, King Charles said, "I leave all in better hands than mine. *Ille Faciet* —Gustav Adolf will do it well."

JOHN SMITH, SIGHTSEER IN ITALY

THE YEAR 1600 was a Holy Year celebrated by the Roman Church. Catholic pilgrims by the thousands were on their way to Rome. One group of pilgrims who had embarked at the French port of Marseilles found the weather so stormy and bad on the Mediterranean that they looked for some reason why they should be punished by God, and lo and behold, they found a Protestant on board! Aha! they exclaimed, they would never have fair weather with that evil creature on deck. They seized him and threw him overboard.

124

This story is from the book, *True Adventures and Observations of Captain John Smith in Europe Asia Afrika and America.* For it was John Smith, on his way to fight the Turks, who was dumped overboard and who crawled up half-drowned and dripping wet onto a little island in the Mediterranean.

"The next morning," he says, "he espied two more ships, put on by the storm that fetched him aboard and so kindly used him that he was well contented to try the rest of his fortune with them. With the next faire wind they sailed along the coast of Corsica and Sardinia and crossing the gulf of Tunis along the African shore for Alexandria in Egypt. There they delivered their freight and then, keeping their course by Cyprus, and the coast of Africa, sailing by Rhodes, they came to the entrance of the Adriatic Sea."

There they met a ship from Venice and a desperate sea fight followed until the Venetian ship was shot so full of holes that she was about to sink and had to surrender. Then the victorious crew proceeded to rifle her and the "silkes velvets gold and silver they unloaded in twenty hours," John Smith declared, "was wonderful." He was set ashore in Piedmont with a comfortable sum of money. "Being glad," he said, "to have such opportunitie and means to better his experience of Italy, he embarked himself for Leghorn and having passed Tuscany and the country of Sienna and many other cities he came back to Rome. [There] it was his chance to see Pope Clement with many Cardinalls creep up the holy stayres brought from Jerusalem. A little distant in the ancient church of Saint John de Laterane he saw Pope Clement VIII say Masse. Having satisfied himself with the rarities of Rome, he went down the Tiber River, where he embarked himself to satisfie his eye with the faire Citie of Naples and her Kingdomes nobilitie. Returning by Capua, Rome and Sienna, he passed by that admired Citie of Florence, the Cities of Bologna, Mantua Padua and Venice." Then at last John Smith, through with sightseeing in Italy, crossed the Adriatic and proceeded to Hungary and to war with the Turks, where he was to have two years of spectacular adventures equal to those of a medieval knight.

125

GALILEO

IN PADUA, on one of Italy's soft summer evenings, Signor Galileo, a young professor at the University of Padua, finished tying up a rose bush in his garden. Then, as it was still light enough to read, he sat down on a bench and opened a new book which he had just received from the author, the German mathematician and astronomer Johann Kepler. He had barely finished the preface when he was interrupted by a laughing group of boys coming toward him across the lawn. They were his private pupils, who lived with him and whom he thoroughly enjoyed.

They were talking about the crazy notion of a certain Copernicus that the earth might be whirling around the sun! And how people would go flying off into space if that were true. Who was this Copernicus anyway?

Galileo closed the book quietly, smiled and listened to them. Then, without divulging his opinion, he said that Copernicus was a Polish astronomer who had lived about a hundred years ago, and had taken up some half-forgotten theories of the ancient Greeks. He had believed that the apparent rising and setting of the sun was an optical illusion. However there was as yet no experiment to prove it. . . . That satisfied the boys, who passed on to a variety of subjects—why wine fermented, why seeds sprouted—and then ended the day singing ballads while Galileo played his lute, until a small crescent moon slid around the tall square chimney and the stars came out.

Later that evening in the candlelight, Galileo wrote a letter which showed why he had been cautious about expressing his opinion regarding Copernicus, even to the boys.

The letter, dated August 4, 1597, was addressed to Johann Kepler. "I have as yet read nothing beyond the preface of your book from which however I catch a glimpse of your meaning, and feel great joy on meeting with so powerful an associate in the pursuit of truth. Many years ago I became a convert to the opinions of Copernicus and by his theory have succeeded in explaining many phenomena, [which] I have not yet dared to publish, fearing the fate of our master Copernicus, who although he has earned immortal fame among a few, yet by an infinite number (for so only can the number of fools be measured) is hissed and derided."

He signed the letter by his full name, GALILEO GALILEI.

Galileo had learned by sad experience to be cautious. He had had difficulty in getting this position at Padua, and he did not propose to lose it by attacking the ideas of Ptolemy, especially since he had no experiment to prove that they were false. He also needed the salary.

Galileo belonged to a noble family of Florence, but he could never remember the time when they were not in need of money. His father,

Vincenzo Galilei, was a charming, cultured gentleman with an inquiring mind, an accomplished musician, and a mathematician by profession. This he considered such unprofitable work that he kept his son from learning mathematics. In 1581, young Galileo, who was then sixteen, was entered in the University of Pisa to study medicine. There his inquiring mind, which he had inherited from his father and been trained to use, made him a misfit in that school where professors taught without questioning what the ancient Greeks had taught.

Aristotle, who had lived in 350 B.C., had known everything that was ever to be known about the natural sciences. Hippocrates, who had lived a half-century earlier, and Galen, who belonged to the time of Ptolemy, had said all there was to say about medicine. All a professor had to do was to repeat what they said, and all a student had to do was to memorize and repeat what the professor had said, and ask no questions. When Galileo asked embarrassing questions, trying to understand what the professors themselves did not understand, they told him "to understand was unnecessary, to contradict was blasphemy." But being a true scientist, the boy could no more stop inquiring, looking, and thinking than he could stop breathing. One day in the cathedral at Pisa, he happened to see an attendant lighting a bronze lamp hanging from the roof. It started swinging. Galileo watched it swinging back and forth till, fascinated by the rhythm, he timed it by his pulse and discovered the principle of the pendulum. Why could not physicians use this to test the rate and regularity of the heartbeat? And soon he had perfected what he called his *Pulsi-logia,* Galileo's first practical invention.

Keeping his ears and eyes open also led Galileo to another discovery—something which his father had never intended him to discover—the fascination of mathematics.

That year, according to custom, the Medici family of the Grand Duke, who was the ruler of Tuscany, and members of his court were spending the winter months in Pisa instead of in Florence. And they had brought a tutor for the pages by the name of Ostilio Ricci.

One day Galileo happened to hear the tutor Ricci giving the boys a lesson from Euclid's geometry, and was so fascinated that he went day after day to listen. He then got Ricci to instruct him privately and finally persuaded his father to let him stop the study of medicine and return to Florence. There Galileo went on, with Ricci, from the study of mathematics to that of mechanics, and made certain discoveries for which he was soon called the "Archimedes of his Time," being compared to the great Greek mathematician and inventor. He was also presented personally to the Grand Duke, Fernando de Medici. All this was very flattering, but Galileo had to eat.

He was giving private lessons in Florence and Sienna, but what he really needed was a professorship in one of the universities. He applied at Bologna, Rome and Padua, but was turned away. Finally when he was practically in despair, a position in his own University of Pisa was awarded him! He was to be Professor of Mathematics, which included Geometry, Astronomy, and Military Engineering. And he was to teach exactly the way he himself had been taught, and exactly what he had been taught, and raise no questions. In physics, he was to pass on word for word what Aristotle had written two thousand years ago, and uphold it as the truth, because "Aristotle said so." One thing Aristotle said was that if two objects of different size made of the *same* material were dropped from the same height, the larger one would reach the ground first. Galileo questioned this and decided to make a test. How and where he did this is not known.

According to an old legend, he climbed to the top of the Leaning Tower of Pisa, taking with him a ten-pound ball of lead and a one-pound ball of lead. The professors and students watched from below, just waiting to see Galileo make a fool of himself, never doubting that the big ten-pound ball would fall ten times faster than the one-pound ball, because "Aristotle said so." Galileo dropped the balls, and with their own eyes the embarrassed professors saw the two balls hit the ground at exactly the same time—and still they refused to admit that Aristotle was wrong. They were eager to be rid of this disturbing troublemaker, and to their aid came now another furiously embarrassed man. This was a member of the Medici family who was governor of Leghorn, a port city which the Grand Duke Fernando was trying to make into a great harbor. The governor, who fancied himself an engineer, designed a hugh dredging machine. The model was sent to be approved by Galileo, who said it was useless. The machine proved to be just that. And the inventor gladly joined the professors in making Galileo so miserable at Pisa that he had to resign in the middle of the year. It was 1592. That year his father Vincenzo Galilei, died. Never had Galileo been so miserable and so poor. Everything he owned was in one small trunk when he went once more to apply for the professorship of mathematics at Padua, where the teaching was much more liberal and progressive. And this time he received the appointment, left his native state of Tuscany, and took up his work at Padua, in the Republic of Venice.

So here he was, spending what he was to look back on as the happiest days of his life, seeing his lectures grow more and more popular, enjoying his home and his pupils, working in his garden and in his workshop, where he manufactured the geometrical compass and various other drawing instruments which he designed.

And in 1600, the *Pulsi Logia,* the first instrument he had ever made, was being used in the School of Medicine in Padua. One of the young students enrolled in medicine was William Harvey from England. He used the *Pulsi Logia* to measure the pulse, but could not understand what happened to the blood, whether it went in and out of the heart like air in the lungs, or where it went when the heart beat. Naturally no one could tell him because no one knew until 1627, when William Harvey himself was to discover and explain the circulation of the blood.

By 1600 Galileo's fame as a teacher had become so widespread that foreign students flocked from England, Germany, and France to attend his lectures. Galileo himself never quite got over feeling like a foreigner in Padua. He was always a trifle homesick for Tuscany, his "native land," and went home every summer vacation to Florence, where he enjoyed tutoring the Grand Duke Fernando's young son, Cosimo.

A ROYAL WEDDING

A MOST IMPORTANT WEDDING took place in Florence, in the fall of 1600. During his summer holidays, while Galileo was tutoring twelve-year-old Cosimo, the Pitti Palace of the Grand Duke was astir with preparations for the coming event. Brocades and jewels were being selected, velvet and satin gowns were being embroidered in gold, trimmed in ermine, encrusted with pearls and fitted to the bride, who was Cosimo's cousin Maria.

On October 6, Maria de' Medici, niece of the Grand Duke Fernando, was to marry Henry IV, the king of France. The fact that Henry was forty-seven, almost the age of her uncle, mattered little to Maria. It made her feel young, even though she was twenty-six, very old for an Italian girl to be still unmarried. That her uncle Fernando was far richer than her bridegroom-to-be also made Maria very comfortable. The Medici family had much more money than the King of France. Her trousseau was magnificent, and her dowry said to be greater even than that of Catherine de' Medici, the first of the family to become a French queen.

Henry IV had been married before, to be sure. Marguerite, his first wife, Catherine's daughter, was still living, but that did not matter. She and Henry IV had not lived together for many years, and Uncle Fernando had prevailed upon the Pope to declare the marriage null and void, so that the French King might marry again.

The French were also eager for the marriage, in order that there might be an heir to the throne. High-spirited Henry, however, who had a charming way with the ladies and whose love affairs were many, was reluctant to be tied by a second marriage, fearing that it would prove to be no better than the first. When he actually heard from the Duke of Sully, who came rushing into his apartment, that the marriage agreement had been signed, Henry jumped up as if he had been struck, then began pacing back and forth.

"Eh bien," he said finally, throwing up his hands in mock surrender, "if I must marry for the good of France, then I must marry!" Having accepted the fact, Henry entered into the preparations in his naturally gay, light-hearted way. Learning that Maria was very fond of clothes, he wrote in one of his letters: "I am told that you desire models of the fashionable dress in France. I am sending you some dressed dolls and will send you a tailor."

"Hasten your arrival," he wrote in another letter to her, and though he had never laid eyes upon her, gallantly added, "If it were fashionable for one to be in love with one's wife, I would tell you how much I am in love with you!"

The wedding celebration in the Pitti Palace was a gala occasion, attended by dukes, duchesses, archdukes and cardinals, a handsome

French duke representing the King, and Maria in her gold-encrusted wedding gown sparkling with jewels. On October 17, in an equally elaborate traveling costume, the new Queen took ship at Leghorn for France, escorted by seventeen galleys and an army of seven thousand men.

Henry IV, who had been at war during the summer and early fall, met her later at Lyons, at the chateau where she was waiting for him. He came directly from military headquarters, wearing his steel helmet and breastplate, booted and spurred. As it was dark when he arrived at the castle, he found the gate barred and the drawbridge up. Almost an hour passed before he could make himself heard, torches could be brought, and the drawbridge lowered. Then he clattered into the gallery where Maria was being served her dinner alone, took one long look at her with his sparkling black eyes, and found her far more pink and white and fair than he had anticipated. She rose, fell to her knees before her lord and master, then hastily retired to her own apartment. He followed and, without further ado, swept her into his arms and kissed her. She was amazed to find him so young and impetuous, in spite of his gray beard. They could not speak together, for he knew no Italian and she understood no French. It was just as well, perhaps, that he should not have been disillusioned at once.

Later Maria proved herself utterly boring to him. She had no wit, no sense of humor, nothing interesting to say. Added to that, she objected harshly to the attention he paid to his other lady loves, a thing which he felt she should have taken as a matter of course.

So, as he had feared, the marriage was a failure, except for their children. Henry adored his children. The birth of a son in 1601 threw him into such excitement that hardly had the puny little fellow been made to utter his first cry, than the King flung open the Queen's bedchamber and, at that late hour of the night, invited all the court nobles waiting outside to enter and behold the miracle—a Dauphin—the first son born to a King of France in nearly fifty years. Here he was—behold him—the royal prince, the Dauphin, their next king—Louis XIII!

GRAND OPERA AND THE VIOLIN

IN OCTOBER 1600, at the wedding celebration of Henry IV and Maria
de' Medici in the Pitti Palace in Florence, a new style of music was
heard for the first time. That night saw the opening performance of
what was to be known as Grand Opera.

Two plays or dramas were performed, in which the words were
set to music and the music used to emphasize meaning and emotion.
Both of these ideas were new and startling. Up to this time there had
existed only church music and madrigals, choral music written for
many parts, very formal and unemotional, unaccompanied by any instrument. The greatest composer of this old formal type of music was

Palestrina, who died in 1594, in Rome, leaving many beautiful compositions which are still used today in the Catholic mass.

Galileo's father, Vincenzo Galilei, was a pioneer in the new exciting form of music. For some years before his death, he had belonged to a group of amateur musicians who met in Florence and began to experiment with musical drama, trying to express in sounds the feeling of a story or poem. One evening Vincenzo sang the tragic story of Ugolino, a Tuscan nobleman, to the accompaniment of his lute. This inspired two other members of the group, which was called "La Camerata," to join forces—a poet and a composer. They wrote a musical drama called *Daphne*, which they also performed for the group. That was in 1594. Five years later the same two men, the musician and the poet, produced a second musical drama, *Eurydice*.

These were the two music-dramas that were played for the Medici and their wedding guests that evening in Florence. The operas were not particularly good, but they were a beginning, an opening of the curtain, a striking of the notes that fired the imagination of other, better musicians. Most important of these was Claudio Monteverde, who is spoken of as the first composer of modern music.

Monteverde, then a young man about the age of Galileo, was the viol player to the Duke of Mantua, and it is most likely that he accompanied the Duke to the wedding. He heard the music, caught up the new idea, and with his genius and imagination put the breath of life into it. To gain his effects, he introduced the use of dischords, and so broke the rigid laws of harmony which had bound the old music.

Monteverde's first opera, *Ariana*, produced in 1607, was also presented for the first time at a wedding, the marriage of Francesco, young son of Monteverde's patron, the Duke of Mantua.

As Monteverde continued writing, he made more use of instrumental music as a background for the voice. For this, a new instrument was needed, stronger and more resonant than the feeble flat-backed viol then in use. Fortunately at this time in the town of Cremona, which was Monteverde's birthplace, the Amati family had begun to make just such a new and wonderful instrument, the violin.

JOHN SMITH AND THE "TERRIBLE TURKS"

THE STORY of John Smith's adventures in the next two years, from the time he entered Hungary in 1601 until he emerged late in 1603 with the right to show three Turks' heads on his coat of arms, sounded so fantastic, when told by him in his *True Travels,* that some people thought he must have invented a tall tale. But most of the strangely spelled names of people and places have been identified. And the tangled events that sounded so incredible fit with actual history. No one who had not been there could have comprehended the confusion in Hungary and the dreadful plight of the Hungarians. Once a proud, independent nation, Hungary was literally being torn apart, in danger not only from the Turks but also from the Germans. Not only were the armies of the German Emperor, aided by Christians from all over Europe, fighting to hold back the Turks—who already held all the eastern part of Hungary—but the Emperor of Germany was fighting to take the western part of Hungary for himself. Hungarians who only wanted their independence could be found fighting on both sides, preferring, if need be, the milder rule of the Turks.

John Smith was assigned to a Hungarian regiment fighting for the Emperor. Their first assignment was to relieve the commander inside the walls of the fortified town of Oberlimbach that was being attacked by the Turks. The newcomer, fresh from the west and full of energy, was permitted to try ideas he had seen used in the Netherlands. One was to signal with lights from a high hill and spell out messages to the commander inside the city. Another trick was to light two or three thousand pieces of fuse, and fool the Turks as to the size of the army. Both tricks worked to perfection. The army inside met the army outside of the town and together they drove off the bewildered Turks. And as a reward for this spectacular beginning John Smith was given a commission. He was now Captain John Smith!

A captain of cavalry with 250 horsemen under his command, John Smith rode off under a Polish colonel to help a French duke who was trying to capture the Hungarian town of Szekesfehvar, long held by Turkish troops.

"New and sudden thynges make armies afrayde," thought the newly commissioned Captain, remembering *The Art of War* by Machiavelli, which he read in his hut of boughs beside the brook.

Acting on that principle he introduced a weapon—new to the Turks —called a "Fiery Dragon." This was a pot filled with gunpowder and musket balls, covered with burning pitch and catapulted over the walls into a town.

"It was a fearful sight to see the short flaming course of their flight in the aire," said Smith. "But presently after their fall the lamentable noise of the miserable slayghtered Turkes was most wonderfull to heare."

The taking of Szekesfehvar, which had been held by the Turks for fifty years, was a tremendous victory, a good ending to the year, for by then it was winter and fighting stopped.

Spring came. Captain John Smith went with his regiment to Transylvania to join the troops of Prince Sigismundus Bathory, a native Hungarian prince with a sweeping mustache and a pompadour. All spring there was fighting. By June they were digging trenches outside of a city called Regall, held by the Turks, but they were so slow about it that the Turks, watching from inside the walls, got bored waiting for them to attack. At length, to relieve the monotony, one of them, called Turbashaw, sent a challenge to any Christian captain to meet him in single combat. And who accepted the challenge? Who else but Captain John Smith? Here at least was one place in the world where knightly combat had not yet died out! Here was a chance for John Smith to put to use all that he had learned at Tattersall Castle about riding a horse and handling a lance, for the challenge which the Turk had flung out was to combat with him *"for his head."*

Oboes sounded. Out onto the field rode Turbashaw with a great pair of wings made of eagle feathers edged with gold attached to his shoulders. A Janissary preceded him carrying his lance. Two Janissaries in high bonnets of white felt walked beside his horse.

Trumpets sounded. John Smith rode out in helmet and armor with one page carrying his lance. He took his station facing the Turk.

A charge sounded. Long lances extended, the brave Englishman and "terrible Turk" rode toward each other. With one well-aimed thrust a lance "passed the Turk through the sight of his beaver, face, head and all, that he fell dead to the ground." Smith dismounted, took off the Turk's helmet, cut off his head, and presented it to his General, "who kindly accepted it."

Next day, a friend of the murdered man challenged the champion.

Their lances flew into pieces, they resorted to their pistols and the friend too lost his head.

John Smith sent the next challenge, which was accepted by one called "Bonny Mulgro." They used battleaxes in this contest, and John Smith was almost knocked from his horse. A great shout went up from the ramparts, "but by God's assistance," he said, he was spared, "and having drawn his short curved sword, the Turk lost his head as the rest had done."

"This good success," said John Smith, "gave such great encouragement to the whole armie that with a guard of six thousand, three spare horses, before each a Turkes head on a lance" he was conducted to the General with his "Presents." The General, "embracing him in his armes gave him a faire horse richly furnished, a scimitar worth three hundred ducats and made him Sergeant-Major of the Regiment." After the siege the town was captured, the Turks driven out, and prisoners presented to Prince Sigismundus. "Celebrating thankes to Almightie God in triumph of those victories, hee was made acquainted with the service of John Smith. For which with great honor he gave him three Turkes heads in a Shield for his Armes, by Patent, under his hand and seale . . . his portrait in gold and three hundred Ducats yearely for a Pension."

This meant that John Smith, the tenant farmer's son, now had a coat of arms, the badge of a gentleman, to carry home with him when he returned to England—if he ever did return! . . .

One day in November (November 18, 1602) it was doubtful that he would even live. He lay wounded and groaning among the "slaughtered and dead bodies on a bludy battlefield."

JOHN SMITH, SLAVE

CONSTANTINOPLE stands as a link at the very point where Europe and Asia meet. Founded by Constantine, the first Roman emperor to accept Christianity, it had been the capital of the Roman Empire of the East for over a thousand years. In 1453 it had

been captured by the Turks, and was now the heart of the "Glorious Empire" of the Turks—a Moslem city.

In Santa Sophia, Christian bells no longer rang. The church which Constantine had built was a Moslem mosque, and from a thousand high minarets five times a day rose the voices of muezzins bidding the faithful bow to the ground in prayer, facing the holy City of Mecca.

Into this city of mosques and minarets, on a day early in the year of 1603, came marching a string of weary, footsore prisoners from the war in Hungary. They were chained together in groups of twenty, and in one of the groups was John Smith, no less footsore and weary than all the others after walking 127 miles. Like them, he had been rescued from the battlefield and taken to a slave market on the Danube River, where they had been stripped, examined, and sold like "beasts in the market place." Smith had been purchased by a Turk, called Bashaw Bogall, and sent on as a gift to a high-born young lady whose name was Charatza Traga-bigzanda, but who, with her great black eyes above her veil and her sparkling jewels, must have been more glamorous than her name. This high-born lady could speak Italian, and when John Smith said he was not a Bohemian nobleman, conquered in battle by her friend Bogall, as Bogall had claimed, she called in those who could speak English, French, or

Dutch to test him in all the languages which he spoke, to see if she understood him correctly.

Then, according to the story as he told it later, she "took much compassion on him, but having no use for him, she sent him to her brother," saying that "he should but sojourne there to learne the language and what it was to be a Turke, till time made her master of her selfe."

Whatever that meant. John Smith may have imagined more than he saw in her melting dark eyes. Certainly he expected a welcome from the lady's brother, as he set forth for his castle in the land of the Tartars. His host-to-be was a Timor, that is, a Turkish ruler over a small part of a conquered land. To reach this land, John Smith was taken along the Black Sea coast to Varna, then by ship across the sea, and through the strait into the sea of Azov, up a river six or seven days' journey to a place north of the Caucasus Mountains south of the River Don. Here they came, he said, "to a vast stonie Castle with many great Courts about it, environed with high stone walls." Coming through this unfamiliar semi-wild land of the Tartars, he observed the people and how they lived.

"The better sort of Tartars," he said, "were attired like Turks but the plaine Tartar hath a blacke sheepe skinne over his backe, and two of the legs tied about his necke, another over his belly and the legs tied behind him, two more serveth him for breeches, with a close cap to his skull of black felt, . . . They move from country to country, driving with them infinite troops of black sheep and cattle."

The Timor was not in evidence when John Smith entered the "vast stonie castle." Nor was his welcome.

Within an hour after his arrival John Smith was stripped naked, his head and beard shaved as bare as his hand, and "a great ring of iron rivetted about his neck with a long stalke bowed like a sickle." He had a coat of haircloth tied with a piece of skin, and "being last of the slaves to arrive was slave of slaves to them all. And all treated in a manner so miserable a dog could hardly have lived to endure." At harvest time, he was put to threshing in a field, several miles from the Timor's house. The Timor came by, and began to beat and curse him, until, Smith said,

141

"forgetting all reason he beat out the Timor's braines with his threshing bat, clothed himself in the Timor's clothes, hid his body under the straw, filled his knapsacke with corne, mounted his horse and rode off into the desert." After two or three days of fearfully wandering he knew not whither, "he came to a great road, and a great sign post, with markers pointing to various places—one marked with a crescent or half-moon, toward the Crimea—if toward Persia, with a blacke man with white dots —if toward China, a picture of the sun—and one with the sign of the cross pointed toward Muscovy [or Russia]." He chose the cross pointing to Muscovy.

Sixteen days he traveled in torment and fear of being caught and sent back, till he reached a garrison, or border fortress, of the Russians on the River Don. "There," he said, "the governor, after due examination, took off his irons, and treated him so kindly he thought himself newly risen from the dead." The good Lady Callamata largely supplied all his wants. He stayed there till a convoy was going west to the next fort. "Travelling through the poor devastated countryside, passing tiny lonely villages with houses made of logs, he finally reached Hernsstadt in Transylvania. Being thus glutted with content and neere drowned with joy," he passed through Hungary to Prague in Behemia, and then into the German city of Leipsig. There he found the most gracious Prince Sigismundus, who, on December 9, 1603, confirmed the coat of arms and made him a gift of sixteen hundred ducats of gold. With his precious coat of arms, for which he chose the motto "To overcome is to live," John Smith now set out on a tour of Germany.

Still not satisfied with sight-seeing, he went down the Rhine to Strasbourg, through France by way of Paris, down the Loire River to Brittany, and there embarked for the Spanish port of Bilboa on the Bay of Biscay, eager to see Madrid, the Escorial built by Philip II, Toledo and all the places in Spain he had heard about.

"Being thus satisfied with Europe and Asia," as he admits himself, but still ready for more war and more brave adventures, our hero "sailed from Gibraltar for North Africa."

ABOUT THE TIME our "knight," John Smith, passed through Spain in search of further adventure, a fictitious knight by the name of Don Quixote was being brought to life by an old soldier of Spain whose name was Miguel Cervantes. Cervantes was now old, but he too had once been young, had read books on chivalry and dreamed of having the great and improbable adventures of a knight. In 1571, he had been in the famous naval battle of Lepanto. He had been struck by two missiles in the leg and in his left hand, crippling it for life. Then the ship taking him back to Spain was captured by pirates of Algiers. It was five years before he was ransomed. Back in Spain, he had received an appointment by the King to be buyer of oil and grain for the Armada. And what a job it had been to avoid rancid oil and rotten flour. Well, the upshot was that the clerks said his accounts were all wrong. The judge ordered him to "refund to the king's treasury" such a huge sum that he laughed out loud. And so he was sentenced as an insolent as well as a dishonest servant of King Philip and sent to the dungeons of Seville. What an ending to high hopes and knightly dreams of adventure. Then came to him the idea of a satire on stories of knighthood, which he had loved as a youth.

And the knight grew in his mind, thin, tall, spare—Don Quixote, riding off on a raw-boned horse, tilting with windmills, followed by his faithful servant Sancho Panza on a donkey. And so we see them traveling the roads to Spain, of Cervantes' day—two immortal figures.

BORIS GODUNOV

JOHN SMITH was "satisfied with Europe and Asia," yet he had not
been to Moscow. He had touched only the southern edge of Russia,
that wide sprawling country that belonged both to Europe and to
Asia. Probably he thought there was nothing of interest to anyone
but fur-traders in that backward land that had been under the brutal rule

of Mongols or Tartars for more than two hundred years. It was only a little over a hundred years since Russia had been freed from Mongol rule and Moscow had become the center of an independent state. This had been accomplished by Ivan III, grandfather of Ivan the Terrible.

The first European to penetrate the backward land was an Austrian, sent on a mission to the Tsar. He returned with such a shocking report that the King of Poland agreed with the Emperor of Germany that they should keep the barbarian Muscovites locked up in their own country and have no dealings with them.

The English had brought Russia into touch with Europe—those Englishmen searching for a northwest passage to China and India who in 1553, had gone inland to Moscow and returned with a message from Ivan the Terrible to Queen Elizabeth. After that the Muscovy Trading Company had been founded. Ambassadors had been exchanged. All was pleasant, until Ivan suggested that Elizabeth form an alliance with him against Sweden, Poland, and Turkey and also let him marry her cousin. Elizabeth refused, considering Russia useful only as a market for grain and an overland route to China and India.

Then Ivan the Terrible, who considered the Great Mogul of India, the Shah of Persia, and the Grand Turk rulers of real importance in the world, expressed in no uncertain terms his low opinion of the rulers of western Europe, such as the Queen of England, who allowed their subjects to have a hand in the government.

To the Russian people, all foreigners were equally feared. Ignorant and isolated so long, they looked upon all of them, whether they came from Asia or Europe, with a kind of superstitious horror. Moslems, Mongols, Turks, Germans, English, Poles, Protestants, or Catholics—all were infidels—all who did not belong to the Orthodox community of "Holy Russia."

In 1603, when John Smith was being so carefully examined at the forts on the Russian border, Ivan the Terrible was dead. He had been dead for nineteen years. The Tsar was Boris Godunov. By his orders all roads leading into Russia were carefully guarded. All foreigners entering were being carefully investigated, lest a mysterious person should slip through. A young man about nineteen, who was supposed to have been safely murdered many years ago, was reported to be still alive. . . . Spies had told Boris Godunov that he was coming in from Poland.

Boris Godunov was afraid. He was the Tsar, but by birth he had no right to be. He was not related to Ivan the Terrible nor was he descended from old Rurik, the first Tsar. He was of a Tartar family that had originally come with the Mongol conquerors into Russia. The mysterious young man coming in from Poland, supposed to have been murdered many years ago, was the rightful heir—the youngest son of Ivan the Terrible—Dimitri Ivanovitch.

Dimitri. Surely he was an imposter, this man they said was Dimitri —Dimitri could not have risen from the dead . . . As the winter wore on, Boris Godunov could not bear the sound of that name—he forbade anyone to speak the name Dimitri—yet it was forever in his mind.

Boris Godunov was a strong man, an intelligent man, but he was made almost helpless by fear. As the dark and gloom of a winter day in Moscow was closing in around him, he paced the floor of the palace, then stopped to look out upon the dark encircling walls of the Kremlin, the three-sided fortress rising from the river. Deep clanging of bells began in the cathedral of Saint Basil, whose many onion-shaped towers rose like tongues of flame beyond the dark edge of the wall. Still deeper clanging of bells came from the tall tower of Ivan the Terrible. The clang and clangor of bells broke in upon one another from all the surrounding churches, until the air was filled with the noise. It rang in his ears like the sound of doom, long after it had died away.

On the wall, Boris could see the guards in their long coats and bayonets, black against a sky streaked blood-red in the sunset. What would they see, those guards, when the night grew black? Would they see again a ghostly carriage drawn by six horses flying through the air above them? Would the driver, dressed like a Pole, strike the Kremlin walls with his long whip—as he again passed over yelling like a madman?

In 1603 it was five years since Boris Godunov had been crowned, but each year had increased his agony and fear. He should have made an excellent ruler. He had intelligence, ability, and years of experience.

As a young man at court, Boris had attracted the attention of Ivan the Terrible and become his chief adviser, promoted by him to the rank of nobleman, or Boyar, which the old boyars furiously resented. On his deathbed Ivan, who in a fit of rage had killed his oldest son, appointed Boris Godunov as guardian of his second son Feodor, who, though feeble in mind and body, was to be the next Tsar. This further enraged the boyars. Feodor, who just wanted to spend his time ringing church bells, turned the government completely over to Boris Godunov. This also infuriated the boyars. They staged a rebellion in favor of Feodor's infant half-brother Dimitri, who had been born the year that his father died. The rebellion was put down, but when he was seven, Dimitri, out playing with his friends, was murdered. At least a boy of his age was stabbed with a knife and fell in a pool of blood. Agents of Boris Godunov were blamed for the murder and practically torn to pieces by the infuriated mob. But was it the real Dimitri who had been murdered, or had another boy been substituted for him? Had Dimitri been spirited away? No one knew—or ever was to know. . . .

Seven years passed, while Feodor rang church bells and Boris Godunov ran the government. Then one day, Feodor lay in a dark breathless room heavy with incense. Ikons were lighted by flickering lamps and candles on the walls. Ikons at his head and feet, a cross in his hands, and an empty crown on the pillow above his head. An empty crown! Who was to wear it?

Boris Godunov. But not immediately. He had his eyes on that crown, but he closed them devoutly, retired to a monastery to pray for the soul of the deceased and await the information from his spies. Word soon came that certain boyars were talking of a limited monarchy like that of Poland. . . . Boris Godunov, as Tsar, did not propose to be limited by a Council of Boyars, with their ignorant backward ideas. He turned to his prayers again.

The Patriarch, then the head of the church of Russia, indebted to

Boris for promotion from Metropolitan to Patriarch, joined by many others who owed their positions to Boris, begged him to accept the crown and continue to rule the land. The Ikon of Our Lady of Vladimir was brought to persuade him. There was a church parade. Boris turned his head away—begged to be left alone to pray. It was not enough for him that just those who were indebted to him should offer him the holy crown. He continued his prayerful waiting until he heard that a National Assembly composed of common people—merchants, magistrates, priests and monks—had cried out for him and cheered when the Patriarch named Boris Godunov as Tsar. Moscow was then filled with armed men, Cossacks, archers, and musketeers, to see that the boyars also took the oath of allegiance. And Boris Godunov was crowned Tsar in a magnificent ceremony on September 1, 1598. The English ambassador described him as a tall, athletic man with coppery skin and clean-shaven face, like a European, in contrast to the long black beards of the Russian boyars.

Unlike those boyars, who were satisfied with "Holy Russia" as it was, Boris was eager to bring the backward people up to the standard of Europe. He was illiterate himself, but he sent for the best teachers to give his son and daughter a European education. For the beautiful dark-eyed Xenia he sought a bridegroom from one of the royal houses of Europe. The first choice was the son of a former King of Sweden. That fell through, he swallowed his disappointment and approached Duke John, prince of Denmark—youngest brother of King Christian IV. Young John came, handsome and charming. He was met at the border with a magnificent reception. But before he had even seen the beautiful Xenia, he was stricken by a mysterious illness that proved to be fatal. Boris wept aloud.

Disaster had piled upon disaster. The stars were against him—even the heavens. There had been no rain . . . the crops had failed, and famine was sweeping over the land. Thousands and thousands of people were dying. Ragged miserable creatures crowded the streets of Moscow. Famine meant to the people a sign of God's anger. God was punishing them, they began to say, for having accepted as Tsar one who had not been chosen by God. They began to remember and repeat the old story of how Dimitri, the Tsarevitch, the rightful heir to the throne had been murdered, by the order of Boris Godunov. No, said others, speaking in a hoarse whisper, Dimitri was not dead. All these years he had been in hiding. Now he was coming back, to take the throne that was his and drive out the imposter.

"Imposter, imposter!" cried Boris Godunov. "He is the imposter—he who claims to be the true Dimitri," for now his spies brought the Tsar word that a young man claiming to be Dimitri was leaving Poland and approaching the Russian border. He headed an army that had been raised by Polish noblemen to help him. One Russian city had opened its gates and met him with the bread and salt of hospitality and acclaimed him as their ruler. Then another city and another. . . .

"Magic—black magic!" cried Boris as the reports came in to him. "Sorcery." In desperation he consulted a famous sorcerer, but the magic spells did not work—they did not stop the imposter.

Boris consulted a soothsayer, a toothless old woman who lived in a dirty underground cell. "You ask what is coming?" she said. "This." His eyes followed her finger, pointing to a small piece of wood over which two other weird creatures were wailing a dirge.

Death, then, let it come! He did not wish to live. Outwardly he remained the same, and life within the Kremlin continued with the same gluttonous round of feasting and celebrating, though the people were starving.

In the early afternoon of April 13, 1605, Boris, handsome as ever and perfectly well, had been dining with many guests in the reception hall of the palace. He went to the lookout window and stood gazing out over Moscow and the walls of the Kremlin. Suddenly he turned and fell, writhing and screaming with pain. His face turned black, as if from poison. The court doctor came rushing in, followed by the Patriarch. He administered the last sacrament and had the dying Tsar shorn as a monk, that he should not face the Last Judgment, on the day of Doom, burdened by a crown.

THE QUEEN IS DEAD

QUEEN ELIZABETH was in her seventieth year when she died. She had ruled England for forty-five years, with absolute devotion and with such skill that she had raised an insignificant island country into a position of power among the nations of Europe.

Two years before she died, she had appeared before Parliament still full of her dynamic magical charm and told them that the glory of her crown had been that she had reigned with their love.

For many days after she became ill she refused to go to bed. When she finally did, she lay for hours staring at the heavy brocaded hangings, a finger in her mouth. One day she called for music, "as if to die as gayly as she lived," said the French Ambassador.

The night of March 23, 1603, she called for the Archbishop of Canterbury and he knelt by her bed and said prayer after prayer. He stopped a moment, and her hand moved. He continued the prayers, watching the white fingers that hung below the cover until they were quiet, and he saw that she had gone without waking.

It was three o'clock in the morning when the lady-in-waiting went to the window and threw something down to her brother, standing booted and spurred beside his horse. It was a blue ring, sent by James of Scotland to be used as a signal. The man caught it, mounted his steed, and was off on his way north to summon the new king.

The Elizabethan Age was ended.

KING JAMES I

A T LAST, after years of hoping and waiting, word came to James VI of Scotland that he was to be King James I of England. He was now thirty-seven years old and a no more attractive figure of a man than he had ever been. Anne, somewhat heavier at twenty-nine than as a bride of fifteen, had never possessed any mark of beauty except a good complexion. But, oddly enough, the two older children were beautiful—Prince Henry, who was nine, and Princess Elizabeth, who was seven. The third, poor sickly little Charles, who was three, had big dark eyes like those of his ill-fated grandmother Mary of Scots, and weak wobbly legs like his father. It seemed best to leave him behind for a while with his lady nurse while the others left for England.

James would have started at once, if he had had the money. He had to send for enough to make the trip. He also sent for the crown jewels (possibly urged on by his queen, who looked forward to all kinds of glittering festivities now that they were leaving grim, poverty-stricken Scotland behind). The jewels did not come with the necessary money. As soon as that arrived, James was off down the highway toward the "Promised Land," accompanied by what seemed a suitable retinue of Scottish courtiers and attendants, though they were to strike the English as a rather numerous string of hangers-on.

Now that he was on his way, there was great curiosity among the English people to see their new king—the first King of England in almost fifty years! There was much speculation as to what he would be like, what his policies would be. All kinds of questions arose. What about Spain—would he want war or peace? What about Puritans? What about Catholics? Would he favor them, or persecute them? How did he feel about the theatre? How would he respond to Parliament? Unable to wait till he arrived, people of all kinds hastened to meet him on the way and make their views known. A delegation of Puritan clergymen met him with a petition. Members of the government who wanted to make their positions secure, as well as those who had no position but hoped for a change of fortune, rushed to make themselves known to the new King and gain his favor. James, glorying in this unaccustomed sense of importance, began to distribute honors and titles right and left. Before he reached London he had created 250 new knights and by the end of three months, over 700.

On the outskirts of London, which he reached on the seventh of May, he was met and ushered in by the Lord Mayor, in long red gown and massive gold chain, flanked by other pompous dignitaries of the city. Ten days after his arrival, the happy King set his stamp of approval on the theatre by designating a company of actors to be known as the King's Men. Anne and the two older children reached London late in June, having been greeted by pageants and poetry at all the country houses where they stopped on the way from Scotland. By then every tradesman in the city, from Shoreditch to Cheapside, was working overtime preparing for the magnificent coronation scheduled for July 25.

Black rats and fleas, however, had also been working overtime in London's dark filthy alleys, and the plague came before the coronation. By July 13 there were fifteen hundred people dying each week. The King was hastily crowned in Westminster Abbey. The public was not admitted. All public buildings were closed. The royal family left for the palace of Hampton Court, miles from the city, accompanied by so many courtiers that these had to be housed in tents. There they spent the first winter.

THE GLOBE THEATRE

THE GLOBE was the newest theatre in London. It had been built and was owned by the company of actors, now known as the King's Men, to which Shakespeare belonged. It had all the most modern equipment of the day, the latest in trap doors, balconies, pulleys, wires, and overhead machinery. The year that it was finished, 1599, Shakespeare had his new play, *Hamlet,* written and ready to be produced.

In 1603, like all the other theatres, bear-baiting arenas, and places of amusement, the Globe was closed during the plague and the King's Men went on tour.

Shakespeare was then thirty-nine, just two years older than King James. He had written twenty plays, all of them successful. But he was still an actor, perfectly willing to take part in plays written by other people—just as modest and unassuming and thoroughly likable as he had ever been. Two years before the Globe was built he had saved enough money to buy a new home in Stratford for his family—Anne and the two daughters (Hamnet had died when he was eleven). It was a large house of brick and timber opposite the old Guild Hall, and was called simply New Place. Shakespeare may very probably have paid a

visit to Stratford during the summer of the plague. But by December he was back with the King's Men, at the country house where they acted for King James the first play that he saw in England.

The week before Christmas the actors were at Hampton Court to present more plays for the royal family, who all loved the theatre as much as the King, though there were times when he had eaten so much that he could not keep his eyes open or his mouth shut.

A Midsummer Night's Dream was the favorite play of the prince and princess. Handsome nine-year-old Henry laughed till he almost cried over Bottom, Quince, and Snout the Tinker. Little Elizabeth, who looked like a fairy herself, especially loved Titania, the Fairy Queen, with her sparkling wand.

The entire holiday season of this first Christmas spent in England by the royal family was filled with new delights never experienced in Scotland. King James, almost beside himself with the rare joy of spending money, kept handing out gifts in a lavish manner. Queen Anne was in a flurry of excitement over her part in the masque which was to be given on Christmas Day. This was a play which had been written especially for her by a poet of her choice. She and the ladies of the court spent days rehearsing their parts and rapturous hours rummaging through Queen Elizabeth's immense wardrobe for suitable and becoming costumes. The day came. The curtain rose, revealing Queen Anne in blue velvet and jeweled buckskins. In the role of Athena, she was greeted with tremendous applause. The author of the masque, pleasantly self-conscious, beamed with satisfaction over the success of his creation. Frankly, he said later, "Impartial beholders declared it was up to the best Masque ever presented in Christendom."

One beholder, not so impartial, fairly snorted his disapproval. As the performance continued, the man caused such a rumpus that he had to be marched out forcibly by the Lord Chamberlain, who was on hand to keep order. This rambunctious disturber of the peace was a poet and playwright who had been furiously disappointed at not being given the honor of writing the masque. His name was Ben Jonson.

BEN JONSON

BEN JOHNSON was a poet and a playwright. He had also been an actor, but he was officially listed in London as "citizen and bricklayer." Among friends and acquaintances he was known to be a warm-hearted fellow, but very pugnacious and opinionated. He had a positive idea as to how poetry should be written and plays constructed. Any one who did not follow the rules and regulations he laid down would hear sharp words from Ben Jonson.

Shakespeare, for example. Will Shakespeare was a friend of his. Ben Jonson liked Will personally, as everybody did, but he considered his plays a disorderly hodgepodge. Tragedy was so mixed with comedy, kings with fairies, night with day, that it was plain to see that Shakespeare gave no thought to the proper laws of Greek and Roman drama.

Apparently he just let his characters speak for themselves without exerting upon any of his plays the "grave and learned toil" Jonson himself recommended. And the worst of it was that all of them were popular.

About the time Shakespeare came to London to learn to be an actor, Ben Jonson, fourteen years old, was learning to spread mortar on a brick, and hating it. His own father had been a minister, but after he died Ben's mother had married a bricklayer, and the boy had grown up in a miserable alley leading down to the river, not far from Westminster Abbey. Next to the Abbey was Whitehall, the royal palace. The little boy from the alley passed it every day on his way to the Westminster School, looking up at the tall windows of the Banqueting Hall, which he never expected to enter. At school, for which a friend of the family paid the tuition, Ben, like all schoolboys in England, began the study of Latin grammar. And unlike most of them, he loved it. He dreamed of going to Oxford or Cambridge and becoming a famous scholar in Greek and Latin. But when the time came, there was no one to pay his way, and he went to laying bricks. But though he had a trowel in his hand, he had a book in his pocket, determined that nothing was going to keep him from becoming a learned man.

Before he had finished his seven years as an apprentice at the distasteful job, he was sent off to war in the Netherlands. As soon as he came back from war to bricklaying, he got married, though as an apprentice he was not allowed to marry until he was twenty-four. By the time he was twenty-four he was no longer laying bricks. He had become an actor at a new theatre called the Swan. Before the year was up he had been thrown into prison for having helped to write a play that the Privy Council called slanderous. He was released after two months and went back to writing poetry and plays. In 1598, he finished his first play— the popular comedy called *Every Man in His Humor,* in which Shakespeare had acted. Soon after the opening night at the Curtain in Shoreditch, Jonson got into a hot-headed argument with an actor friend, fought a duel with him in Hog's End Field near the theatre, and killed him. Duels were common enough, but killing a man was murder, and

Jonson was locked in Newgate Prison to be tried, and, if found guilty, to be hanged. Taking advantage of an old law, he was released, but came out permanently branded on the thumb. He had his freedom, but not for long. He was in debt, with no money to pay his debts, so he was promptly sent to debtor's prison, where he not only had no chance to make any money, but was charged for food, bed, even his handcuffs and chains. All quite according to the custom of the day. Finally he was bailed out by one of his friends, of which he had many more than he had enemies, and went back to writing poetry and plays.

Shakespeare's popular new play *Julius Caesar* was then playing at the Globe. As a Roman tragedy, Ben Jonson said, it was not at all what it ought to be. After a wrangle with a couple of other playwrights he announced that he was going to retire "High and Aloof" and write a Roman tragedy, properly, the way it should be written. The play he produced was so dull and boring that people in the audience booed and hissed and stamped their feet. It was played at the Globe theatre in 1603, the year of the plague, and also of the performance of the Christmas masque at which the disappointed playwright had been evicted by the scruff of the neck.

The next Christmas Ben Jonson was the man of the year. The Queen had commissioned him to write the masque. And it was to be given at Whitehall, in the very Banqueting Hall which as little Ben from the alley he had passed each morning on the way to school, but never dreamed of entering. It was called the *Masque of Blackness* and Queen Anne painted her arms black to the elbows, to play the part of a "Black-amoor." It was a complete success. From then on, Ben Jonson was *the* court poet.

The King's Men were also on hand for the holidays at Whitehall, and produced seven of Shakespeare's plays. Among them was *Othello,* for which Shakespeare had borrowed a description of the "headless men" from Sir Walter Raleigh. Raleigh, unfortunately, was not there at Whitehall to hear the speech or see the play. He was a prisoner in the Tower of London.

... from an old print

SIR WALTER RALEIGH—A PRISONER

ONE OF THE SLYEST, keenest and busiest in currying favor with the new King was Robert Cecil, the "crooked-backed" son of Lord Burghley, who upon his father's death had become the

Queen's most trusted minister. Cecil had rushed to meet the King, make his own position secure, and poison the King's mind against those whom he did not favor. One of these was Sir Walter Raleigh, who also went to meet the King, and who received an icy stare from His Majesty together with a bad pun.

"Rawley?" said he. "On my soul, I have Rawley heard of thee, mon!" Though the pun was bad, Raleigh's future was worse.

One morning early in July, Raleigh was walking on the terrace at Windsor Castle, when someone came up behind him and tapped him on the shoulder. It was Cecil, who said that the King's Council desired Raleigh to appear before them at once to be questioned.

The fact was that Cecil, always sniffing around for trouble, had brought in what he called "fearsome tidings of a surprising treason." He had discovered a vague, ill-formed plot by certain Catholic and Puritan nobles to seize the new king on the way to London and lock him in the Tower of London, until he had agreed to sign concessions they desired concerning religion. One of the conspirators who had been seized and questioned had mentioned the name of Raleigh. Later he wrote a letter apologizing to Raleigh for having accused him unjustly, then turned about and repeated his accusation to the Privy Council. Amid all the lies and dishonest accusations, it has never been discovered what, if anything, Raleigh knew about the plot or had to do with it. But in July he was one of those men who were arrested and held to be tried for treason, for which the punishment was death.

The trial was postponed because of the plague until November. Then, at Winchester, Raleigh was brought before the bar. As he entered the courtroom, he caught the eye of Cecil, and, looking about, could see that there would be no justice. The jury was "packed" with his enemies. There was no lawyer to speak in his defense. And the Attorney General who was to prosecute him was one of the most experienced lawyers in all England, Sir Edward Coke.

Raleigh knew little about the law. But since, according to the custom of the day, he had to plead his own case, he rose when he was called upon, faced his accusers, and declared his innocence.

Coke jumped to his feet, glared at him. "Thou art a monster," he cried in a harsh rasping voice. "The most notorious traitor that ever came before the bar!"

"You speak barbarously sir, and uncivilly," replied Raleigh, who again declared his innocence, and pled so eloquently for the jury to believe his words and spare his life that even Cecil, it was said, had tears in his eyes.

There was no effect upon the jury or the Attorney General.

"You are an odious fellow," roared Coke, "hateful to all England!"

The jury, after a fifteen-minute absence, returned the verdict of guilty. The Lord Chief Justice pronounced the death sentence. The trial was over, but the reaction in Raleigh's favor, and against the injustice of his sentence, was so overwhelming that James began to weaken about having it carried out. Queen Anne pleaded with him not to sign the death warrant. James himself did not want to start his reign by being blamed for injustice, yet he wavered.

Meanwhile, day after day, Raleigh, looking out through the bars of his window and seeing the other prisoners being led off to their fate, wondered when his own turn would come. Finally, two weeks before Christmas, 1603, a letter was handed to him bearing the royal seal. He opened it, and read that his life was to be saved by mercy of His Majesty the King.

That did not mean he was to be given his freedom. Raleigh was taken to the Tower of London, where presumably he was to remain a prisoner for the rest of his life.

Sir Edward Coke, the Attorney General, who appeared so unfavorably at the trial, was later to uphold justice in such a courageous way as to make his name famous in the history of English law.

Coke was then to be opposed by Sir Francis Bacon, a younger lawyer, now just scrambling up to a place of prominence at court with the help of his cousin Cecil.

SIR FRANCIS BACON "RINGS THE BELL"

THIS IS Francis Bacon. This thin face with the pointed beard and sharp eyes is that of a most ambitious man, whose fame rests not upon his deeds but upon his words—his written words.

In 1604, at almost any hour of the day or night, in his lonely lodgings at Gray's Inn, Bacon might have been seen covering page after page with his nervous writing. There was not a sound in the room but the continual scratching of his quill. He was then at work on the third book written and dedicated to His Majesty James I, so ambitious was this man of words to prove himself worthy of advancement.

Before the King reached London, Bacon had written letters to his cousin Cecil and to other influential acquaintances who might speak well of him to the King. Enclosed in one of them was a letter for delivery to the King himself, which he called *An Offer of Service to His Majesty King James Upon His First Coming In*. It began with a solemn quotation in Latin, followed by much flattery and extravagant praise, and ending with a recommendation of himself in these words: "Therefore, most high and mighty King, my most dear and dread sovereign lord, . . . I think there is no subject of your Majesty's whose heart is not set on fire, not only to bring you peace offering but to sacrifice himself a burnt offering to your Majesty's service amongst which number no man's fire shall be more pure and fervent than mine. But how far forth it shall blaze out, that resteth in your Majesty's employment. . . . I must leave all to the trial of further time and so thirsting after the happiness of kissing your royal hand, continue ever to be . . . etc, etc. FR. BACON"

This letter, with Cecil's recommendation, brought immediate results. In July, 1603, before the coronation, Francis Bacon was knighted with three hundred others at Whitehall. He would have been far more pleased if, as he wrote Cecil, he had not been one "of a troop." Nevertheless he was content to have the honor, such as it was, because, as he said, "I have three new knights in my mess in Gray's Inn commons; and because I have found out an alderman's daughter, a handsome maiden to my liking . . ."

The marriage to the handsome maiden was reported by one of the wedding guests in a letter of May 11, 1606. He says:

"Sir Francis Bacon was married yesterday to his young wench in Maribone Chapel. He was clad from top to toe in purple and hath made himself and his wife such a store of fine raiments of cloth of silver and gold that it draws deep into her portion. The dinner was kept at his father-in-law's lodging over against Savoy. . . ."

Sir Francis Bacon, the bridegroom of the young wench, was then forty-five years old, as slow about entering matrimony as he was at rising to a place of prominence at court.

For many years he had been ambitious for the post of Attorney General. Shortly after his marriage, Sir Edward Coke was promoted to Chief Justice of the Court of Common Pleas, leaving the old post vacant. The new Attorney General appointed was *not* Sir Francis Bacon, which might make one suspect Cecil's sincerity about wanting to help his

163

cousin. However, the help he had thus far given was far more than Bacon had ever received from Cecil's father, Lord Burghley.

The year that Sir Walter Raleigh had captured the favor of Queen Elizabeth, Francis Bacon, then a sickly lad of nineteen, a law student at Gray's Inn, had applied for help to his uncle, and been refused. Lord Burghley had not only scolded his nephew for his arrogance, but told the Queen that he was an overly ambitious and dangerous young man. As long as Elizabeth was on the throne, there had been no chance for Francis Bacon.

Under James I his fortune had immediately improved, largely due to the fact that he bombarded the king with words. Knowing that James prided himself on being a scholar, Bacon wrote on every subject he thought would be of particular interest to the King.

First. James was a Scotsman. It was known that he desired Scotland and England to be united. So Bacon wrote *A Brief Discourse Touching the Happy Union of the Kingdoms of England and Scotland.* Although the union was not to be formed until a hundred years later, in 1604 James I took the title suggested by Bacon, "King of Great Britany" shortened to "Great Britain."

Second. James as King of England was head of the Church, and Bacon next wrote on *Certain Considerations Touching the Church of England.*

Third. He wrote a book on a subject in which he was passionately interested himself and deeply concerned. It was called *The Advancement of Learning.* Published in 1605, it was one of the most famous books of its day. It was so well written, so widely read, that it had an enormous influence in changing the methods of science from the old medieval way of memorizing to the modern way of experiment. This was a subject on which Francis Bacon had been wanting to speak his mind since he was fifteen years old. As a student at Cambridge he had chafed under the same kind of teaching as Galileo had at Pisa. He too had had to repeat what the great Greek Aristotle had said, and believe it because Aristotle had said it. As if, protested Bacon, the world had reached a peak in the Golden Age of Greece and had discovered everything that it was ever possible to know. How absurd!

"There is nothing in nature," he declared, "except individual bodies performing individual acts according to fixed laws, the discovery and explanation of which are the foundations of science, pure and simple."

This idea did not originate with Francis Bacon. Individual scientists here and there were secretly using experiments to test the old statements and discover new truths. Thinking men everywhere were beginning to find fault with the old method. The idea was in the air. Someone was needed to put it into words.

Francis Bacon did just that. He summed up the faults of the old medieval system. He described the modern way in which science should be taught, by observation and experiment. And he did this so eloquently and well that he has been called the Father of Experimental Science. His fame rests not upon his deeds but upon his words. He made no great discoveries, but he inspired others. That, he said himself, was his true work: "the ringing of a bell to call the wits together—the rallying of men of science to a new way of learning."

The time was ripe for change, but such changes come at a snail's pace. As late as 1750, over a hundred years after Bacon's book was published, no one could graduate from Oxford University who questioned a single one of Aristotle's statements. And what happened to a scientist, in Bacon's own day and age, who dared to challenge one of those long-cherished ideas, would soon be seen in the case of Galileo.

Nevertheless, the break had been made. The new way of learning had been announced. Francis Bacon had been "ringing the bell."

HAMPTON COURT

THE KING JAMES BIBLE

ON A JANUARY DAY of 1604, a delegation of twenty solemn men in black might have been seen filing into Hampton Court, their long robes blown by the chill winter wind that swept about its rambling red brick walls and leaded window. They were all ministers of the Church of England summoned to a conference by James I, who as king was also head of the Church, and who likewise fancied himself an authority on all matters of religion. He was prepared to settle the dissension that had arisen within the Church and he proposed to deal harshly with the Dissenters, that group of reforming ministers known as Puritans—a name taken from the fact that they wanted to simplify the church ritual and change its government, or in other words "purify" the church.

The delegation of Puritans who had gone to meet James on his way to London presented him with a petition signed by a thousand ministers. It was their desire that the church should no longer be "Episcopal,"—governed by bishops and archbishops. It was their hope that James, brought up in Scotland where the Presbyterian Church was governed by the "presbyters," or ministers and elders, would favor a similar reform in the Church of England.

They were sadly mistaken. If anything made James turn purple in the face, it was the thought of those Presbyterian ministers in Scotland trying to run the state as well as the church.

"If ye aim at Scottish Presbyterianism, I tell ye," he said, "it agreeth no better wi' monarchy than God with the Devil."

He saw very well what democracy in religion would lead to, and he would have none of it. People who thought they could get along without bishops would soon be thinking they could do without kings.

On the first day of the conference, he opened the proceedings and then began to speak. He spoke on and on for three hours, spellbound by his own voice and the rapt attention of the audience. There was not a murmur of dissent, because there were no Dissenters present. The four Puritan churchmen, from Oxford and Cambridge, had not been invited to attend the first meeting. They were outside in the anteroom seated around a long oak table. Only the eighteen bishops and archbishops, who naturally were conformers, listened to the King's three-hour speech. When it was over, the Bishop of London flung himself on his knees before James and exclaimed that his heart melted for joy that God had given them such a king. The Archbishop of Canterbury declared that His Majesty must be divinely inspired. Such praise merely convinced James of what he already chose to believe—that a king took his power directly from God.

The second day, the four dissenting churchmen from Oxford and Cambridge were allowed to attend the session and present their arguments. James shuffled in, feeling more than ready to "confound" the Dissenters, and afterward congratulated himself on the outcome.

167

"I peppered the dissenters roundly," he boasted, "they fled me from argument to argument like a pack of school boys."

One proposal, strangely enough made by the Puritans whom King James so resented, was to give long-lasting prominence to his otherwise well-forgotten name.

"Your Majesty," said Dr. Reynolds, president of Corpus Christi College, Oxford, "it is our opinion that such English versions of the Bible as now exist are unlike the originals in Hebrew and Greek." To this James, as a self-acknowledged student of the Bible, was obliged to agree. He also consented to the learned doctor's proposal that a new translation should be undertaken.

"And let it be done," he said, "by the best learned scholars in both Universities, Oxford and Cambridge, reviewed by bishops and ratified by my authority."

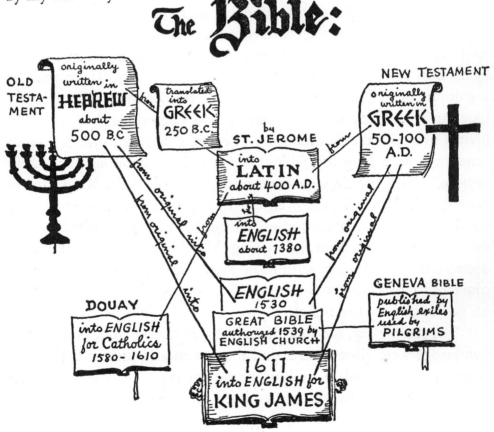

The Bible:

Forty-seven learned men then set to work on the translation that was to take seven years. And so it was that out of this great age of poets and writers came the very beautiful King James Version of the Bible.

The third day of the conference James could no longer keep his mind on what was being said and soon got up and shuffled out of the room. On the whole, he left the conference well satisfied with himself as absolute head of the Church and the King of England who derived his power directly from God.

A shock came with the first meeting of Parliament. King James I appeared in his crown and long purple ermine-trimmed robe. Holding the sceptre as majestically as possible in his hand, he proclaimed the opening of the session, was given what he took to be a cordial ovation, and departed.

The House of Commons then got down to business and proceeded to inform King James just where the power lay. It drew up a document stating that a king of England had no power in himself to alter religion, or make any law whatsoever, without the consent of Parliament. Nor could a king spend more money than the sum to be allotted him by the order of Parliament.

When James heard that his joyful money-spending was to be curtailed, he was so furious that he almost choked on the mutton he was eating. If he was to be cramped for money, he thought, taking a large gulp of ale, he might as well be back in Scotland. The thought of Scotland brought to his mind again the irritating Presbyterian ministers, and the equally irritating Puritans here in England, of which there were far too many. There were too many Puritans in Parliament, too many in the church—too many Puritans everywhere, disturbing the peace. They were not to be tolerated. He issued an order:

Let the ten dissenting Puritans who had met him on his way to London with a petition, be imprisoned by order of the King. As for all other Puritans, he declared that he would drive them out of England if they did not conform. And he kept repeating it.

"I will make the Puritans conform or harry them out of the land."

GUY FAWKES AND THE GUNPOWDER PLOT

CATHOLICS were as disappointed in the new King as the Puritans had been. It had been reported that James, as son of Mary Queen of Scots, had vowed that he would be lenient toward the followers of his mother's religion. It had also been reported that he intended to make peace with Spain, which led them to hope that England might even be turned back into a Catholic nation. Added to this was the report that at the first Christmas masque, the King had been seen deep in conversation with the Spanish ambassador, sounding him out, it was later learned, on the possibility of a future marriage between the two-year-old Spanish princess and eight-year-old Henry, Prince of Wales.

That was true. James I did favor an alliance by marriage with the richest nation in Europe. He appreciated that there might be compromises to be made, but did not anticipate such an arrogant reply as the one he received from Spain.

In case of a future marriage, the Spanish replied, Prince Henry must be educated in Spain. A Spanish cardinal went so far as to send a book of religious instructions to King James himself. This, as head of the Church of England, James considered little short of insulting.

170

He also took it as a warning that he should not be too lenient with the Catholics in England. For years old laws against them had been carelessly disregarded. James I now demanded that all those old laws should be revived and should be strictly enforced. Furthermore, from then on, any person, Protestant or Catholic, refusing to attend the Church of England should be fined, and the fines diligently collected.

In retaliation for this sudden blow, a crazy, wild plot was conceived by a little band of Catholic gentlemen, later looked upon with horror by loyal and responsible English Catholics, of whom there were many.

Guy Fawkes, a young man of good family, was persuaded to lead in the wild plan, which was intended to do away with Parliament and the entire royal family, all at once. The plot was to blow up the House of Parliament at the opening session of the year 1605, when all would be there—King James, young Henry, the Prince of Wales, and sickly little Charles, who had now been brought down from Scotland and been made the Duke of York.

Parliament House stood about fifty feet from the Thames River. The small house next door was to be rented, and a passage tunneled through the cellar wall in which to lay the train of gunpowder. February 5 was the opening date. By Christmas, they had begun their work. While rehearsals for the Masque by Ben Jonson were going on at Whitehall, not too far away, the conspirators were quietly digging in the dark, slimy cellar. They had laid in an ample supply of food, and each day Guy Fawkes, disguised as a servant, brought in a little more gunpowder. For various reasons they missed the February date, but after the summer recess they were ready and waiting for the reopening of Parliament on November 5, 1605.

During all those months, others had been told of the plan but sworn to secrecy. Yet as the time grew nearer and nearer, it seemed too horrible not to warn innocent friends and relatives who might be in Parliament that day and blown up without warning. So before November 5, the secret had leaked out.

On Saturday night, October 26, a certain Lord Monteagle was

handed a peculiar letter by his footman, who had had it slipped into his hand by a tall fellow who vanished in the dark.

The letter read: "I advise you, as you tender your life to devise some excuse to shift your attendance at this Parliament. . . . Retire into the country. They shall receive a terrible blow, this Parliament, and they shall not see who hurts them." Lord Monteagle rushed to Whitehall at once, gave the letter to Cecil, who immediately ran with it to the Lord Chamberlain, the Lord Admiral, and two other members of the Privy Council. The King himself was not there to be advised or consulted. He had gone hunting and would not be back in London until Friday. The Privy Council concluded that the vaulted cellar under the House of Lords should be searched. They agreed that this should not be done until the night before the meeting so as not to frighten the "base knaves out of their dark corners." They must be caught red-handed.

It was a little after midnight, not yet one o'clock of the morning of November 5, 1605, when Guy Fawkes, carrying a dark lantern, went back to the cellar where the gunpowder was stored, to wait for the appointed moment when he was to light the fuse. He had barely pushed open the huge, creaking oaken door—when he was seized by soldiers and the Justice of the Peace for Westminster. They marched him to Whitehall, to the anteroom of the King's bedchamber, where the sluggish, sleepy king, the bright-eyed Cecil, and other members of the Privy Council, roused from their sleep, were gathered in the dim foggy light of early morning.

"How could ye conceive so hideous a treason?" queried the King, as he squinted up at the prisoner. "Do ye not regret it?"

Guy Fawkes staring down at him with hard eyes, made this reply: "I regret nothing but that it was not carried out."

All the conspirators were arrested or slain. Thanksgiving for the discovery of the Gunpowder Plot was included in the Book of Common Prayer, and November 5 was to be long celebrated with fireworks and bonfires as a national holiday, Guy Fawkes Day.

"Trust in the Lord with all thine heart
   and lean not unto thine own
   understanding
In all thy ways acknowledge him
And he shall direct thy paths."

A MEETING IN SCROOBY VILLAGE

WILLIAM BREWSTER closed the Bible, and slipped it slowly back in place among the many books on the wall behind him. Then he turned and stood thoughtfully looking about the comfortable room with its open fireplace and gleaming brass fenders. It was an apartment in the large Manor House of Scrooby Village, which, as royal postmaster, William Brewster was privileged to occupy with his wife and family. Now the serious decision he had to make might cause him to lose his position and all that it entailed. William Brewster was in his late thirties, but as he stood there the lines in his forehead and the touch of gray at his temples made him look older than he was. It was eighteen years since he had left his post at the court of Queen Elizabeth and come home to Scrooby. Those years had been pleasant ones here in the tiny village where most of the people were his friends. For the past nine or ten years he had been the royal postmaster. Now the question was; should he obey the King, conform to his demands in matters of religion, or should he obey his conscience, withdraw from the Church of England, and join an Independent or Separatist congregation?

The decision he made was that of many others. The threat of James I that he would harry the nonconforming Puritans out of the land did not have the desired effect of making them conform. Rather, it caused some, like William Brewster, to withdraw quietly from the Church of England and form independent congregations—true Congregational

173

churches governed by the people themselves—the kind that James feared would lead, as it eventually did, to a government of the people in a land without a king.

The small independent congregation in the village of Scrooby met in the home of William Brewster. There to attend the meeting one day in 1606 came a tall lean young man by the name of William Bradford.

In 1603, when James I became King of England, William Bradford was thirteen and had never dreamed of knowing so cultured a gentleman as William Brewster. Nor had he ever thought of finding anyone who would teach him and talk to him and treat him as if he were his own son. William was an orphan. He lived with his uncles, Thomas and Robert Bradford, about two miles from Scrooby in the village of Austerfield.

Almost any summer day, the boy might have been seen tending his sheep on the hills surrounding the village. Sometimes, seated on a large stone, he read from his Bible, or with the book closed said aloud to himself the Twenty-third Psalm or some other verses he knew by heart. The words always made William feel stronger, more able to bear the scornful look in the eyes of his uncles, who seemed to blame him for having had a long sickness and still being "weakly."

Thomas and Robert Bradford were farmers, good strong hearty yeomen. They worked hard plowing, harrowing, shearing sheep, shoveling manure, and sat down to hearty meals of meat, bread, ale, cheese, and good Yorkshire pudding. They couldn't see why William couldn't eat what they did. Then he'd be able to work, and not always have his nose in a book. Reading, that was queer business, especially reading the Bible. That sounded like Puritans to them. They wanted no Puritans in Austerfield. The Bradfords were important people in their little community—honest, upstanding people. Every Sunday, rain or shine, they were in their pew in St. Helen's Church, accepting as a matter of course that which Henry VIII had long ago decreed should be the Church of England. They obeyed and prayed without question, as their forefathers had done.

Every Sunday William also sat squeezed in between his uncles, aunts, and cousins in the family pew, listening but also questioning and thinking, wanting so much to understand what every word meant. Later he often searched his Bible for some of the things that were said and done, but could find no mention of them. The puzzling questions remained. One Saturday night as he was driving his sheep home from the hills, he was thinking that the next day, Sunday, might bring some of the answers. For he was about to do a daring thing. He had a new friend, and he was going to church with him at Babworth to hear a Puritan minister preach. The village of Babworth was eight miles away, so he would have to get up early and slip out before the uncles were awake. . . .

Sunday came. Before sunup, while the grass was still wet, William was on his way. Monday morning his uncles made him confess where he had been. He had to admit that although Mr. Richard Clyfton, whom he had gone to hear, was still a minister of the Church of England, he was a Puritan. They were furious. They forbade him ever to go again. It was a shame and a disgrace to the family.

William listened quietly—but his mouth was firm. In spite of all their threats, he went with trembling heart to hear the minister again and again, until he found himself no longer afraid of his uncles when they stormed and ranted at him. When Richard Clyfton withdrew from the Church of England and joined an Independent Congregation, young William Bradford followed him and became a member also.

That was more than the Bradford family could endure. One and all rose to prevent the stubborn young dissenter from disgracing them. Then, in the midst of their protest, a terrifying thing happened. One of them was stricken dead. They looked at one another with frightened eyes, believing it was the hand of God. From then on they said no more, but let William go his way.

And now it was becoming a dangerous way. Many Separatists were being thrown into prison. Everywhere they were scoffed at and scorned, hunted out and persecuted. The King's decree against all nonconformists was being carried out. As conditions grew worse, more than half of the congregation to which William belonged left everything behind and fled the country. The smaller group, with Richard Clyfton as minister, went to Scrooby village, where it was found that they could hold their meetings in a part of the manor house occupied by William Brewster, the postmaster. And so William Bradford and William Brewster met, and a life-long friendship began.

The Independents went in and out of the manor as secretly as possible, but Scrooby village was such a tiny place that the meetings soon aroused suspicion and were reported to agents of the King. Toward the end of the year William Brewster and four other members of the congregation received a summons to appear before the Commissioners of the Province of York, and were charged with "disobedience in matters of religion."

Fortunately William Brewster was allowed to return to Scrooby, but the postmastership had already been taken from him, and he could no longer live in the manor house. So they were faced with the problems of what to do and where to go. Should they try to go to Holland? In Holland, they knew they would not be persecuted. There "religion was free to all men," as it was not in England. Yet to leave England—leave their farms and friends for a strange land where they could not speak the language—how could they do it? But how could they do otherwise? They had joined together to walk in the Lord's way as free people regardless of the cost. So they made their plans to leave, but when they tried to go they found the way barred by officers of the King.

They had hired a ship at the port of Boston and made an agreement with the master, but he no sooner had them and their goods on board than he betrayed them. Searchers and other officers stripped them of their money and books and held them in prison for a month, until orders came from the Lords of Council to dismiss them and send them home. This was the spring of 1607. The next spring they tried again, hired a Dutch boat, and at length after many trials and troubles they left England behind and crossed the North Sea to Holland.

from a sketch of Spaniards
burning Indians made
by Champlain in Mexico

NEW SPAIN
Mexico.
VERA CRUZ
PANAMA
PORTO BELLO
FLORIDA
ST. AUGUSTINE
PUERTO RICO
PERU
GUIANA
SPANISH MAIN
BRAZIL
STRAITS
OF MAGELLAN

A FRENCHMAN REPORTS ON NEW SPAIN

IT WAS EARLY MORNING in Paris. The vegetable men had barely laid
out their fresh greens, when along the narrow streets came Samuel
de Champlain, a slight, wiry young Frenchman, carrying a large
notebook. He was walking briskly toward the Louvre to keep an appoint-

ment with the King, Henry IV. The King's son, the Dauphin Louis XIII, was then about a year old. Probably in some room of the great rambling palace he was waking up and screaming to be fed, as the brisk young man with the notebook turned into the wide doorway of the Louvre. He proceeded to climb the grand marble staircase leading to the royal apartments on the third floor. Energetic Henry IV was already conferring with the Duc de Sully and signing papers, although it was not yet seven, the hour at which the audiences began. The ante-chamber outside was filled with courtiers waiting to see the king. At one glance they observed that the young man with the notebook was not a Parisian, but from one of the Provinces. This was true.

Samuel de Champlain came from the fishing village of Brouage on the east coast of France, south of Brittany. Although he did not expect the King to remember the fact, he had been an officer in the King's army, had fought against the Spaniards in Brittany and helped to defeat them. As Henry IV never forgot to be grateful to the soldiers who had fought for him, the young man knew he would be well received, and allowed to present his notebook. This contained many of his own sketches, and a description of a visit he had made to Spain's colonies in the New World, which he knew would be of interest to the King, because no other Frenchman had ever made such a visit.

Although the French had long been envious of the great wealth Spain drew from the New World, France, like England, had as yet no colony in America. It was this young man waiting to see the King who was to found the city of Quebec and become the "Father of New France."

After the Spanish troops had been defeated in Brittany and the French soldiers discharged, Champlain had returned to his home, the fishing village of Brouage. Walking idly along the wharf watching the fishing schooners coming in from the Banks of Newfoundland and Labrador, the urge came upon him to take a voyage on the sea. Not to the north with the fishing fleet, but south to the West Indies to visit Spain's colonies in the New World. So long as France was at war with Spain, this would not have been possible for a Frenchman. But now that the war was over, Champlain believed that if his Uncle Provençal could help him get to Spain, he might manage to make the voyage. Uncle Provençal was a sea captain, now employed in taking home Spanish troops that were being evacuated from Brittany. Champlain found his uncle, who agreeably took him along on his troopship, the *Saint Julien.* They sailed to Cadiz, where the soldiers disembarked, and from there they went to the port of Seville.

A Spanish admiral who was gathering a fleet for a voyage to New Spain arranged with Uncle Provençal to charter the *Saint Julien* and was happy to have the French captain's nephew aboard.

So, early in February 1599, Champlain boarded the *Saint Julien,* one of a fleet of ten ships leaving Spain for the New World. His hope was to be realized, his curiosity satisfied. He was going to see with his own eyes what Christopher Columbus had seen, what Balboa had seen, and Cortez and Pizarro. He had bought a fresh notebook in which to write descriptions, and he had paints and brushes with him to make sketches of everything he saw—fruits, flowers, vegetables, animals, as well as the native people.

The Spanish admiral, Don Francisco Coloma, kept the fleet united for safety against English pirates until they reached the harbor of San Juan in Puerto Rico. There he divided the ships, taking four large vessels with him to the Spanish Main (the north coast of South America), sending three to Portobello with goods for Panama and Peru, and the three remaining to Mexico. Champlain's ship was one of these. After an encounter with some English, Dutch, and French pirate ships, it arrived safely at the harbor of Vera Cruz. Two weeks later Champlain was on his way to Mexico City.

It was a journey of about 250 miles up from Vera Cruz, along a winding mountain road—the very road, Champlain was thinking, that Cortez had traveled ninety years before. Up this narrow, steep road, Cortez had led his soldiers to the high city, then the capital of the Aztecs. After being graciously received by the great Aztec Emperor

Montezuma, Cortez had captured the city, conquered the people, made himself governor and captain-general of Mexico.

Champlain was amazed when he entered and found that it was now a magnificent Spanish city. "I had not thought it to be," he said, "so superbly built of fine temples, palaces and beautiful houses—the streets so well laid out, with fine and large shops with all kinds of rich merchandise . . ."

There was also in the City of Mexico, though he does not mention it, a university—the first one in North America—founded in 1551, just five years after Philip II had become King of Spain. Also, on the site of the old temple to the Aztec god of war, Mexitli, stood a great Spanish cathedral, topped by a cross of gold.

Champlain estimated that there were about fifteen thousand Spaniards in the city, about six times as many Christian Indians, and a large number of Negro slaves. He pitied the Indians, and describes in these words the cruel way in which they had been treated in the name of religion: "At the beginning of the King of Spain's conquests, he had established the Inquisition among the Indians, and enslaved them or caused them to die in such great numbers that the mere story of it rouses one's pity. If the Spanish still wanted to punish them according to the Inquisition they would cause them all to die by fire . . ." (This burning of the Indians he illustrated with a sketch) "Now," he says, "the Spanish rule is milder, and each village priest calls the roll before Mass and any Indians who are absent are sought out and given thirty to forty blows with a stick."

Even that, Champlain thought, was no way to bring anyone to a knowledge of God and belief in the Church.

After a month spent in Mexico City, Champlain returned to the fleet at Vera Cruz. Finding that he still had time for another side trip, he went to Portobello on the Isthmus of Panama. There he saw the possibility of a canal being cut through the narrow strip of land. "So that from Panama to the Straits of Magellan would be one island, and from Panama to the Newfound-lands and other island, so that all America would be two islands."

The idea was not new. Though he did not know it, the possibilities had been investigated in 1534 by a commission appointed by Charles V and the report made that the obstacles were then insurmountable.

After leaving Vera Cruz, the fleet sailed for Havana and from there eastward across the Atlantic. According to Champlain's own reckoning, the journey ended in Seville in March, 1601. Some months later he was back in France, and within a year was on his way to Paris, hoping for a job and trusting that the report on his Mexican adventures would serve as a recommendation to the king.

Henry IV responded to Champlain's story with his natural enthusiasm. He felt that France as well as Spain should have colonies in the New World. He spoke of the possibility of finding a northwest passage to India and China. He mentioned the name of Jacques Cartier, the Breton fisherman who had set sail for Newfoundland in 1534, hoping to find a channel to the Pacific Ocean. Jacques Cartier had planted the flag on the Gaspé Peninsula, and claimed all of Canada for France. Since that time little had been done—nothing in the last sixty years. Religious wars had made that impossible. But now! Now France must plant colonies. France must share in the wealth of the New World!

The Duke of Sully did not echo his sovereign's enthusiasm. "The true source of the wealth for France, Sire, lies here, at home in the pastures and fields of our own country. As for Canada! No! Never will we take great wealth from that country so far to the north. Never voluntarily will I give support to such a foolish adventure, as to plant a French colony in Canada!"

SANTA FE, NEW MEXICO

ABOUT THREE YEARS before Champlain was born, Huguenot refugees from France tried to form a settlement in Florida. They were wiped out by the Spaniards, who built a fort there the following year, 1565, to protect their "Land-of-Flowers" from all future intruders. They called it St. Augustine. Thirty-three years later, as Champlain was starting from France on his visit to Spain and Mexico, a group of Spanish settlers were leaving Mexico for that colorful desert land where they were to found Santa Fe.

That high land of brilliant sun, purple shadows, turquoise sky and white clouds was long known to the Spaniards as having been the site of a great ancient civilization such as they had found in Mexico and Peru. For fifty years bold Spanish explorers had set out to find a fabulous lake of gold, and to discover marvelous cities, described as having houses whose doors "were studded with turquoise as if feathers from the sky had flown down and clung to them." All of these conquistadors, like the tireless Coronado, had marched far and wide across the country but found only desert land, dreary pueblos, and half-naked Indians. Their failure, however, had never kept others from believing

182

that the gold was there to be found and setting forth in search of it. And always, along with the adventurers searching for gold, went monks and priests just as eagerly searching for souls to be saved among the Indians.

Before he died, Philip II, undisturbed as usual by failure, ordered the Viceroy of Mexico to find some one who would explore, conquer, and establish a colony in that land north of the Rio Grande to be known as "New Mexico." The volunteers must pay all expenses, raise an army, enlist colonists, furnish provisions and equipment. In spite of this, the chance of gain was so dazzling that many offered to take the gamble. Volunteers actually plotted and schemed and connived to be given the contract, which caused much delay and confusion. In the midst of all the wrangling, one man stood quietly waiting, a gentleman of wealth and prominence, of equal patience and courage, and a loyal subject of his king. In the end he was to be founder of New Mexico, Don Juan de Oñate. The contract bearing the royal signature was handed to him by the Viceroy.

Oñate took the King's letter, kissed it, placed it on his head for a moment as a sign of obedience. Three years passed before he was allowed to start on the expedition. By then it was 1598, the year that

Philip II died, as well as the year in which Champlain started the voyage which would lead him to Mexico City. That year, also, Oñate had been saddened by the death of his beautiful wife, who was both Indian and Spanish, being the grand-daughter of Cortez and the great-grand-daughter of Montezuma.

At last, in February, Oñate and his company broke camp in Mexico and started for the Land of the Pueblos. There were four hundred soldiers in their shining steel helmets, 130 colonists with their families, seven thousand cattle, sheep, goats, mares, and oxen, and eighty-three carts filled with tools, iron, provisions, seeds, medicines, and garlic. The heavy wooden wheels creaked and groaned with every turn. Three days' march through the desert, covered with sage brush and greasewood and cut by deep arroyos brought them to the Rio San Pedro. There they were met by a band of Franciscan monks, which completed the caravan.

April 30 they reached the Rio Grande, and there (a few miles south of El Paso, Texas) they halted for a ceremony. One of the brothers preached a sermon, and prayed while the circle knelt about him in the sand. He blessed the royal standard. Oñate then stepped forward. He planted the standard in the ground and formally took possession of the land in the name of His Sanctified Majesty, the King of Spain.

Then came the fiesta! There was feasting and dancing. Men wore their best velvet jackets, braided in gold. Dark-eyed women, with red flowers in their hair, and wide, many-ruffled skirts, went whirling about to the clatter of castanets and strumming of guitars.

In the morning they broke camp and the trek began again. During the next four hot, dusty months the caravan crawled through the Rio Grande valley. Oñate rode ahead with part of the army. He visited the pueblos and explained to the Indians what great good fortune had come to them. They now belonged to the King of Spain, who would protect them from their enemies, if they obeyed him. And if they prayed to the God of the King, they would all be saved. From what? The seven chiefs who listened at Santo Domingo pueblo did not know, but the man had a kind voice and good face, so they knelt and kissed his hands.

184

A few miles farther on, the Rio Grande joined the Cham river at the foot of a black mesa, or tableland. An Indian pueblo, with its houses of sun-baked adobe, stood on each side of the river.

Oñate took the one on the east for the Spaniards, naming it for his own patron saint, San Juan. By the middle of August, the long trail of settlers, soldiers, and animals came dragging in, utterly exhausted and disgusted. What barren land was this that he had led them through! They would have starved, they said, if they had not been able to take the corn the Indians had stored up for the winter. And what was this miserable place? Were they going to stop here? Where was the gold?

Oñate's ears rang with their grumbling. August was too late to plant crops. So to keep them busy, he began building a church—a little church of sun-baked adobe, with a rough-hewn wooden cross and bronze bell. When it was finished they had a ceremony.

The Indians from the pueblo across the river were invited. They sat in a circle while, for their amazement and amusement, the Spaniards with their steel helmets and long lances performed a sham battle. Then in solemn procession, Oñate, the monks, and the Indian chiefs descended one by one through a small opening in the ground into a Kiva. This was a small jug-like underground chamber where the Indians held councils. Here, after the monks had explained to them how they could be saved from some disaster, the Indians bowed to the white man's God, to the faraway King, and to Oñate, who represented the King. Then there was a fiesta, a wild gay glorious fiesta, when no one thought of anything but dancing and singing, as long as it lasted.

The black cloud of gloom and despair that followed the fiesta's bright moment lasted all winter. Grumbling against Oñate increased when spring came, and the settlers were told to plow the soil and plant seeds. What? they said. They had not come here to do what they did at home. Plow and plant? They were now *hidalgos* . . . Had not every settler who agreed to come been made an hidalgo, a gentleman? Well, then, who ever heard of an hidalgo working, tilling the soil, degrading himself? They might better go home. A third of the colony plotted to steal away and return to Mexico. The plot was discovered and thwarted.

The missionaries had also been having trouble converting the Indians, who had starved through the winter because the Spaniards had eaten their corn. They were more intereseted in being saved from starvation than from some future misery.

Oñate grew desperate. The soil was fertile. All it needed was water. Where irrigation ditches had been dug, the grain and vegetables grew luxuriantly. All that was needed was a little work. But the hidalgos could not be made to work. "They want to find gold lying on the ground," he reported to the Viceroy.

And there was no gold to be found. Oñate rode in every direction from the colony, east as far as Kansas, west to the Grand Canyon and the Gulf of Mexico, exploring the country. On his return from one of the expeditions he found three-fourths of the colony gone, taking tools and equipment with them. Enough loyal friends had remained to keep the colony alive. It had now been moved to the pueblo on the west side of the river—and given the new name of San Gabriel.

Meanwhile the settlers who had revolted were back in Mexico City denouncing Oñate to the Viceroy. Officers who were still jealous of Oñate for having been granted the contract joined in plotting against him. Their plots succeeded. After keeping the colony alive for eleven years, Oñate was recalled.

There was some talk in the Council meeting that the colony of New Mexico should be abandoned. But the good monks protested in all sincerity. What was to be done about the Christian Indians? They could not abandon them. So if the monks were determined to stay, it was decided to keep the colony alive. However, it must no longer be under the rule of one man, but supported and ruled by the Spanish government.

Early in 1609, Don Pedro Penalta was appointed to succeed Oñate. Following orders, he proceeded at once to the pueblo of San Gabriel and there founded a town, or *villa—La Villa Real de Santa Fé de San Francisco*—in short, Santa Fe.

CHAMPLAIN VISITS CANADA

CHAMPLAIN made his first trip to Canada in the spring of 1603, the year that James I became King of England. The ship on which he sailed from France was going, as it did each spring, to bring back a load of furs. The captain was an old, experienced fur-trader. Every spring he left the French port of Honfleur, with his ship, the *Bonne Renommée,* loaded with axes, knives, tin pans, beads, and other articles for trading, sailed to Tadoussac on the St. Lawrence River,

187

met the Indians there who came down the river every spring in their canoes heaped with the winter's catch. He returned in the late summer, his ship loaded with beautiful furs to be sold in France.

Champlain went on the voyage as observer and map-maker, for this particular expedition was to bring back facts as well as furs. Henry IV was asking for facts about this wild land of his yet to be settled, and about the valuable fur trade which had been going on for years but never properly regulated. Since the first Breton fishermen had gone to Newfoundland for cod and begun trading trinkets with the Indians, Frenchmen had been bringing home furs to be sold in France. Most prized of all was the beaver. Gentlemen of the court clamored for fashionable beaver hats. Hatters needed the fine skins. Beaver or any other furs, purchased so cheaply in Canada, brought tremendous profit in France.

Splendid indeed it seemed to Henry IV to own a land that yielded such a valuable product. How could that land be settled? How should the fur trade be handled? Should it be open to all, or should one man be given the monopoly? If so, on what terms?

These were the questions, Champlain understood, that his observations must answer. As map-maker and observer, he must also bring the King word of any lake or river that might be the undiscovered northwest passage to the far sea.

Fortified with a royal letter of introduction, Champlain went to the port of Honfleur, found the ship, and presented himself to the captain, sturdy, good-humoured Captain Pontgravé.

"Ah, Champlain!" roared the captain in a loud hearty voice, clapping a friendly hand on the younger man's thin shoulder and making him feel welcome at once. "Ho!" he called, "ho, ho!" and two Indians at some distance turned about. "*Mes amis,* come here," he shouted, beckoning. Indians from Canada, he explained to Champlain, Algonquins—he had brought them back on his last voyage, to learn French and act as interpreters. They answered in French as Pontgravé introduced them, and nodded agreement as the captain told how they had been to Paris to see the sights and meet the King. They would bring back a report to their Sagamore (or chief).

It was March when the ship sailed from Honfleur. It was May when it was anchored at Tadoussac, and Champlain set foot for the first time on the land where he was to spend almost all the rest of his life. First land to be sighted had been the shores of Newfoundland, then came the wide mouth of the St. Lawrence with the mountains of the Gaspé Peninsula to their left, and at last, to their right, the mouth of another river, the Saguenay, joining the St. Lawrence. And there, said Captain Pontgravé, pointing to the shore, was Tadoussac!

Grim gray granite rocks rose from the water, edged by a narrow sandy beach. Many birch-bark canoes were drawn up along the shore. There was the smell of pines in the air, mingled with that of wood smoke from many fires. As the captain, the two Indians and Champlain approached the shore in a small boat, strange half-naked savages came into sight, looking like painted devils to the man who was seeing Indians in their warpaint for the first time. They landed and went to the lodge of the great Sagamore named Anadabijou, to whom the two Indians with them were to make their report.

There, that day of May 27, 1603, an alliance was to be formed, a friendship established between the French and the Indians that was to remain unbroken as long as the French held Canada.

"We found [the great Sagamore]," said Champlain, "and some eighty of his companions, making *tabagie* (that is to say, a feast). He received us very well . . . and made us sit down beside him, while all the savages ranged themselves one next to the other on both sides of the lodge. One of the savages whom we had brought began to make his oration, of the good reception that the King had given them, and of the good entertainment they had received in France, and that . . . His Majesty . . . desired to people their country, and to make peace with their enemies (who are the Iroquois) or send forces to vanquish them.

". . . then . . . Grand Sagamore Anadabijou, who had listened

189

to him attentively, began to smoke tobacco, and to pass on his pipe to Monsieur du Pontgravé of Saint Malo, and to me, and to . . . other Sagamores who were near him. After smoking some time, he began to address the whole gathering, speaking with gravity . . . saying to them that in truth they ought to be very glad to have His Majesty for their great friend . . . that he was well content that His said Majesty should people their country and make war on their enemies. . . .

"When he had ended his speech, we went out of his lodge, and they began to hold their *tabagie* or feast, which they make with the flesh of moose, which is like beef, with that of bear, seal, and beaver, and with great quantities of wild fowl. They had eight or ten kettles full of meats . . . each on its own fire. The men sat . . . each with his porringer made of the bark of a tree; . . . out of which they feed very filthily, for when their hands are greasy they rub them on their hair, or else on the hair of their dogs, of which they have many for hunting. . . . Then when they had ended their feast, they began to dance, taking in their hands . . . the scalps of their enemies, which hung behind them. . . .

"They were celebrating this triumph for a victory they had won over the Iroquois, of whom they had slain about a hundred."

The celebration over, the Indians removed their warpaint and the fur-trading began. Two weeks were spent in talking and fur-trading, giving Champlain a different impression of these primitive people to whom he was to become so deeply attached. "I think," he said, "that if anyone should show them how to live. . . and to till the ground . . . they would learn very well . . . I think they would speedily be . . . good Christians, if their country were colonized . . ." This, he was to discover, was largely wishful thinking.

The fur-trading over, the exploration began. In mid-June Champlain, Pontgravé, and the Indian guides started up the St. Lawrence in a pinnace which they had brought with them on the ship. Four days from Tadoussac brought them to the narrows of Quebec. They sailed on to the mouth of the Iroquois River, and then turned south and followed the river into what was to became New York State. The Algonquin guides told of a lake farther south and beyond that another lake where dwelt the terrible Iroquois. Beyond that was a river flowing south.

"And what lies to the west?" asked Champlain.

"A great waterfall," the Indians told him, and beyond that "still waters so great that no man had seen the end." Without doubt, thought Champlain, this could be nothing other than an entrance to the South Sea—the northwest passage to India and China!

In mid-August the *Bonne Renommée* sailed for Honfleur, with its cargo of furs. This time the captain was taking back a small Indian boy, the son of an Algonquin Sagamore, whose father was sending him to be educated in Paris. The journey home was made in the record speed of eighteen days, and Champlain was busy every minute preparing maps and writing his report for the King. What a disappointment, when the ship docked at Honfleur, to find that Henry IV and Queen Marie had been there only the week before. Champlain hastened to Paris, only to find that the royal family had then gone to the palace of Fontainebleau, twenty miles from Paris. So Champlain went to Fontainebleau, with his maps, minerals, and various curiosities—including the little Indian boy, decked out in a French blue coat and bonnet. Louis the Dauphin, now three years old, was wild about the little brown boy, whom he called his Canada. He would send him jelly and cake and soup from the nursery. But poor little Canada would not eat. He was homesick, sick all over . . . and he died the following June.

Henry IV was delighted with Champlain's report of the possibilities of establishing a "New France" in Canada. He agreed with Champlain that the fur trade should not be open to all. Some one should be given a monopoly, as a reward for planting a colony.

Sully shook his head in disapproval. "The French, I regret," he said, "have neither the nature nor mind for such matters. A colony separated from us by foreign seas will be nothing but a useless burden."

For once the great minister's judgment was to be overruled. Next spring Champlain would help plant a French colony in America.

15 MILES FROM LONDON TO THE MOUTH OF THE

OFF TO VIRGINIA

LATE IN THE YEAR 1605, John Smith was on a ship sailing into the Thames. *Captain* John Smith now, he was coming home to England, with a pocket full of ducats, a new coat of arms, the right to call himself a "gentleman," and a tale of adventure more than equal to any he was to hear. On his right, as the ship approached the arches of London Bridge, he looked up at the grim gray stone walls of the Tower of London. And from a parapet high on those walls, Sir Walter Raleigh, looking down, may have seen the ship pass, quite unaware that on that ship was a small Captain who was to fulfill Raleigh's dream of establishing a colony in Virginia.

It is possible that, having stepped outside the gloomy Tower room in which he was imprisoned, Sir Walter Raleigh may have been pacing back and forth in the open air, as he was allowed to do, watching from a distance all that he was able to see of the outside world in which he no longer had a part. As he watched, prison-bound, his imagination carried him away and his spirits soared in anticipation of dreams to be realized when he was free again—dreams of an empire for England—a

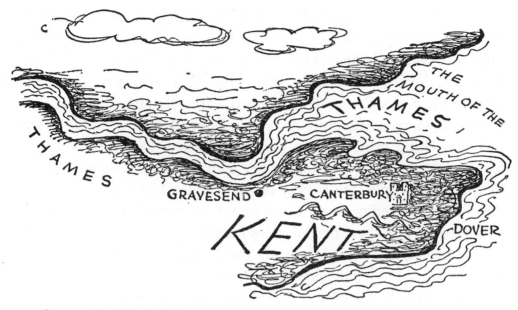

settlement in Virginia!

Twenty years had passed since Queen Elizabeth had granted her young favorite permission to send explorers to that wonderful virgin country which had been named for her. It was three years later, in 1585, that he had financed and equipped an expedition, a colony had been founded on the island of Roanoke, and then, because of the Spanish Armada, had been left to its uncertain fate. After Governor White had failed to find the "Lost Colony" in the summer of 1591, Raleigh still did not give up hope. He sent out five more expeditions in the next thirteen years.

"I shall yet see Virginia an English nation," he kept saying. The year 1602, in which he sent his final expedition, was the last year of Queen Elizabeth's life, and the last of his own freedom. The next year had brought James I to the throne, and sent Raleigh to the Tower.

Lady Raleigh, his wife, his son, and two servants were with him, and his life in prison was made as bearable as possible by the sympathetic jailer. Guests were allowed to come freely, and all kinds of interesting and varied people came to see him, ranging from Guiana Indians to Queen Anne.

However, he was financially ruined, his lands and income and all his colonizing rights in Virginia taken from him. Yet he did not lose heart, nor cease to hope that he could regain his fortune. He spoke and wrote continually to those at court who might secure his freedom. Among these was Cecil, who had proved friendly after the trial, and Queen Anne, who often brought young Prince Henry with her to see this stimulating man. He was such a contrast to her royal husband, whose slobbery slovenliness filled her with loathing. Raleigh showed the prince his books, the History of the World which he was writing, the chemical experiments on which he was at work. To the Queen he spoke continually about regaining his freedom, and also about the new Virginia Company which was being formed and the possibility of his being permitted to join its first expedition.

The Virginia Company was a stock company formed in 1605 by gentlemen who had been associated with Raleigh before his imprisonment. They had petitioned the King and received the right to settle Virginia. Actually there were two companies, the Virginia Company of Plymouth, which was to colonize the northern part, and the Virginia Company of London, which was to colonize the southern part. The Plymouth Company did not become active until later, but the London Company planned to start at once on this business venture in which the King was to share. One-third of all gold or precious metals they should find were to be his—and the colony was to be named James Town, in his honor. The colony was to be governed by a council in Virginia, composed of seven of the settlers. They were to take orders from a council in London, composed of stockholders, who in turn were to take orders from the King. All this had been arranged by April, 1606. After that, money had to be raised, ships procured, seamen hired, crews and settlers signed up. This took several months more, during which Raleigh clung to the hope that his plea to join the expedition might be granted.

His nephew Ralph (Sir Humphrey Gilbert's son) was permitted to go, but not Raleigh himself. He was still in the Tower when the three small three-masted ships that were to make the voyage passed by down the Thames to be tied up not far from the spicy wharves of the East India Company. There they were loaded with sea beef, salt pork, dried peas, beer, cheese, and other supplies needed for the voyage. The ships were anchored, Raleigh knew, just beyond the place where Drake's *Golden Hind* was still on display. If they followed the custom of the day, the Captain and his men would plan to dine the night before sailing on the famous old ship, to bring them luck on the voyage.

It was late in December, 1606 when, with 105 aboard (all men—no women) the three small ships, the *Sarah Constant,* the *Goodspeed,* and the *Discovery,* were ready to sail.

Captain Christopher Newport was admiral and commander-in-chief of the little fleet. As he went aboard he carried a sealed box in which was a list of the seven men who had been chosen as councillors to govern Virginia. During the long journey no one was to know who the seven men were. John Smith and many another might hope his name had been included, but the sealed box was not to be opened until they reached the New World. Till then the bearer of the box, Captain Christopher Newport, was in command.

Allowing six weeks for crossing, February would see them in Virginia. In February they were still in sight of England. The wind had failed as they reached the mouth of the Thames. For over six weeks they were held up, anchored off the coast of Kent, waiting for the wind to change. A miserable, seasick crew they were, as the anchored ships rolled and pitched and tossed incessantly. Then came dysentery and scurvy to increase the misery. The chaplain, Robert Hunt, became so ill that he was not expected to live, but his uncomplaining spirit, his example of courage and endurance (said John Smith later) kept the project from being abandoned altogether.

Finally, when they had almost despaired of having a favorable wind, it was there, filling their sails, and they were off—the *Sarah Constant,* the *Goodspeed,* and the *Discovery,* three tiny ships on a tremendous gray ocean.

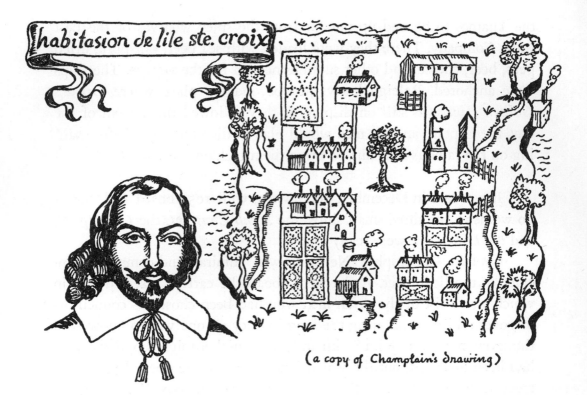

habitasion de lile ste. croix

(a copy of Champlain's drawing)

NEW FRANCE: THE FIRST COLONY

THE LAND IN AMERICA to which the King of France laid claim
extended roughly from the Gulf of St. Lawrence down to Delaware Bay. In March, 1604, a party of seventy-nine left for the
New World to plant the first colony in this vast area which they happily
considered "New France." Champlain had been appointed geographer
for the expedition. The leader was the Sieur (Sir) de Monts, an old
military friend of Henry IV. De Monts had been granted the monopoly
of the fur trade for ten years. In return for this he was to explore the
country, establish a colony, and convert the Indians to Christianity.

The first settlement they made was on an island in the river which
now marks the borderline between Maine and Canada. Champlain's
idea had been to settle somewhere along the St. Lawrence, but de Monts

196

insisted on finding a spot farther south. After exploring the Atlantic coast line until June, they finally turned into the broad mouth of a river to be called the St. Croix. Half a dozen miles upstream they came to a small island that looked so inviting and pleasant between summer sky and blue water that they gave no thought to what it might be in winter when icy winds swept down upon it out of the northwest. With light hearts they went ashore to build a settlement, unloading doors and woodwork they had brought on the ship, cutting down all the trees on the island. They erected first a storehouse fifty feet long, then a house for de Monts, one for Champlain, one for the priest, a chapel, a kitchen, a forge, an oven, and a hand mill for grinding corn. All looked tidy.

Early in October, snow began to fall and winter set in. The wind blew fiercely around the cabins and whistled through the cracks. Soon the firewood was almost gone; so were all the trees on the island. The water was filled with cakes of ice so that they could not cross to the mainland for more wood to burn; there was not even enough to cook the food; they had to eat it frozen or else starve. Scurvy broke out. Thirty-five out of the seventy-nine died before spring suns melted the snow and ice. The Indians then came wandering in, to trade fresh meat for whatever struck their fancy—and Pontgravé, good Pontgravé, bless him, arrived from France with supplies.

During the summer Champlain went with de Monts to chart the coast to the south, going as far as Plymouth harbor; and then turned north again to choose a better spot to spend the coming winter.

Port Royal, on the west coast of Nova Scotia, was the place they chose. Only Champlain and two other survivors of the first winter remained on, joined by newcomers from France. The rest went home with de Monts, who felt he must appear in Paris, interview Sully and Henry IV, and try to protect his fur-trading interests from his jealous rivals.

The second and third winters, spent at Port Royal, the settlers were warm, comfortable, and well fed. There were always Indians about the camp, coming and going and treated as friends, and missed by the French when they were gone for a while.

"Whenever the Sagamores or chiefs came to us," said one of the Frenchmen, "they sat at table eating and drinking as we did; and we took pleasure in seeing them, as contrariwise their absence was irksome to us."

This friendship between the French and Indians was to last. Theirs was a very different feeling toward the natives from that of the Spaniards, who oppressed and enslaved the Indians, and different too from that of the English, who drove them back so they might cut down their forests to make fields and villages.

Lescarbot, a former Parisian lawyer who spent the winter at Port Royal, even questioned whether Europeans had any right to occupy land which belonged to these original Americans. He concluded that the only excuse could be on grounds of religion, and recommended that the Mass should be said in the native languages.

"I am driven to think," he says, "that the lack of devotion which is seen throughout almost the whole Church springs from lack of understanding of that for which one prays."

Lescarbot was interested in the Indian music. He wrote a history of New France in which can be found what were probably the first words and notes of American Indian music ever written down.

In the spring of 1607, when the supply ship came from France, it brought bad news. The fur-trading monopoly of de Monts had had bad results. The price of fur had gone up so high that the hatters had complained to the government. Sully, who had foreseen just such trouble, canceled the monopoly. De Monts could not support the settlement without the monopoly. So the settlers were told to leave Port Royal and come home. Champlain felt, by that time, that no one individual trader could plant a successful colony. It must be done on a grand scale supported by the government.

It was May 24, 1607, when they left Canada. Just ten days before that, the English had landed at Jamestown to plant a colony, financed not by one but by a company of traders—the Virginia Company of London.

Part III

from 1607:

When Powhatan ruled
in Virginia &
John Smith in Jamestown

PEOPLE who were Living when

QUEBEC was founded in July 1608

JAMESTOWN was founded in 1607 but later abandoned

The Indians about learned GUNS

CHAMPLAIN went with Indians south to the lake that now bears his name.

1609

1607
POCAHONTAS
POWHATAN'S daughter saved JOHN SMITH'S life.

HENRY HUDSON first sailed into the river now called the HUDSON

The HALF MOON

1619

Prince CHARLES added names to the map of what JOHN SMITH called "NEW ENGLAND"

First NEGROES were brought to Virginia.

The HOUSE OF BURGESSES America's first representative Assembly met in Jamestown.

& EVENTS that took Place

John Smith was an Explorer

A Dutch spectacle maker happened upon the telescope

GALILEO perfected the TELESCOPE and explored the Heavens

MICHAEL, first of the ROMANOVS became Tsar of RUSSIA

The PILGRIMS persecuted in England, took refuge in Holland.

1608

1614 First shipment of Virginia Tobacco reached England.

REMBRANDT VAN RIJN, son of a Leyden miller began to paint.

1616 POCAHONTAS with her husband JOHN ROLFE and small son visited England.

between the YEARS 1607-1620

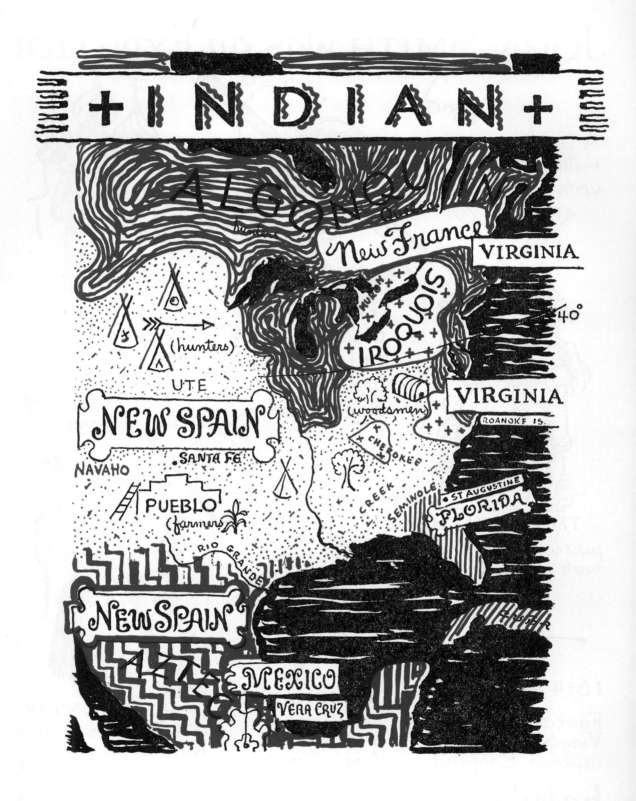

from a drawing by John Smith

THE GREAT CHIEF POWHATAN

POWHATAN, Chief of Chiefs, mighty Algonquin, ruler over many tribes, sat alone in the shadows of his long house, deep in thoughts that were dark and angry.

Outside, warm sun shone on the forty or more houses of his peaceful village by the river Pamunkey, in the land that was to be known as Virginia. It was early summer, time of the Rose Moon. Game was plentiful in the forest. The smell of roasting meat came drifting in to him, and more was drying for the winter. Long leaves of corn standing knee-high in the fields about the village were waving gently in the soft breeze. The old braves dozed in the sun, while the squaws worked quietly and the small brown children played—a scene of peaceful contentment.

There was no peace in the heart of Powhatan. Fifty warriors stood guard about the village. Dark thoughts filled his mind, black as rain clouds shot by flashes of lightning. In all of his sixty years the great chief had faced no such problem as this, now reported by his spies—those "Eyes and Ears" he kept forever roaming through the forest.

White men had settled upon his land, and they carried war sticks filled with thunder and lightning! Powhatan had not yet seen these white men with their deadly sticks, but he felt scornful of all those who could not see that they were enemies.

Foolish ones, Tribe-of-the-wet-sand, had taken them for gods blown across the Big Water in three canoes flying with great wings. They had feasted them with oysters.

Blind ones had taken them for friends—Men of the Blind-Mole-Tribes—living up the Chickahominy River where the white men tied their great canoes and built a village. They had smoked the peace pipe with these pale men. They had taken them a red deer for a feast.

Bah! Foolish ones, blind ones. Powhatan knew these white men were not gods—nor friends. They were enemies, snakes of evil slipping into his land. They would cut down the forests and destroy the hunting grounds. Even now, he was told, they had cut down the trees by the river and stood up the pointed tree trunks side by side, like a circle of warriors to protect their village.

Braves of the Paspageh tribe were not foolish or blind. They had surrounded the circle of logs and shot arrows into it. But the white men inside, using their thunder-sticks, had driven them away; killed them with lightning. The Paspagehs were bold, but they were not wise. Young braves with strong arms and hot blood have yet to learn patience. Men cannot fight with arrows against men who fight with fire and lightning. Powhatan sat motionless on his mat of reeds and buckskin, his eyes half closed, deep in thoughts that were crafty and wise.

In the open doorway behind him the slight figure of a girl appeared. She was a young girl of eleven or twelve in a fringed doeskin skirt, holding a large moccasin in one hand. Three white owl feathers, denoting a princess, were in the back of her blue-black hair, held in by a beaded band. This was his "snowflake"—old Powhatan's favorite daughter, whom he called Mato Ax. She had another name. The "Kila," or Prophet, called the lovely girl-child Pocahontas, meaning "Bright Stream Between the Hills." Pocahontas had been taught by the prophet to listen in silence that she might hear in her heart the voice of the Great Spirit, Mitchi Manitou. And so, as she saw her father sitting in silence, she stopped motionless. Eager as she was to show him his new moccasin she had so richly beaded, she would not disturb him. The silence must not be broken when one is listening to the voice of the Great Spirit.

So, she slipped away, unaware that Powhatan's mind was turning on dark thoughts. He had decided that deceit and treachery were the only defense against the white men who came with smiles, accepted food from people, and then killed them with fire and lightning.

Powhatan was not blind and foolish. He was not young and hasty. He would keep the peace. He would call the white man friend and brother until he had what he needed—the white man's secret. Then he would raise the war club. Then his warriors should paint their faces, shout the war whoop, dance the war dance. But when they started on the warpath, they would be carrying the deadly new thunder-stick that killed with fire and lightning. And they would fall upon the white man's fort and drive him out of the land which he had stolen—out of the Indian hunting ground.

This was Powhatan, chief of the land in which the English had now made their settlement, and against whom John Smith was soon obliged to match wits.

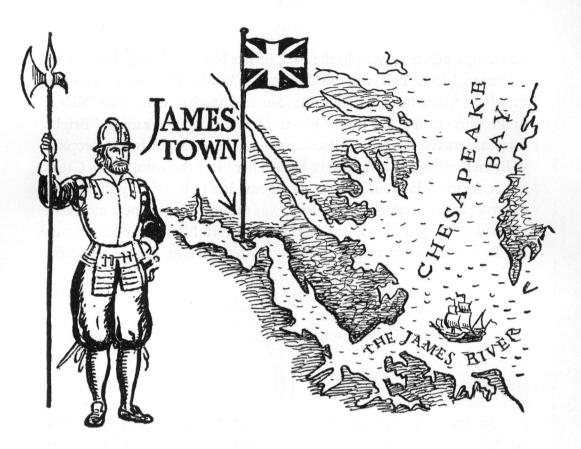

JAMES TOWN

CHESAPEAKE BAY

THE JAMES RIVER

JOHN SMITH—AT JAMESTOWN

ON THAT DAY in late April, 1607, when the *Sarah Constant,* the *Goodspeed,* and the *Discovery* came in sight of Virginia at the end of their long journey from England, John Smith was a prisoner. As the English settlers gazed for the first time upon the broad sandy mouth of the river which they were to call the James, John Smith was below decks locked up. He had been held prisoner all the way across the Atlantic Ocean from the time they left the Canary Islands. He had been accused of mutiny. What he did or said to arouse the suspicion or envy of those who complained to Captain Newport, has never been clearly understood. It is only known that some of the chief men, among them the pompous, haughty Maria Wingfield, told Captain Newport that the young man who called himself *Captain* John Smith, intended to usurp the government in Virginia and make himself King!

206

THE FORT

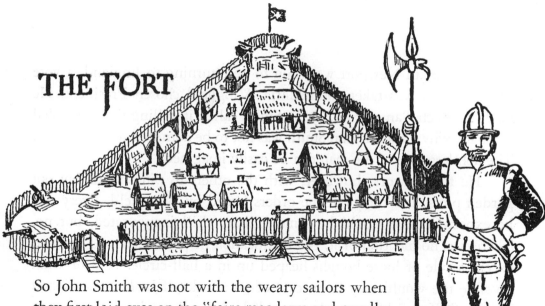

So John Smith was not with the weary sailors when they first laid eyes on the "faire meadows and goodly tall trees" of the new land.

John Smith was not with the thirty or more men who rowed ashore that first day, after the ships were anchored in the bay. Nor was he in the circle of men on deck that evening when Captain Newport took out the all-important small box, unlocked it and read the names of the seven men who were to form the governing council in Virginia. He did not see the faces of the other six when they heard that the seventh name was that of their prisoner—John Smith.

They refused to accept him. They did not include him in the small exploring party that went up the river to find a place for a permanent settlement—one that would fit the specifications given them by the London Council. It must be a hundred miles up some river, on a place easy to defend from land or sea, and not inhabited by savages, where ships could anchor near shore, and where it would be healthy to live. A peninsula in the river forty miles from the mouth was agreed upon as the best spot they could find. By May 14 the three ships were anchored in the middle of the river, and men and supplies were being carried in small boats to the shore. This was to be Jamestown, the center of the new Virginia colony.

As Captain Newport was soon to be returning to England, a vote of some kind was taken, and Maria Wingfield chosen President. He made a speech, "an oration," John Smith called it, telling the assembled company why Captain John Smith was not to be admitted to the council. The helpless rage of the man can be easily imagined.

He fell to work, however, with the others to pitch tents, lay out garden plots, and carry out the orders issued by Wingfield. Every day he expected there would be some military drill inaugurated, but no. There was no mention of it. No fortification or protection was planned except a pile of loose boughs heaped up in a half-circle. And of what possible use would they be in case of an attack? If he had mentioned the word "fort," however, he would doubtless have been laughed to scorn. Where, pray, would you get stones in this stoneless land to construct a fort? John Smith could have told them, had they asked him, of forts he had seen in the backwoods of Poland and Hungary built entirely of logs.

About ten days later, the settlement was attacked by Indians, and President Maria Wingfield had an arrow shot through his beard. This considerably altered his viewpoint.

John Smith was not there at the time, nor was Captain Newport. They had gone with twenty others in small open boats to explore and to discover if they could, the source of the Chickahominy River, which emptied into the James. They found the Indians friendly, especially one named Navirans, who acted as a guide and drew a map of the river, and then in some way aroused the suspicions of Captain Newport that all was not well. They hurried back to Jamestown, and found that the day before, while the men were at work, with their guns stored in fat to keep them from rusting, the settlement had been attacked by Indians. Seventeen men were hurt, one boy killed, and if a shot had not been fired from the ship's cannon, which scared off the attackers, there would have been an end to the plantation.

President Wingfield, who had felt the arrow whiz through his beard, was "contented," as John Smith said, "that a palisade of logs should be built, the guns mounted at each of the corners and the men armed, exercised and drilled." On June 10, just five days before the fort was finished, John Smith was admitted to the council, due, he said, "to the good doctrine of our Preacher, Mr. Hunt." The next day all received Communion; the following day the Indians voluntarily desired peace, and Captain Newport returned to England.

It was June. One hundred settlers were left in Virginia. By mid-September fifty of them were dead, and most of the others so weak from malaria and typhoid fever that they could scarcely bury the dead. Only the President was well. They were then living on sturgeon and sea crabs, half a pint of wheat a day and half a pint of barley boiled with water. The grain had been in the ship's hold and contained as many worms as kernels. Only the President, Wingfield, was obviously well fed. The dissatisfaction with him was so great that the three remaining members of the council deposed him, and while one of the other two got the title, John Smith became the natural leader of the colony. He took six or seven men down the river with some beads and hatchets to trade, and came back with food—oysters, venison, wild turkey, and sixteen bushels of corn. He set to work with the men and got them to build houses and thatch them. He tried to keep them from blaming the London Council for their starvation, misery, and lack of supplies.

"First," he said, "the fault of our going was our owne. What could bee thought fitting or necessary wee had, but what wee should finde, what we should want, where we shoulde bee, we were all ignorant. Supposing to make our passage in two monthes . . . we weare at sea five months, where we both spent our victuals and lost the opportunity of the time and season to plant.

"Such actions have ever since the worlds beginning beene subject to such accidents and every thing of worth is found full of difficulties, but nothing so difficult as to establish a commonwealth so farre remote from men and meanes . . ."

And now the small, weakly established "commonwealth" was facing its first winter.

A COMPASS AND "TALKING PAPER"

IT WAS DECEMBER, Moon of the Great Frost. Snow lay softly white upon the ground and houses of Powhatan's village. Pocahontas wore her winter leggings.

Powhatan lay, when he slept, beneath many bear skins, while his two favorite squaws, who sat on watch at his head and feet, hugged themselves against the cold. The great chief slept little, his vigorous mind and body needing little rest.

One day terrific war whoops and the beating of drums were heard from the braves on guard about the village, announcing the approach of a stranger. This proved to be a Pamunkey warrior, with a message from his chief, who was Powhatan's brother Opekankano.

"We have taken the great white warrior, the one they call Smith." He grinned as he spoke. His face was painted yellow, his stiff black brush of hair bristled with porcupine quills. The scalp of a white man was dangling from his belt. It was not Smith's? No. Opekankano would not let them kill Smith. He was a man of magic. This scalp belonged to one of two other white men they found sleeping by a fire. Smith was not there. They walked further, the warrior explained, before they saw Smith. He was with two Indian guides. Quickly he stepped behind one Indian to shield himself from their arrows. He shot with his fire-stick. They drove him back into the swamp. He sank in the freezing water but he did not give up. He was brave. He kept them away with his fire-stick. He could stand the cold no longer. He threw the stick away. They pulled him from the mud. They took him to a fire and rubbed the legs of the brave one until they were warm again.

John Smith could speak to them in Algonquin words. He asked to see Opekankano, and gave him a present—a thing of magic. A round thing it was, with an arrow that always pointed to the One Star in the sky that does not move. One could see the arrow, but not touch it, because over it was something clear and hard like ice. He had called it glass, and the whole thing was a compass.

What was now to be done with the white warrior, the man of magic, Opekankano wished to know.

"Bring him," answered Powhatan. "Bring the white man to me."

The messenger left at once for the village where the captive was being held. There he found that Smith had further proved himself a man of magic, with his "Talking Paper."

After his rescue the Indians had taken John Smith to a village on the north side of the swamp, displayed him triumphantly to the braves and squaws who came running to see him, yelling and screeching and dancing round him in a circle. Then they feasted him so well that he almost feared they were fattening him to eat, though he actually did not believe them to be cannibals. They proposed a bargain. They would set him free. They would give him wives. They would give him land, if he would help them attack Jamestown. He told them they could not do it because of the guns, and believed he had persuaded them not to try, but was still wondering how to send a warning to the settlers when the way opened up.

There happened to be a sick Indian whom they wanted him to cure. What he needed for that, he told them, was in Jamestown. Would they send messengers to get it for him? They nodded and stood by while he tore a sheet of paper from his notebook, made a few scratches on it and told them what to do with it. Mystified, they went off, dropped it near the fort where it would be picked up, and then fled. Three days later they returned and there where the paper had been were the things Smith needed! And nobody but the paper had said anything! How did he make paper talk? Truly he was a man of magic. They took him from village to village proudly exhibiting this amazing, short, blond-bearded white man whom they had captured. Finally they reached the village of Powhatan, where the most famous event in John Smith's life was to take place.

King Powhatan comands C. Smith to be slaine, his daughter Pokahontas beggs his life . . .

POCAHONTAS AND JOHN SMITH

AT WORD that John Smith had arrived, Powhatan put on his crown of eagle feathers, his robe of raccoon skins trimmed with many tails, long strings of pearls, all of his most regal attire. He seated himself at the end of the long house, and gave a signal.

John Smith was led in. Coming from the white outside, the long, dark room with its rounded roof looked dim and shadowy. It was filled with people. On each side sat two rows of men, with women standing behind them, their heads and shoulders painted red and wearing long strings of white beads. At the far end, beyond the fire which lighted up his stern face, sat the great chief between two beautiful young women, their heads decorated with white down.

In a moment John Smith, a young man of twenty-seven in a filthy mud-stained uniform, stood before the Indian chieftain. But he stood squarely on both feet, with his head up. And there was a brave look in his eyes that touched the heart of the young girl in white doeskin, standing not too far from her father. She looked from one face to the other.

She watched as hot water was brought for the prisoner to wash his hands, then a bunch of feathers to dry them. Then platters were set before him heaped with food. After that the interrogation began—the first round in a match of wits between the young white man and the old Indian chieftain that was to last as long as John Smith stayed in Virginia.

Why had the white men come, Powhatan asked.

They had been chased by their enemies the Spaniards and had to find a safe harbor, was the answer.

How long did they need to stay?

Until their great chief, Captain Newport, came to take them away.

And when was that?

Very soon—within the moon—the great chief Captain Newport would be at Jamestown, said John Smith, hazarding a guess.

Powhatan nodded, and after more questioning he turned to his council of braves and a long consultation was held. In conclusion this is what happened to John Smith, as told in his own words:

"Two great stones were brought before Powhatan—then as many as could lay hands on him dragged him to [the stones] and thereon laid his head, and being ready with their clubs, to beat out his brains, Pocahontas, the Chief's dearest daughter, when no entreaty could prevail, got his head in her arms and laid her own upon his to save him from death."

That is the original version of what has been called the first and best-known folktale of North America. The story of the little Indian princess who saved the life of the brave white settler—the story of Pocahontas and John Smith.

Some people have tried to explain the story by saying that it was part of Powhatan's strategy in handling his councillors. He condemned Smith to death to satisfy those who wanted him to be killed, then took this way that the Indians had of setting the death sentence aside. Who can say what went on in the head of that wise and wily old man? Perhaps he was waiting to see the white man's "father," as he called him, the great chief, Captain Newport, who was so soon to come and who, he was assured by John Smith, would immediately make him a visit. At the same time he had other plans in his head for this man whose life he had spared. He had decided to make him his son. Two days later the ceremony took place. John Smith, not knowing what was to happen, was led to a long house in the woods and left alone. After some anxious moments, there was a fearful noise, and in came two hundred painted braves, dancing wildly and yelling like so many devils. Then Powhatan spoke. They were now friends, he said to John Smith. They would be father and son. His name should be Nantaquoud, and he should call Powhatan his "Father."

Now he was free to go back to Jamestown. Twelve guides would go with him. As gifts to carry back to Powhatan, John Smith was to give the Indian guides two cannons, such as Powhatan had been told, stood at each corner of the white man's fort. Also a grindstone.

John Smith readily agreed to the request. It was an easy promise to make, since the cannons were too heavy for the Indians to carry back, and a grindstone was a cheap price to pay for his freedom.

They spent the first night on the way, and an hour after sunrise were walking into the little three-cornered fort at Jamestown. A few days later the Indians were back in the village of Powhatan without the cannons but with the grindstone and other presents and also further proof of the uncanny magic of the white man. Just as he foretold,

214

the very day they got there the great chief, Captain Newport, had blown in from over the Big Water in his winged canoe.

Captain Newport's arrival, however, was not an unmixed blessing. On his first visit to Powhatan, he made trading with the Indians more difficult for John Smith. This visit was attended with much ceremony on both sides, exchange of gifts, and other proofs of friendship. Indians chanted a welcome, a trumpeter preceded Captain Newport into the house of the chieftain who presented each of the thirty or forty English guards with five pounds of bread. A suit of red cloth, a white greyhound, and a hat were presented to Powhatan, who laughed when he asked John Smith about the cannon he didn't get. He seemed to enjoy the joke on himself.

John Smith, who spoke easily in the musical Algonquin, asked for Pocahontas. "Kehaten pokahontas," he said. "Bid Pokahontas bring two little baskets and I will give her white beads to make her a chain."

He also promised that Captain Newport would leave an English boy to live with Powhatan as a seal of their friendship. Powhatan greatly pleased, pronounced Smith a chief of the tribe, and declared the English no longer strangers, adding that "the Corne, Women and Country should be (to them) as to his own people."

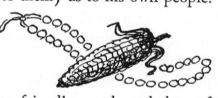

After all the fine friendly words and days of feasting came the trading. It was careful, exact trading, one thing for another—such-and-such an article for so much corn, as John Smith knew it had to be if the English were not to run out of articles to trade. This method irked Powhatan. Turning to Captain Newport he said:

"It is not agreeable to my greatness to trade for trifles in this piddling manner. You are also a great chief. Lay down all your commodities together; what I like I will take, and give you what I think fitting their value."

Newport agreed, spread out the goods, and John Smith saw the price of corn doubling and tripling. This could not go on. He reached in his pocket and drew out a few blue beads the color of the sky. Powhatan saw them at once and offered two pecks of corn. So little, queried John Smith, for this rare sky-blue, worn only by kings? In the end, the exchange was made. Powhatan had two pounds of blue beads. John Smith had two hundred bushels of corn to take back to Jamestown.

It was then the ninth of March. Captain Newport had come the seventh of January. He had brought food and supplies, and he had also brought sixty new settlers who had to be fed. And he stayed two months instead of two weeks as he had expected, while his crew aboard ship ate up the food meant for the settlers. He remained still another month, the reason being that he felt he must have something to show when he made his report to the London Company. After all, this was a business venture, in which the stockholders were to share with the King one-fifth of all the gold and precious metal they should find. Certainly he must have at least a lump or two of gold to display. So he stayed on, and no one dared to complain. John Smith fumed inwardly as he saw the crew eating up the beef, pork, oil, butter, and cheese which had been sent to the colony, while Newport and his men did nothing but "dig gold, wash gold, refine gold, load gold." And it was not gold, just "gilded dirt," worthless stuff with which they loaded the ship down and finally sailed away.

In addition to finding gold, another order given the Virginia settlers by the council in London was to explore the country and discover, if possible, a passage through to the great western sea. This appealed to John Smith far more than grubbing for gold. Every river lured him on to discover its source. He had been trying to find the source of the Chickahominy River, mapping the turns as he went, when he had been captured in the swamp and taken to Powhatan. All of the summer of 1608 was spent in exploring Chesapeake Bay and drawing his very perfect Map of Virginia.

JOHN SMITH DRAWS A MAP OF VIRGINIA

CAPTAIN NEWPORT had barely left for England when John Smith set out with a small company for Chesapeake Bay in an open barge. There were six gentlemen, four soldiers, one doctor, one blacksmith, one fishmonger, and one fisherman. In the next two weeks, they had crossed the great bay, passed the capes named for the King's sons, Henry and Charles, passed the islands still called Smith, and were as far north as Baltimore. By that time, the men were heartily sick of the open barge. They were blown by the wind, soaked to the skin with rain, tired of rowing and sick at their stomachs from the wet moldy bread and rotten watersoaked food. They had had enough. They begged Smith to return. Return? John Smith would not hear of it. According to his own account, this is what he said:

"Gentlemen, if you would remember the story of Sir Ralph Lane, how his company urged him to proceed, saying they yet had a dog, that being boiled with Sassafras leaves would feed them on their return; what shame would it be for you to force me to return with a month's provision, scarce able to say where we have bin, nor yet heard of that we were sent to seek. . . . As for your fears that I will lose myself in these unknown large waters, or be swallowed up in some stormie gust, abandon these childish fears, for worse than is past cannot happen and there is as much danger to return as to proceed forward. Regain therefore your old spirits; for return I will not (if God assist me) till I have found the Potomac, at the head of this great water. . . ."

And so they went on sailing up the Potomac as far as possible, then, turning about, entered the Rappahannock. There John Smith came so near to dying that he pointed out the place where they should dig his grave and bury him. In this place there were so many fish among the weeds that the men had amused themselves by spearing them to the ground with their swords, catching in an hour all they could eat. The last fish John Smith had lifted off his sword was a sting ray, which plunged its poisonous tail so deep into his wrist that his arm, shoulder, and part of his body became badly swollen. They had no surgeon, but Dr. Russel had some oil which he applied, and the dying man not only lived, but managed to eat a piece of the fish for his supper.

They returned to Jamestown, stayed three days, and then set out again with eight of the original men in a party of twelve, all buoyed on with the good hope that, as the Indians had said, the great bay stretched to the South Sea.

As they traveled, John Smith made his careful, accurate map of Virginia which he brought back with him to Jamestown, and then sent home in November to the London Company.

Before that, in August, while he was somewhere on the Potomac River or in Chesapeake Bay, his first published writing was being printed in London at Stationer's Hall. It was entitled *A True Relation by Captain John Smith*. This was explained on the title page as being "A True Relation of such occurrences and accidents of noate as hath happened in Virginia since the first planting of that colony . . . Written by Captain Smith, Coronell of said Collony, to a worshipful friend of his in England . . . to be solde at the Greyhound in Paules-Church-yard, 1608."

218

"HALF MOON" ON THE HUDSON RIVER

O N A FOGGY LONDON DAY in the fall of the year 1608, Henry
Hudson, an English seaman, was walking along the bank of
the Thames reading a letter. A ship from Virginia had just
come in with letters from the Jamestown settlers to friends and relatives at home. Hudson's letter was from Captain John Smith, who suggested that his friend Hudson "try for a northwest passage around forty
degrees"—where he himself had had to leave off.

Northwest! To sail northwest instead of northeast again. That was

exactly what Henry Hudson had in mind. He was "out of heart," he
had said, with seeking for a passage to the east. He had just returned
from the second of two voyages he had made for the Muscovy Company (of London) in search of a northeast passage, which had taken
him well up into the Arctic Circle. Hudson was ready to sign another
contract with the Muscovy Company or any other company of merchants that might engage him. It would not be difficult for him to find
employment. Henry Hudson was a mariner by trade, with an honorable
reputation. Sailors who returned with him from those uncharted icy
seas north of Siberia, where the sun shone all night and there were no
stars to steer by, declared he had a very "nose for the sea" and a "compass in his head."

The English Muscovy Company had no further funds to spend at
this time on exploration. The Dutch East India Company, extremely
prosperous, asked Henry Hudson to come to Amsterdam to consider
making a voyage for them. Ortelius, one of the most famous map-
makers of the day, acted as interpreter. At this time Hudson was also
approached by an agent of Henry IV about making a voyage for the
French. This caused the Dutch directors of the Company to make up
their minds in a hurry and sign the contract with "Heindrik Huitson,"
as they pronounced his name. They were to furnish the ship. He was
to deliver his log books, journals and charts to them at the end of the
voyage. For this voyage, the directors were to pay said Hudson for his
outfit and for the support of his wife and children the sum of eight
hundred guilders. Hudson had three sons. John, the middle one, went
with his father on the voyage. The crew was divided between Dutch
and English sailors. The ship was called the *Half Moon*.

When Hudson left the harbor of Amsterdam his orders were to
sail northeast, and if a northeast passage was not found, to return to
Amsterdam. Henry Hudson disobeyed those orders. He sailed northwest. And so, as it happened, he secured Manhattan Island for the
Dutch and sailed up the river that was to be known as the Hudson.

This is how it happened. He sailed northeast first, according to orders—into the cold north seas, until the Dutch sailors began to complain. They had been used to sailing the warm southern seas around the tip of Africa. They could not endure the piercing cold, in which the sails were frozen stiff and ropes covered with ice. In the middle of May, which was like the dead of winter, they mutinied. They refused to go farther. Hudson could not control them. He was forced to ask them where they *would* go. Certainly they would not go back to Amsterdam—to be punished for mutiny.

Where else then could they go but northwest? Just what Hudson had wanted to do—sail northwest and "try for a passage around forty degrees"—that would be somewhere between Newfoundland and Chesapeake Bay. So they swung about and the *Half Moon* sailed west.

July 1, they were off the banks of Newfoundland among the Frenchmen fishing for cod.

July 15, they were coasting along the rocky, foggy shores of Maine catching lobsters.

July 22, they passed Cape Cod, where the English had tried and failed to make a settlement.

August 15 found them passing Chesapeake Bay not far from Jamestown. Hudson did not stop to see his friend John Smith. No one knows why.

Not far from the Island of Roanoke, he turned north again. At sunrise on the second day of September, 1609, he saw the low, flat, shining curve of Sandy Hook, then the outline of Long Island. Soon he was sailing into the broad harbor where the Indians' wide "river of steep hills" came down to meet the sea, and anchored on the "island of hills" which the Indians called Manahatin. The *Half Moon* rode at anchor that night near the present ferryboat landing at Forty-second Street, just north of where the great ocean liners from Europe dock today.

It seemed to Henry Hudson that this broad beautiful "North River" might lead to the passage he was looking for. He explored as far up the river as Albany. From there on, the channel grew so much narrower and shallower that Hudson realized that it could not be the entrance to the far sea, and turned back.

Up near a place which the Indians called Schenectady—"the place you reach through piney woods"—Hudson entertained some of the Indians on board ship, and introduced them to "fire water." One old chief became dead drunk, which so terrified the others that they fled in panic from the ship. Next day they returned with strings of shells, to pay the white man if he would cure their poor friend of his spell. And so Hudson and his sailors were introduced to the money of the Indians, which they called *wampum*.

It was suggested, as they were again passing Manhattan Island and leaving the harbor where the great Hudson River meets the sea, that it might be sensible to spend the winter in Newfoundland and so be ready when spring came to try again to find a northwest passage. Hudson did not dare to risk the chance of another mutiny when the weather became bitter cold and the food rations short, so they sailed east, across the Atlantic, and a little over a month later entered the English harbor of Dartmouth. Hudson wrote immediately to his Dutch employers, suggesting that he spend the winter where he was and be ready to set out again in the spring. The Dutch directors preferred that he come to Amsterdam, as agreed, bringing his log books, journals, and charts.

He was forbidden to do so. Henry Hudson was an Englishman. As such, King James and the Privy Council forbade him and all other English members of his crew to leave the country. The voyage he had just made was pronounced "to the detriment of his own country," and in the future, said the King, "If you sail, you sail for me."

"Many persons thought it rather unfair that these sailors should have been prevented from laying their reports before their employers." Those are the mild words of the Dutch Consul in England, a very studious and dignified old gentleman by the name of Van Meteren—a cousin of the great geographer and map-maker, Ortelius.

"The English are not vindictive," he said, "but very suspicious, especially of foreigners, whom they despise."

ABITATION DE QUEBECQ

DOVE COTE

SUNDIAL

Lodging for workmen

Storage

Draw bridge

MOAT

CHAMPLAIN'S LODGING

Cannon

Champlain's GARDEN

THE ST. LAWRENCE RIVER

FRENCH AND INDIANS ON LAKE CHAMPLAIN

IN SEPTEMBER 1609, Henry Hudson had been at Albany on the river to be known as the Hudson. In July Samuel Champlain, less than a hundred miles up the river, had come down from Canada and reached Lake Champlain. There he had helped the Algonquins and Hurons defeat the Iroquois in a famous first battle, as part of an alliance that was to last until the end of the French and Indian War, 150 years later.

In the spring of 1607, when Champlain had returned to France, he had found his old friend de Monts in despair over having lost the monopoly of the fur trade. This was indeed sad, because Champlain had returned filled with enthusiasm over a new project. He wished to build a trading post farther up the river at Quebec, so that the Indians would not have to paddle all the way to Tadoussac with their furs. Also, at Quebec the rock wall rose high from the river and would be a fort to protect them from the terrible Iroquois, as the French had promised to do.

A good idea, said de Monts, *oui,* but impossible! He had no money —the monopoly of the fur trade was no longer his. However, let them go together, he and Champlain, to Paris to consult the King. Henry IV's interest was aroused at once. Charmed to see Champlain again, and, as always, to see de Monts. Regretted that it had been necessary to cancel the monopoly, and proposed a compromise. The monopoly would be renewed for one year, the coming season of 1608. De Monts and Champlain would found the fort at Quebec, as a permanent French settlement in America.

Quebec. It was on July 3, 1608, that Champlain landed there. Just above the river, between the water and the high rock wall, there was a shelf of land, and there he built what he called his "Habitation." Since Jamestown was later to be abandoned, this was the founding of the oldest French or English city in the New World, the city of Quebec.

Here he and twenty-three men spent the winter with such bad food, what there was of it, that when spring came sixteen had died of scurvy, and only seven besides the wiry small leader himself remained alive. His black eyes were bright, his mind alert and filled with plans for the coming summer.

The first thing the French must do was to keep their promise to the Algonquins and help them against their enemies the Iroquois. He went to consult old Pontgravé, then on board his ship at Tadoussac. From there Champlain returned in an open boat with twenty men. He stopped at Quebec and continued up the river for about seventy miles. There he found a camp of two or three hundred Indians on their way to Quebec to help their French friends explore the country of the Iroquois. With the Algonquins was another tribe of Indians, tall, well-built men called Hurons. The ridge of coarse black hair on their shaven heads had reminded the first Frenchmen who saw them of wild boars, or in French, "huron." These Hurons were great traders, bringing furs in to the trading post from as far west as Lake Superior and nearly as far north as James Bay. Champlain knew this and was glad to smoke the peace pipe with the Huron chief introduced by the Algonquins.

The Algonquin chief asked "as a token of friendship and rejoicing" to have the muskets and arquebuses fired off for the amazement of the Hurons, who uttered shouts of astonishment.

The Algonquin chief also wished to continue on to Quebec to show the Huron chief the White Man's wonderful "Habitation." So they all went back to Quebec, and spent five or six days in feasting and dancing before they finally set out for the land of the Iroquois. About sixty Algonquins and Hurons in skins and war paint, with their powerful bows and arrows, and eleven Frenchmen in steel armor and helmets, carrying their muskets—murderous new weapons about to be formally introduced into Indian warfare.

Champlain had been led to believe that it would be possible to sail south up the Richelieu River from the St. Lawrence to the Lake of the Iroquois. But about halfway there they reached the roaring Chambly rapids. It was impossible to go on in the shallop, but equally impossible for Champlain to turn back, so intense was his desire to see the long lake of the Iroquois and the North River beyond—to see if by any chance this might be the way through to the far sea. Which of the Frenchmen, he asked, would volunteer to go with him? Two stepped forward. The other eight returned in the shallop to Quebec.

That left a party of sixty Indians in twenty-four canoes with Champlain and his two Frenchmen to continue on down into New York State. Marching through the dense woods until they could again launch their canoes, they were preceded by a few scouts who went ahead looking for marks on trees and other signs of the enemy, while hunters spread out on both sides to bring back plenty of game.

Every night as the Indians sat about, the medicine man made a prediction. For this he built a wigwam covered with beaver skin.

Then, said Champlain telling of it later, "he gets inside . . . seizes one of the poles of the tent and shakes it, whilst he mumbles

225

between his teeth certain words, with which he declares he is invoking the devil, who appears to him in the form of a stone and tells him whether his friends will come upon their enemies and kill many of them. [He] will lie flat upon the ground, without moving . . . suddenly he will rise to his feet, speaking and writhing so that he is all in a perspiration, though stark naked. The whole tribe will be about the tent sitting on their buttocks like monkeys. They often told me the shaking of the tent was caused by the devil. . . . I pointed out to them that what they did was pure folly, and that they ought not to believe in such things."

One soft summer evening, in the hush that comes after the sun has set, the invading party, paddling cautiously along the Richelieu River, came to a place where the river widened into a long shining lake. The shores were richly wooded, and in the distance were the hazy blue tops of the Adirondack Mountains. They were now in the land of the Iroquois, so they travelled by night and slept by day, hidden in the deep woods. Summer nights were beautiful on the silent lake, with the stars reflected in the water, and no sound but the occasional drip of the paddles. This lake of the Iroquois seemed so beautiful to Champlain that he felt it must be his, he must claim it as his own, give it his name. It should be Lake Champlain!

Two weeks later, they were still paddling softly southward on the edge of night, when the silence was shattered by loud yells and shouts. It was a war party of the Iroquois. Soon the dark shapes of their canoes were visible, much clumsier and heavier than those of the Algonquins. Catching sight of the invaders, the Iroquois pulled into shore, where they began building a barricade of trees, while the Algonquins and Hurons on the water lashed their canoes together with long poles. Soon two Iroquois canoes paddled out, to hold a parley. Did the Algonquins wish to fight, they asked. If so, as soon as the sun should rise they would have the battle. To this the Algonquins and Hurons agreed. It was almost like a gentlemen's agreement.

All night the Iroquois danced and sang on shore and exchanged insults and boasts of victory with the Indians on the river. Just before dawn, the Algonquins, the Hurons, and the three Frenchmen went ashore. As soon as the sun rose the Iroquois—two hundred of them, Champlain said—"came slowly to meet us with a gravity and calm which I admired; and at their head were three chiefs. Our Indians . . . told me that those who had the three big plumes were the chiefs, and that there were only these three . . . and I was to do what I could to kill them. I promised to do all in my power.

As soon as we landed our Indians began to run . . . toward their enemies who stood firm . . . Our Indians began to call to me with loud cries; and to make way for me they divided into two groups . . . and I marched on until I was within some thirty yards of the enemy,

(from Champlain's drawing)

who as soon as they caught sight of me halted and gazed at me and I at them. When I saw them make a move to draw their bows upon us, I took aim . . . and shot straight at one of the three chiefs, and with this shot two fell to the ground. . . . The Iroquois were much astonished that two men should have been killed so quickly, although they were provided with shields made of cotton thread woven together and wood, which were proof against their arrows. . . . As I was reloading my arquebus, one of my companions fired a shot from . . . the woods, which astonished them again so much that, seeing their chiefs dead, they lost courage and took to flight, abandoning the field and their fort, and fleeing into the depths of the forest . . ."

There on that day Champlain planted in the minds of the Indians conflicting and never-to-be-forgotten opinions of the French. To the Algonquins and Hurons a Frenchman was a brave friend who kept his word. To the Iroquois, all Frenchmen were treacherous.

In October, Champlain had to return to France to make a report to De Monts and to His Majesty Henry IV at Fontainebleau. He described the Habitation, the French settlement at Quebec, and told of the alliance with the Indians and the battle on Lake Champlain. In all this the King, he said, "took pleasure and satisfaction."

At the end of April, Champlain sailed from France on his fifth voyage to Canada. Earlier that same month, Henry Hudson sailed from England on what was to be the last voyage of his life. Not to be outdone by the Dutch, Sir Thomas Smith, the greatest merchant in London, principal officer in the East India Company, the Muscovy Company, and the Virginia Company, formed another company with several other promoters and engaged Hudson to look for a northwest passage.

Hudson sailed away on a small ship called the *Discovery*. And again in the Arctic Sea, when the cold was bitter and the food supply so low it had to be doled out, the crew mutinied. Hudson was bound, thrown into a small boat with his son John and six other sailors, and then set adrift, while the *Discovery* sailed away.

FOR ONE YEAR, from September, 1608, to September, 1609, John Smith was *President* of the Virginia Colony. It was the most responsible position he was ever to hold.

His idea was to put everybody to work—"gentlemen" and all.

"He that will not worke shall not eate," he said. He had a notice board put up, recording on it each day what each man had accomplished. They had to work six hours and then spend the rest in "Pastime and merry exercises."

The first work he had them do was to extend the fort, double the size of Jamestown and make it five-sided instead of three. He kept a guard on duty day and night. To the west he had a drill field leveled off and held drill every Saturday. Indians came, a hundred at a time, to watch the musketeers shoot for a mark set up on a tree.

He had been President but a month when Newport was back again, bringing what John Smith considered more "fool" orders from the London Company. The most ridiculous order was that they were to crown Powhatan! For this absurd affair, Newport had brought a scarlet cloak, a crown, and many gifts. John Smith was almost speechless with annoyance. They could not all go to Powhatan's—it would take too many men from the fort. So John Smith went himself with four men to invite Powhatan to come to Jamestown for the ceremony and presents.

"This is my land," the old chieftain replied. "I am a King. If your King has sent me presents, let your 'Father' come to me, not I to him."

That was the way it was done. John Smith, Captain Newport, and fifty soldiers went by land. The presents were sent by water. These included a bed, complete with furnishings, which was set up in the long house. Then the coronation took place. Powhatan stood tall and straight in the new scarlet robe. He would not kneel to be crowned. So they reached up, one of them pulled on his shoulders to make him stoop, and then clapped the crown on his head. Suddenly there was a pistol shot, and guns boomed from the ships in the river. Powhatan was alarmed. What was all this? A trick? Were he and his people to be murdered? No, said John Smith, it was a friendly salute in honor of his coronation. Powhatan was reassured, and presented his old skin robe and moccasins to Newport, who took them back for display in England. They may still be seen in the museum at Oxford.

That was that. The next order to be carried out was to get a glass factory going. Newport had brought experienced glass blowers—Poles and Hollanders and seventy other workmen. And he was to return to England with pitch, tar, and clapboards. Clapboards were possible, but pitch and tar! Here in Virginia there were almost no trees that would provide pitch and tar. But orders were orders. Taking thirty gentlemen with him, Smith went down the river to make clapboards. Unused to such labors, the men's hands became sore and blistered. They cursed and swore. John Smith did not swear. Never as a boy had he heard Lord Willoughby swear. No gentlemen should swear. He decreed that a can of water should be poured down each man's sleeve for every oath he uttered. So the work went on. The clapboards were ready when Newport departed.

Also ready to go was a blunt letter from President John Smith to the council in London. He did not like the orders they issued and he told them so. Also he had made as great discoveries as Newport, at far less cost, and he enclosed a map to prove it.

The winter was a difficult one. Only John Smith's courage and common sense in dealing with the Indians kept the colony alive. He secured corn. He had a well dug. He had twenty more houses built, thirty or forty more acres of land cleared, and a blockhouse fort built farther down the river. And he kept law and order. He refused to listen to the disillusioned settlers who demanded that he let them abandon the colony and go back to England.

230

And then, when the winter was over and summer came, there arrived a letter from the council in London, criticizing him for dealing too harshly with the Indians and for not sending back ships loaded with pitch, tar, and other commodities. It also informed him that a new charter had been granted by the King. A new governor had been appointed for the colony—Lord de la Warr. And supplies were on the way. A month later four ships with a few supplies came. But the *Sea Adventure* with the large store of provision did not come with the rest. Three men with whom John Smith had quarreled were back again, however, to make trouble for him.

"It would be too tedious, too strange and almost incredible," said one of Smith's loyal friends, "should I relate the infinite dangers and plots Smith daily escaped amongst this factious crew." On the way over, he said, they had poisoned the minds of the newcomers against him, but not all . . . "Men of better reason and experience, hearing the general good report of his old soldiers, and seeing with their eyes his actions so well managed—ever rested his faithful friends."

Though he knew he was to be deposed, John Smith had to stay on until the end of his term. Even then he might not have returned to England, had it not been for a serious accident. The gunpowder bag which he wore on his belt was touched off and exploded, his thigh and side were horribly burned, and there was no surgeon in Jamestown. So in mid-September, he stood on shipboard looking back at the land where he had spent over two years and to which he had become so deeply devoted that it seemed like home to him.

On his return to London, he had to face charges made by his enemies to the London Council. Though he also had friends among the council members, he never worked for the Virginia Company of London again.

John Smith then began writing his book about Virginia. In it he gave a "Description of the Country, and the Proceedings of the English Colonie." It was published in 1612 in Oxford, and was the best account, so far, of the Virginia Indians and their customs.

231

STARVATION AND SHIPWRECK

THE WINTER after John Smith left Jamestown was known as the "Starvation Time." It was such a dreadful nightmare of suffering that the colony of 490 persons was practically wiped out. "And he had left us," wrote one of his friends, "with commodities to trade, the harvest newly gathered, ten weeks provision in the store, six mares, a horse, five to six hundred swine, hens, chickens, goats, and sheep . . . twenty-four pieces of ordnance, 300 muskets, pikes, swords, nets for fishing, tools of all sorts." Yet everything went to sixes and sevens; it was so badly managed, with the officers quarreling, nobody on guard, Indians stealing the animals, everyone eating out of the common supply of food, that they were reduced to living on herbs and roots, acorns and rats. As the famine grew worse and people died of starvation, the living were driven to horrible lengths. One dead Indian was dug up and eaten. One wretched half-mad man killed his own wife, preserved her body in salt, and had eaten part of it before the crime was discovered.

"What shall I say," continued one of John Smith's friends, "but that we lost him, John Smith, that, in all his proceedings, made Justice his first guide, and experience his second; . . . whose adventures were our lives and whose loss our deathes."

The *Sea Adventure,* the ship with the large supply of provisions, had never been heard from. A terrible hurricane had driven it to the shores of Bermuda where it had been completely wrecked. On board were one hundred and fifty new settlers, and among them at least one woman to join the two or three others then living in Jamestown. She was the wife of young John Rolfe, who, of all those on the ill-fated *Sea Adventure,* was to be the most important to Virginia. They spent the winter in Bermuda, building a new ship, so that it was spring before they reached Jamestown and the sixty starving creatures still alive.

"When those noble knights did see our miseries," said one of the survivors, "and being strangers to the country could not understand the cause, they took us aboard ship with themselves, and abandoning James Towne, set sail for England. But yet God would not have it, for ere wee left the river we met the Lord de-la Ware, governor for the countrie, with three ships well furnished, who again returned us to the abandoned Jamestown, the 9th of June, 1610. But his Lordship had such an encounter with scurvy sickness, so that after eight months, he was forced to save his life by his return for England."

John Rolfe's young wife died very soon, as did their baby, who had been christened Bermuda. The widower was to marry Pocahontas, but not until four years later. John Rolfe heard of the Indian princess who had come to Jamestown during the time of John Smith, but he did not see her. Often she had brought messages from her father Powhatan. Once she had run through the dark woods to warn Smith of her father's plan to attack and kill him. But after John Smith was gone, Pocahontas did not come any more.

URING his first years there, John Rolfe was occupied in changing the future of Jamestown and the history of Virginia. He began cultivating tobacco, as he had seen it being grown in Bermuda. He experimented with it in one small field, then in a larger field. More and more fields were planted each year, until all about the settlement fields were green with tobacco plants. Soon they were shipping it to England, where, ever since Sir Walter Raleigh had introduced the smoking of tobacco, it had grown increasingly popular.

King James hated the "vile stinking habit." In 1604, the year he had blasted out against the Puritans, he had sounded off against the loathsome habit of smoking the vile stinking weed in an essay, entitled *A Counterblast to Tobacco*.

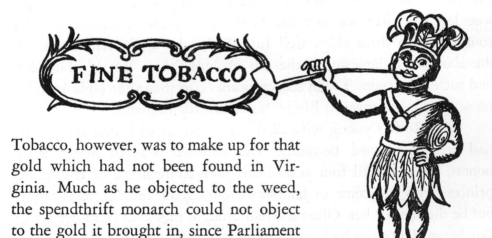

FINE TOBACCO

Tobacco, however, was to make up for that gold which had not been found in Virginia. Much as he objected to the weed, the spendthrift monarch could not object to the gold it brought in, since Parliament kept him on what he considered a starvation allowance.

THE YEAR that John Smith was President of the Virginia colony was the first year that the little group from Scrooby village spent in Holland. By early fall of 1608 they were in Amsterdam, all of those who had been courageous and determined enough to reach this land of religious freedom.

Here they were in the teeming city of Amsterdam, a small, bewildered group of country people from a foreign land. All about them were citizens in strange dress, speaking strange words, bustling about their business, paying them no heed. The streets were canals, crossed by little bridges, filled with boats and faced by rows of tall buildings, their flat fronts and richly carved roof lines making rippled upside-down patterns in the narrow waterways.

"It seemed," said William Bradford, "they were come into a new world, all so far differing from that of the plain country villages wherein they were bred and had so long lived."

Where should they go? What should they do for a living, these plain farmers set down in this, the busiest metropolis in Europe?

Only to Mr. Brewster, the "Elder" of the company, were this land and city not entirely strange. And yet Amsterdam had grown and changed in the twenty-four years since he had come here for the first time. He was then seventeen. William of Orange, that hero of Holland who had led the Netherlands in declaring their independence from Spain, had just been assassinated.

Since that time refugees of all faiths, persecuted in their own lands, had come in large numbers to the Netherlands. The country had grown and profited, for many were the finest scholars, the most skilled textile workers and craftsmen, the most successful merchants in the countries from which they came.

Protestants had fled north into Holland from Antwerp and what is now Belgium. That southern part of the Netherlands had not held out, but had given up and were still under the rule of Spain.

There were also Huguenot refugees from France. One of these, a skilled weaver of silk, gave young William Bradford employment.

Another group of persecuted people who came bringing their contribution of wealth and skills were the Jews from Portugal. A new synagogue, called the "Habitation of Peace," the second one in Amsterdam, was being built the year the Scrooby pilgrims arrived. To them the Jews were a strange people. The English knew little about Jews outside of what they read in the Bible. There were few, if any, Jews living in England. They had been driven out in the Middle Ages, when they had also been driven out of France. But they had remained in Spain, because Spain was too busy trying to drive out the Moslems. In 1492, when that had been accomplished, the Spaniards had turned to the task of ridding their country of the Jews—all except those who were willing to be baptized as Christians.

As they fled from Spain the Jews went to various countries. Some went to Italy, especially to the cities of Genoa and Venice. Some fled to Constantinople, and found a happy home among the Turks, who never demanded of their subjects that they surrender their religion.

Many Jews had gone from Spain into Portugal, where they lived

outwardly as Christians and were known as Marranos. Year after year they had lived in this false position, unable to profess their own faith or teach it to their children, until they had almost forgotten the prayers, symbols and outward forms of worship of their ancient religion. Portugal was later ruled by Spain. So long as the Netherlands was also ruled by Spain, there was no nearby land to which they could escape. When the Netherlands became an independent republic, it seemed to the Jews like a second Promised Land. They waited until after the defeat of the Spanish Armada; then a ship carrying sixteen Marranos sailed from Portugal headed for Amsterdam.

Storms swept their ship out of its course, and blew it into the port of Emden, Germany. There they saw a house or shop with a sign above the door written in characters that seemed vaguely familiar. Could it possibly be Hebrew? From a few cautious questions at the inn, they discovered that it was the home of a learned Jew named Moses Uri.

Jacob Tirado, their leader, who looked like any elegant Portuguese gentleman, slim, dark, and smooth-shaven, stepped into the house of Moses Uri, and saw before him a very different kind of Jew than he had ever known. There stood a short, blue-eyed, full-bearded man, in a long black robe, a high black skull cap—a German Jew from the Ghetto. Moses Uri, looking quizzically up at Tirado, did not recognize the richly clothed, handsome stranger as one of his own people. Who was this man? What did he want? With some difficulty Tirado made him-

237

self known as one of a group of Marranos from Portugal, who wished to be instructed in their old religion. Moses Uri said he dare not take the risk of converting Christians there in Emden. The town was too small. But should they go to Amsterdam, then he, Moses Uri, would follow them, and teach them the Hebrew prayers and the Law of Moses and receive them into the Covenant. The promise was kept.

The small group of Marranos went to Amsterdam. To avoid attention, scarcely believing they would not be persecuted, they chose a poor marshy street to settle in, known as Vloijenburg or "Fleatown." Moses Uri came, rented a house on Jonkerstraat and turned one of the upper rooms into a synagogue. For four years the Jews passed unnoticed, and the settlement grew. Then someone saw them gathering for the Feast of the Atonement and suspected them of being Spanish conspirators, and since the war with Spain was still going on, reported them to the government. Jacob Tirado, who could speak Latin, went before the Burgomeisters and assured them that, far from being conspirators, they were fugitives from the rule of Spain. They were Marranos from Portugal. Many others of their nation would also come and bring wealth to Holland, if they were permitted to live in peace. And they were. The Dutch granted them permission to build a synagogue. Jacob Tirado donated the site, and it was named Beth Jacob—the House of Jacob.

The colony grew and prospered. Many came of all classes, from the wealthy and educated to the poor and ignorant who sorted rags for a living. One Portuguese family who took a house in Fleatown were the Espinozas. Their son, Baruch Espinoza, born there in 1632, was to become one of the world's great philosophers—Spinoza.

One would think that the Jews, having found this land where they were allowed to live in peace, would have been able to live in peace with one another. It was not so. Jews from various countries differed too much in the languages they spoke, in their customs and mannerisms, as Moses Uri differed from Jacob Tirado. And so the break came, and another synagogue was being built in 1608, the year that the English refugees from Scrooby village arrived in Amsterdam.

238

AT HOME IN LEYDEN

THE GROUP from Scrooby village were not the first English people to seek refuge in Holland. They found, as they expected, two other congregations of Separatists living in Amsterdam. One group had been part of their own old congregation which had fled to Holland when they themselves had gone to Scrooby village. The other group had come in the days of Queen Elizabeth and were known as the "Ancient Brethren."

As in the case of the Jews, one might think that these English Separatists who had escaped to Holland, where they could live in peace and worship as they saw fit, might have been able to live in peace with one another. It was not so. The pilgrims from Scrooby found the two older congregations wrangling and quarreling.

William Bradford wrote about it later, telling how after "they had lived in Amsterdam about a year their pastor, Mr. John Robinson, a gentle and moderate man, seeing that he could do nothing to cure the strife and trouble, thought it best to leave Amsterdam rather than become involved in it." William Brewster, who was to be the "elder," or assistant to the pastor, and others of the congregation approved of making the move, even though it meant they would suffer financially by having to make a new start, trying to find work in a smaller city where there would be less opportunity.

Pastor Robinson went to ask permission of the Burgomeisters of Leyden, a beautiful city at the mouth of the Rhine, which they had chosen for their new home. Leyden was the seat of a great university where there would be lectures that a young man such as William Bradford might attend, even though he could not afford to enroll as a regular student. And of course it would have a fine library.

Pastor Robinson returned, pleased to report that he and his flock would be most welcome in Leyden, in spite of the fact that the English ambassador had orders from James I to prevent the city fathers from receiving them. So plans were made to leave.

William Bradford finished the last yard of silk he was to weave in Amsterdam, rose from the loom, and bade a grave goodbye to his employer, speaking in French as he had learned to do. Next day he was bidding farewell to other friends, among them little Dorothy May, who would not be going. Her father belonged to the Ancient Brethren. Dorothy was only eleven, but William took with him the memory of her sweet, sad, appealing little face.

The pilgrims went by boat, gliding through flat green pastures and near fields toward a perfectly level horizon, broken only by the widespread arms of windmills, slowly turning. In Leyden, an ancient fortress topped by a circular tower was the first building they saw, then the spires of the guild halls and the bell tower of St. Peter's church. A church of their own was the first building they planned to purchase. They could have had one free of rent or taxes, furnished by the Dutch government. This offer had been made to Pastor Robinson when he had come to see if they would be welcome.

240

A group of Puritans from England living in Leyden had gladly taken advantage of this offer, which the Dutch made to all Protestant refugees. But this little group of independent people were a special type of Puritan. They were Separatists. They believed in the separation of church and state, of politics and religion. In this they were far ahead of other Puritans. Poor as they were, they did not accept help from the government. Instead they bought a house to serve as a home for Pastor Robinson and used the parlor for their meeting-house. It was on Bell Alley, a neat little brick-paved street, across from St. Peter's church and near the University. Surrounding the parsonage was a large lot on which they built twenty-one smaller houses for their families. The men worked as carpenters, bricklayers, masons, coopers, brewers, weavers and dyers—whatever they could do to earn a living.

William Bradford used his experience and became a weaver. He made his home with the Brewster family, which was a real advantage, since Elder Brewster taught Latin and Greek. William was eager to learn these and also Hebrew, so that he could read the Bible in the original language.

Thursday evenings, as well as every Sunday, were spent in the meeting-house. The men sat on one side, the women and children on the other. Sunday service began at eight in the morning, and the sermon was four hours long. After the noon meal (which had been cooked before the Sabbath day of rest) the members of the congregation spoke on new understanding they had gained about the ways of God.

That was their simple desire—to understand and follow the will of God, knowing that "he whose delight is in the law of the Lord shall be like a tree planted by the river of waters and whatsoever he doeth shall prosper."

When he was twenty-two, William had word that his uncle Robert was dead, and that he had inherited a share of his grandfather's property. That made it possible for him to buy a house of his own near the

University. He now spoke Dutch as well as he did English; he was a member of the weavers' guild, a registered citizen of Leyden, a responsible young man. It was time to be married. He went back to Amsterdam for his bride. In the old City Hall in Leyden may still be seen the record, which states that on November 30, 1613, William Bradford married Dorothy May.

THE TELESCOPE

THE TELESCOPE was invented in Holland in 1608, the year that the Pilgrims arrived. As so often happens when the time is ripe for a scientific discovery, the idea occurred to various people independently. It is agreed, however, that the first person to invent a telescope and make it known to the world was Hans Lippershey, a Dutch spectacle-maker of Middelburg.

One day, according to the story, he happened to hold a spectacle lens in each hand and looked through both of them at the same time toward the steeple of a nearby church. To his surprise, the weather-cock appeared much nearer, and as distinct as if it were on the window sill. He looked again, then he found a tube, fitted the lenses the proper distance apart to get the sharpest image, and so he had it—the first telescope.

In October he applied to the States-General for a patent. Soon telescopes were being made in great quantities and shipped all over Europe. In the month of May, 1609, a Frenchman took one to Milan, Italy, and offered it for sale to a count. About that time Galileo happened to be in Venice and heard that such an instrument had been made. The fact that it could be done set his imagination afire. The day after he returned to Padua he had made a telescope.

To the spectacle-maker Hans Lippershey, who had happened on the idea, it was just a "spyglass," a novelty, more or less of a toy. In Galileo's hands it became a key that opened up the heavens.

242

GALILEO AND THE PLANETS

ALL THE WAY HOME from Venice to Padua, Galileo was thinking about the telescope, his thoughts focused on the principle involved, the bending or refraction of the rays of light. What combination of lenses would produce the desired effect?

"It cannot depend on one glass," he thought, for that could be only convex or concave, or plain. Concave diminishes objects, convex enlarges them, but both show them blurred and indistinct . . . plain glass does neither . . . So it must be a combination of the first two . . . The solution came to him in the night—or early dawn. He hurried to his workshop and before sundown Galileo had made his first "spyglass," using a piece of organ pipe.

A few days after that he made a better one, with the two glasses fitted into a leaden tube. This made an object appear three times nearer and so nine times larger! Then, he wrote later:

"As the news reached Venice that I had made such an instrument I was summoned before the Signoria, and exhibited it to them, to the astonishment of the whole Senate. Many of the nobles and senators

243

although of a great age, mounted more than once to the top of the highest church tower (the bell tower of San Marco) in order to see ships that were so far off that it was two hours before they could be seen, steering full sail into the harbor."

In the other direction from the bell tower of San Marco, they could see the bell tower of the church in Padua, twenty-one miles away, the farthest object visible.

"Knowing of what use such an instrument would prove in naval and military operations," continued Galileo, "I resolved to go to the palace and present it as a gift to His Serenity, the Doge. As I was quitting the presence one of the heads of the University of Padua came, and taking me by the hand, said that the Senate, knowing the way in which I had served it for seventeen years at Padua, and my courtesy in making a present of my spyglass, had ordered my election to the Professorship for life, with an increase of salary. . . . So I am bound here for life and can only hope to enjoy a sight of my own country during the recesses . . ."

Galileo continued to improve on his spyglass, making one that enlarged more than sixty times, then another that enlarged four hundred times, and at last perfected one that showed an object nearly a thousand times larger and thirty times nearer.

With the second of these he was able to look at the moon. On a visit to Florence in the fall, he showed it to Cosimo II, "who to his great surprise was able to see that the moon was a body very similar to the earth." He could see depressions and mountains, and that it was not a smooth, polished disc, as the ancients had believed.

"Therefore do I give thanks to God," wrote Galileo, "Who has been pleased to make me the first observer of marvelous things that were unrevealed to bygone ages. I have learned the nature of the Milky Way, which has always been a matter of controversy. But the greatest marvel of all is the discovery of four new planets. . . . These move around another very great star in the same way the other known planets move around the sun."

Jupiter was "the very great star" whose four moons Galileo had been able to see through the telescope which enlarged a thousand times. "It is now," he writes, "not simply a case of one moon revolving around the earth, while the two together make a revolution around the sun, as Copernicus teaches. But four moons revolve around Jupiter as the moon does around the earth, while they all revolve around the sun."

At Easter in 1610, Galileo went home to Florence, where his pupil Cosimo II had become the Grand Duke following his father's death. In honor of the Medici family (Cosimo and his three brothers), Galileo proposed to call the moons of Jupiter the Medicean stars. Cosimo, who was devoted to his tutor, wanted the telescope with which the discovery had been made, and Galileo promised to keep it for him. He could never actually bear to part with what he called his "old discoverer."

Galileo made over a hundred telescopes in the spring of 1610, and they were distributed to princes and scholars all over Europe, causing great excitement. He had a letter from Marie de' Medici, queen of France, saying, "In case you discover any other fine star, call it by the name of the Great Star of France, and if it seems fit to you, by his proper name Henri, than by the family name of Bourbon."

From Prague came a letter from Kepler, enthusiastic over the new discoveries and wishing he might discover moons around Saturn, Mars, Venus and Mercury!

In reply Galileo expressed appreciation of Kepler's belief in him, while he added that the leading professors of philosophy at Padua even refused to look through the telescope. A professor at Pisa said that since the moons of Jupiter could not be seen with the naked eye; they did not exist. Furthermore, there could not be more than seven planets. This was his argument: "The Jews and other ancient nations divided the week into seven days, and named them after the seven planets. Now if we increase the number of the planets, this system falls to the ground." Better to preserve the system than to know the truth. "What is to be done?" Galileo asks in his letter. "I think, my dear Kepler, we will laugh at their stupidity."

The telescope and his discoveries, whether believed or discredited, made Galileo famous. Students flocked to Padua to hear the lectures of the renowned astronomer. The hall seating a thousand was often so crowded that the lectures had to be held out of doors. In fact, his lectures and private lessons took so much time that Galileo had little time for experiments. As always, he was homesick for Florence, and thought if he were there he would have time for his true work. He stated this in a letter to Cosimo's secretary of state. Later in 1610, he was gratified by a reply, summoning him to Florence. He was to be First Mathematician at the University of Pisa and also Philosopher and Mathematician to the Grand Duke Cosimo II.

His delight was so dazzling that he packed up and left Padua in haste, without even notifying the authorities. The heads of the University of Padua had given him a position when he needed it. They had assured him that he was to have the position for life. The Republic of Venice had allowed him freedom that he could find nowhere else in Italy. He left without even giving them a formal notice. It was Galileo's sad mistake. He was to pay for this ingratitude in bitterness and suffering. Years later he would look back on the eighteen years at Padua, now ended, as the happiest years of his life.

Henry IV crowned 1594

Louis XIII

BOURBON

HENRY IV IS DEAD

Less than three weeks after Queen Marie had written Galileo, Henry IV was dead. Murdered, on the streets of Paris.

He was killed by a fanatic, who brooded over what he had heard of the King's latest plan until he was convinced that it was the very work of the Evil One. Others called the plan fantastic, impossible; still others said it was magnificent, the only hope for lasting peace in Europe. Some said it had been thought up by Sully—that Henry IV had nothing to do with it. Others said it was a spendid dream of that first Bourbon, the most liberal monarch that France ever had. It is spoken of in history as the *Grand Design.*

There was to be a Christian Republic of Europe—composed of fifteen equal states. All the rulers, including the Pope and the Emperor of Germany, would submit their disputes to a council of sixty representatives of the united nations meeting in a central city.

The first move toward this goal, as Henry IV saw it, was to weaken Spain and add Belgium to France, so that France would not be entirely surrounded by the Hapsburgs—the king of Spain on one side, the Emperor of Austria on the other. During the winter Henry had made plans for a campaign against Spain, to be carried out in the spring.

Louis was then only nine years old. Queen Marie was to be crowned before Henry IV left, so that she might act as regent and govern during his absence. Her coronation was to be on May 13, 1610. One night she woke in tears from a dream in which she told the King she had seen him stabbed with a knife. A soothsayer had already told her that the coronation would end in mourning. An astrologer had also warned the King that May 14 held danger for him. Even he, not at all superstitious, began to be worried.

Nevertheless, he was as gay as ever at the coronation, which took place in the abbey of St. Denis. He slept at the Louvre that night, waking early as usual. Later in the afternoon he was to go to the Arsenal for a meeting. He bade the Queen farewell a couple of times, kissing her more warmly than usual, then went down the stairs to the courtyard, where a large open carriage was waiting. Also waiting, unseen by the footmen, was a lean, wild-eyed man with a knife in his hand. As the carriage rolled away, he slid along behind it unnoticed. In the Rue St. Honoré, two farm wagons, one loaded with hay, one with kegs of wine, blocked the royal carriage. The footmen went ahead to clear a passage for the King. At that moment the madman leaped up on a curbstone and struck the King with his knife, drew it out and plunged it in again. The King sighed once and was gone. The people of Paris went wild with grief and rage. The body of the assassin was literally torn to pieces by the mob.

"God have pity on us and the state," cried Sully when he heard the news that Henry IV was dead. "France will fall into strange hands."

And so it did—into the fat, foolish hands of Marie de' Medici, who completely reversed the policies of Henry IV. She called off the war against the Hapsburgs and sought favor with Spain. She arranged for her son, nine-year-old Louis III, to marry Anne of Austria, the Spanish infanta, and for his sister Elizabeth to marry the five-year-old Spanish prince who was to be Philip IV.

There was another little French princess, named Henrietta Maria, who was only a year old when her father died, and who was eventually to marry Prince Charles of England, now ten years old. However, Queen Marie was not concerned at this time in arranging a marriage for the baby.

The Duke of Sully was either dismissed, or resigned knowing that his day was over. All the money which he and Henry IV had accumulated and set aside to be used for the improvement of the country, as well as for war, was dipped into and squandered by the Queen.

One prince, accusing the Queen-Mother of shameful waste and bad management, finally demanded that the Estates-General be called. This was a national assembly composed of nobles, clergy, and bourgeois (the wealthy merchants). They made a reasonable request about taxes, which the Queen denied. Next time they went to the assembly hall they found the doors locked and were told that the Queen wanted the hall for a dance. The Estates-General was not called again for 175 years. Since this was 1614, that would be 1789, the beginning of the French Revolution. During the Revolution when Louis XVI, the last of the Bourbon kings, was to be beheaded and the bodies of the others torn from their burial places, the tomb of the first Bourbon king, the maker of modern France, was to remain untouched and respected.

Henry IV represented to the people of France the spirit of liberty. His memory was to be cherished forever.

GALILEO IN ROME

IN ROME, on a clear, starry night in March, 1611, four members of the papal court were gathered in the gardens surrounding the summer palace of the Pope on the Quirinal Hill. They had come to view the heavens through the telescope of their famous guest, the Florentine astronomer, Galileo. Among those present was the aging Jesuit Father Clavius, who had made the new calendar thirty years ago. The entire Roman college, Jesuits and Dominicans, had denied Galileo's discoveries and threatened to outlaw the books of Copernicus. Galileo had come to Rome to give them a demonstration, to let them prove for themselves what was there in the heavens to be seen. As they looked through the telescope, one after another, they were amazed at what it revealed. They had to admit that what they had ridiculed as impossible, "those celestial novelties," as they called the four moons of Jupiter, were actually there. They saw them with their own eyes. The telescope was the wonder of the age! All honors were accorded Galileo. Pope Paul V granted him an audience and assured him of his continuing good will, and one cardinal wrote to Cosimo II:

"I verily believe that if we were still living under the ancient Republic of Rome, there would have been a column erected in his honor."

Galileo returned to Florence elated by his visit to Rome. It is sad that this relationship could not have continued. The story becomes dark and tangled in misunderstanding.

One December day, the Grand Duke, Cosimo II, was dining with his family and guests in the palace at Pisa, where he and his court were spending the winter as usual. One of the guests was Father Castelli, the professor of mathematics at the University of Pisa. The Grand Duke's mother asked him whether the Holy Scripture did not contradict Galileo's theory that the earth moved around the sun. Father Castelli defended Galileo and told him later about the conversation. Galileo was moved by this to write a long letter to his friend, "On Bringing the Holy Scriptures into Scientific Discussions," dated December 21, 1613. He said in it:

"God is a Spirit. From his Divine word, Holy Scripture and Nature do alike proceed. I think in discussing Nature we ought not to begin with texts from the Scripture but with experiment and demonstration. The Holy Scripture cannot err, but its interpreters can."

Castelli saw nothing objectionable in the letter. Nor did a wise Carmelite friar, by the name of Foscarini, who was a student and scientist as well as a deeply religious man. In a letter to the General of his Order, the monk explained how and why, as a devout Catholic, he could and did accept Galileo's discoveries as proof of the theory of Copernicus. He expressed what is now the accepted position of the Catholic Church:

"Holy Church with its visible head, the Pope, assisted by the Holy Spirit, cannot err in questions of faith, but it can err in its judgments of practical questions, in scientific speculations and other matters which are not concerned with our salvation."

Had that been generally understood and accepted in the time of Galileo, all the rest that must now be told would not have happened. Sincere high churchmen would not have made themselves appear ridiculous passing judgment on something they knew nothing about. Galileo would not have denied the divine truth revealed to him through the study of nature, and so have debased himself as a man and perjured himself as a philosopher. But the story continues.

The letter which Galileo had written was circulated, with the thought that it might be enlightening and helpful. And so it fell into the hands of a certain Father Caccini, a Dominican monk whose zeal far exceeded his education.

"I believe there is no greater hatred in the world than the hatred of ignorance for knowledge," Galileo once said. And now came evidence of it. Father Caccini read the letter and preached a violent sermon in Santa Maria Novella in Florence, denouncing Galileo and all that he stood for.

In reply, a Jesuit preacher at the Cathedral in Florence undertook to prove that Copernicus was right, that Galileo and his followers were good Catholic Christians, and pointed out (here was his mistake) that all Dominicans were ignorant fools.

Ignorant fools, indeed! snorted Father Caccini. He gathered up his skirts and betook himself to Rome "to unburden his conscience." In March, 1615, he appeared with blazing eyes before the Inquisition and "unburdened" himself.

"I wish to inform the Holy Office of a public rumor that Galileo holds two propositions to be true.

"1. The earth moves.

"2. The sun does not move.

"According to my conscience and understanding these propositions contradict the Holy Scriptures as they are interpreted by the Holy Fathers, and therefore contradict the faith."

Galileo, hearing rumors that proceedings were beginning against his teaching and the books of Copernicus, sincerely felt that he must go again to Rome and do what he could in the interest of truth. He was ill at the time and his friends warned him to be cautious, but he insisted upon going. "I cannot and must not fail to give what help my knowledge affords. I am bound to do this by my conscience as a zealous and Catholic Christian."

His efforts were as hopeless as those of Don Quixote fighting windmills. The wheels were grinding. The Congregation of Qualifications was turning over two propositions:

1. The sun is the center of the universe.
2. Earth is not.

They brought forth the unanimous decision: "Foolish, absurd and heretical."

On February 26, 1616, Galileo was summoned to appear at the palace of Cardinal Bellarmin, who, following orders, demanded that Galileo give up teaching or discussing such views. If he did not he would be thrown into jail. Galileo submitted weakly and returned to Florence.

The Roman censors also forbade the books of Copernicus to be read or taught until they had been revised by a committee. Three years after the decree was issued, a third edition of the book of Copernicus was published in Holland by a printer of Amsterdam. And the earth kept on moving around the sun. Man's decrees do not alter the ways of God. The ways of God are eternal. Only man's understanding of them changes.

FRENCH MISSIONARIES IN CANADA

Four Franciscan monks, in their long gray robes bound with knotted ropes, followed Champlain to the harbor of Honfleur in 1615, shortly before the fur ship was to sail on its annual spring voyage to Canada. They were welcomed aboard by old Pontgravé in his hearty, friendly fashion. He repeated each name in turn, as Champlain introduced them—Father Joseph, Father Jean, Father Denis, and Brother Pacifique, four friars from the Franciscan monastery at Brouage.

254

Champlain's face was aglow. At last he was to realize his dream of taking missionaries to the Indians. During the meeting of the Estates-General in Paris, he had interviewed every cardinal and bishop separately and told them of the Indians' need for a knowledge of God. Enough money had been raised to send the missionaries, and also to buy a portable altar. Father Jean and Brother Pacifique carried it on board, while Father Joseph rushed joyfully ahead to find a safe place for them to set it down.

Father Joseph's eyes were lighted by a contagious ardor for the missionary work, burning ever brighter as they neared the New World. Father Denis had eyes for the beauties of sea and sky. He followed the flight of gulls as they neared the land. He watched the wild ducks skimming the water and rising in clouds before the ship as they entered the mouth of the St. Lawrence. From Tadoussac, small boats took them on to Quebec. Father Jean and Brother Pacifique began at once to build a little chapel. Father Joseph, eager to be among the savages whom he was to teach, went off up the river in a small boat to the island of Montreal. Champlain, Pontgravé, and Father Denis followed as soon as they could, but before they reached Montreal Father Joseph met them, heading down stream, hurrying back to Quebec to get some furniture for the Mass. He was going to spend the winter with the Hurons—he had met the splendid, wonderful people!

"Not so fast," cried Champlain. "You are not yet seasoned enough for winter in this wilderness among the Indians."

"No matter," replied Father Joseph. "It is necessary for me that I learn the language—that I know the people. As for hardships, is it not the rule of our Order, that one make up his mind to suffer for the glory of God all pains and toils which may present themselves?" On he went down the river, continuing the joyful song he had been singing.

Champlain and Pontgravé reached the Huron camp, and were well along with the fur-trading when Father Joseph returned from Quebec with the altar. It was set up on the river bank. The savages gathered around, and while Father Denis and Father Joseph celebrated the Mass,

255

they sat awe-struck by the ceremony and amazed by the beautiful crucifix and ornaments. From then on, a solemn high Mass was to be part of every annual trading fair.

Champlain had to return to Quebec to make certain arrangements. Father Joseph and twelve Frenchmen set out with the Hurons on their long journey home. They paddled up the Ottawa River to Lake Nipissing, across the lake, past the Manitou Islands—paddled down the French River through a stony land, to Lake Huron—paddled the great fresh-water sea southeast along the shore of Georgian Bay. And there, after paddling for seven hundred seemingly endless miles, they reached Huronia, the land of the Hurons. A week later Champlain made the same journey, taking the hardships as a matter of course; but sympathy for Father Joseph caused him to hope that he had not found the journey too exhausting.

Father Joseph shuddered. His feet were still puffed and rubbed raw by his open-toed sandals. His hot, heavy wool robe, soaked with sandy water, had proved far from comfortable. Later, to a brother in France, he sent a description of this first terrible canoe trip.

"I can hardly tell you the fatigue I suffered. I had to keep a paddle in my hand all day long, and row with all my strength with the Indians. More than a hundred times I walked in the rivers over the sharp rocks, which cut my feet, in the mud, in the woods, where I carried the canoe and my small baggage, in order to avoid the rapids and the frightful waterfalls. And the hunger! We had only a little sagamité, which was dealt out to us morning and evening. Yet I must avow that amid my pains I felt much consolation. For alas! when we see such a great number of infidels, and nothing but a drop of water is needed to make them children of God, one feels an ardour which I cannot express to labour for their conversion and to sacrifice for it one's repose and life."

Champlain, Father Joseph, and the twelve Frenchmen spent the winter with the Hurons, who were hospitable people. Champlain inquired about their laws and religion, but could not discover that they

256

had any in particular, though they lived in harmony—and "with all their wretchedness" he considered them happy. He says:

"Father Joseph and I many times conversed with them on *our* own belief, laws and customs; they listened attentively in their councils saying to us sometimes: 'You say things that pass our understanding and that we cannot comprehend by words. If you would do well by us, you should dwell in our country and bring women and children. When they come to these regions we shall see how you serve This God, whom you worship, and your mode of life with your wives and children, your way of tilling the ground and sowing and how you obey your laws and your manner of feeding animals, and how you manufacture all that we see proceeding from your invention. Seeing this we shall learn more in one year than hearing your discourses in twenty, and if we cannot understand, you shall take our children who will be like your own. Thus judging our life wretched by comparison, it is easy to believe that we shall adopt yours and abandon our own.' Their speech seemed to me natural good sense, showing their desire to know God."

These four Franciscan monks were not the first French missionaries in Canada. Jesuits from France had arrived at Port Royal in 1611—where Champlain had lived for three winters, or until De Monts had lost the monopoly of the fur trade. Four years later, a French noblewoman had "purchased" for the Jesuits from De Monts all of North America from Florida to the St. Lawrence. This, to be sure, was the land which the English claimed as Virginia. The Jesuits worked very hard. They built their chapel and colony on Mount Desert Island in Maine. Then came the English Captain Argall from Virginia, burned the settlement to the ground, and carried off the Jesuit priests to Jamestown.

On the way there Argall stopped off to deal with other interlopers —namely the Dutch, who had built a fort on Manhattan Island, which he also burned to the ground. This was in 1613. In April he was back in Jamestown, ready to deal with Powhatan and the trouble he was causing the English in this new land of theirs.

257

POCAHONTAS IS MARRIED

FOR SOME TIME, Powhatan had been holding seven Englishmen as prisoners and also keeping twenty-five guns that had been stolen from Jamestown. Captain Argall, eager and enterprising, believed that if they could capture Pocahontas and hold her in Jamestown, he could make Powhatan buy his daughter's freedom by sending back the prisoners and the stolen guns. No one knew where Pocahontas was until Captain Argall himself went up the Potomac River to trade for corn. There he heard that the Indian princess was visiting a chieftain named Japazaws.

Argall went to Japazaws and offered him a fine copper kettle if he would persuade Pocahontas to go aboard the English ship. He promised not to hurt her, but only to keep her until they had made peace with her father. Japazaws would do anything for a copper kettle. So he tricked Pocahontas by getting his wife to beg and tease him to take her aboard the ship, provided Pocahontas went with her. On board,

Argall told Pocahontas that she must go with him and try to make peace between her people and the English. At this the Indian and his wife began to howl and cry, and then turning their backs went merrily ashore with their copper kettle, leaving Pocahontas to dry her tears alone and go on with Argall to Jamestown.

A messenger was sent to Powhatan to say that if he wished to ransom his daughter he must return the prisoners and the guns that he had stolen. It was three months before Powhatan returned the seven men, each with a musket that was broken. The English answer was: Send back the rest of the stolen guns and we will send Pocahontas. Many months passed. Early the next year Argall went up the river to the village of Powhatan, to try to settle the matter, but with no success.

All this time Pocahontas was at Jamestown. She was now eighteen, lithe and beautiful and soft-spoken. John Rolfe, try as he might, could not resist her charm. His thoughts and emotions were entangled in such a labyrinth he felt that he could not find the way out. Soon it was John Rolfe who was sent to Powhatan. It was then that he wrote Thomas Dale, the governor of Jamestown, a long letter, saying that he was deeply in love with Pocahontas, and yet did not know whether it was right to marry her. He had never failed, he said, to offer daily and faithful prayers to God for his guidance.

Governor Thomas Dale approved. Why should he not? Aside from being a lovely person with a charming dignity, Pocahontas had learned to speak English, had given up her Indian dress for English clothes, and had been baptized with the Christian name of Rebecca. In April 1614, the marriage of Pocahontas and John Rolfe took place.

Powhatan, to whom Pocahontas had sent word of her desire to marry the white man, sent an old uncle of hers and two of her brothers to witness the ceremony in his place.

Members of the London Council were troubled when they received news of this marriage in Virginia. They debated long and earnestly as to whether John Rolfe, a commoner, had not committed treason by marrying a royal princess, daughter of an "Indian emperor."

THE ROYAL COUPLE

THIS IS A COPY of the painting of the royal couple, Elizabeth, the lovely seventeen-year-old daughter of James I, and the pleasant roundfaced German prince Frederick V, who was just the same age. Their wedding was celebrated on St. Valentine's Day, 1613.

Henry, prince of Wales, Elizabeth's handsome brother, died suddenly soon after the betrothal was announced and the festivities began. That left Prince Charles heir to the throne.

Queen Anne had not been entirely pleased with the choice of her son-in-law. Gustav Adolf of Sweden, however, whose name had also been proposed, had been absolutely out of the question, especially since her brother Christian IV was about to go to war with him over the disputed boundary line between Norway and Sweden.

James I had been inclined toward Gustav Adolf, but had settled on Frederick V, who was also a Protestant and, as ruler of the German Palatinate, was likewise an Elector. That is, was one of seven German princes who elected the Holy Roman Emperor. "Holy Roman Emperor" was a more or less honorary title, since the German states were loosely joined together into a confederation rather than an empire. Each ruler, Catholic or Protestant, was supreme in his own state, but the Emperor, who was a Catholic, was eager to increase his power over all of them. James I felt that the marriage of Elizabeth to Frederick would help to strengthen the Protestant cause.

Queen Anne loved any excuse for a party. After the betrothal was announced, she threw herself into making the festivities as gay as possible for the fun-loving princess.

Elizabeth herself was so winning and altogether lovable that she

Prince Charles

was called the "Queen of Hearts." In her sparkling gown and gold crown, she seemed to lack only a magic wand to be Titania, queen of the fairies, whom she had seen when she was a little girl on her first Christmas in England. She may have seen *Midsummer Night's Dream* again with Frederick at their wedding festivities, for the King's Men were on hand to perform many of Shakespeare's plays, including his latest one, *The Tempest.* This was based on the description of the storm in which the *Sea Adventure,* bound for Jamestown, was wrecked in Bermuda.

John Donne, the preacher-poet, who was also King James's chaplain, wrote a wedding poem for the young couple, entitled:

An Epithalamion, or Marriage Song
On the Lady Elizabeth and Count Palatine Being
Married on St. Valentine's Day, 1613

Up up fair bride and call
Thy stars from out their several boxes, take
Thy rubies, pearls and diamonds forth, and make
Thyself a constellation of them all . . .
Come forth, come forth, and as one florious flame
Meeting another grows the same,
So meet thy Frederick, and so
To an inseparable union grow.

After the glittering fairytale wedding on St. Valentine's Day, the young couple left for Heidelberg, which was the capital of the Palatinate. There they spent six happy years, and the first of thirteen children was born. Then tragedy struck. For the rest of their lives they were to have no home or country they could call their own, but their descendants were to rule over almost every country in Europe. The twelfth of their children, Sophia, married Ernst Augustus, elector of Hanover, and became the mother of George I of England, and so the ancestor of Queen Victoria, Czar Nicholas II of Russia, Kaiser Wilhelm of Germany, Queen Marie of Rumania—and, coming down to the present day, Queen Juliana of Holland, the King and Queen of Greece, Elizabeth II of England and her husband Prince Philip.

KING GUSTAV ADOLF

GUSTAV ADOLF of Sweden was not at all disappointed that he could not marry Princess Elizabeth of England, whom he had never seen. He was in love with darling Ebba Brahe who was right there in Sweden before his eyes. This Swedish general's daughter was the only girl he ever wanted to marry. Queen Kristina, his mother, had higher ambitions for her son. Not that the Queen disliked Ebba; she was fond of her and had had her come to live with them at court after her mother died. But for a daughter-in-law, she wanted to make an alliance with one of the German states and have a German princess for the future Queen of Sweden.

Gustav Adolf's father had suffered a stroke and been paralyzed for some time before he died. His death came on October 30, 1611, and young Gustav Adolf was crowned King of Sweden. Though he was not yet seventeen, the Riksdag decided that, young as he was, he was capable both "by nature and training to have the entire and undivided government of the Kingdom." The Riksdag had also made another

decision which had pleased the boy
even more. They had formally de-
clared that he was "so far arrived at man's estate as to be able to wear
armor and carry weapons." It was his ambition to be as great a general
as his hero, Prince Maurice of the Netherlands. After 1609, when a
truce had been signed between Holland and Spain, many soldiers who
had fought in the long war had come to Sweden. Gustav Adolf had
asked them hundreds of questions about battles and sieges both on land
and sea. What he had learned, he was soon to have a chance to practice.
Before his father died, Christian IV, knowing that he was ill, had decided that this was an opportune time to begin war. Early in 1611 he
crossed over from Denmark to Sweden and seized the fortress of Elfsborg, which gave him control of the entrance to the Baltic Sea.

Gustav Adolf's first year as king was therefore spent in war against
the Danes. It was a terrible year of frontier warfare. He nearly lost his
life in a winter battle by falling with his horse through the ice while
crossing a frozen lake. Swedish peasants of the region rebelled against
being under Danish rule. The nobles of Denmark would not support

Christian IV any further, fearing he would gain more power over them by too much success. The lazy fellow himself was sick of fighting anyway. So the war ended. With James I acting as go-between, peace was made in January, 1613; just before the wedding of Christian IV's niece, the princess Elizabeth. His war with Denmark settled—not too satisfactorily since he had to buy back Elfsborg, but settled nevertheless—Gustav Adolf could turn his attention to Russia, where strange things were happening. There for some years past, both his father, Charles IX, and his cousin Sigismund, King of Poland, had been fighting to get hold of the Russian borderlands. Poland wanted the land on the western border. Sweden wanted the land on the north that would shut Russia off completely from the Baltic Sea . . . The Russian fort of Novgorod had already been captured by Sweden and it was possible that Karl Filip, Gustav Adolf's brother, might be named the next Tsar of Russia! But by February, 1613, the Russian people themselves had made another choice; which was no disappointment to Gustav Adolf, who considered Russia a "barbarous and unruly nation."

RUSSIA'S NEW TSAR—MICHAEL ROMANOV

MICHAEL ROMANOV!" shouted the crowds of Russian people on the Red Square. "Michael Feodorovich for Tsar!"

It was February 21, 1613, one week after the wedding

of Princess Elizabeth, who was also to be an ancestor of the last of Michael Romanov's descendants.

In Moscow, heart of Holy Mother Russia, on Red Square between the market and the Kremlin, crowds of Russians had been gathered together. Standing before them was the Archimandrite of the church in gold dome-shaped hat and embroidered robes, and also a boyar with full black beard, high fur hat, and long fur-trimmed cloak.

"Who shall be Tsar?" asked the Archimandrite. "What is your will?" asked the boyar. The people's answer was unanimous.

"Michael Feodorovich Romanov!"

Michael's great-aunt had been the saintly Anatasia, the first wife of Ivan the Terrible, his grandfather General Nikita Romanov, a great hero of the people. So they shouted for Michael Feodorovich Romanov to be Tsar of Muscovy and the whole state of Russia.

Thus, three hundred years before it was to be wiped out in 1918, the Romanov family was put upon the throne of Russia by the unanimous will of the people. Russia had lived through eight terrible years since the death of Boris Godonov, known as the "Time of Troubles," during which one false Tsar after another had been proclaimed, deposed or murdered. First, the Dimitri who came from Poland claiming to be the youngest son of Ivan the Terrible, had been crowned and then murdered by the anti-Polish boyars, who then crowned one of their own leaders, Shuisky. A revolt against him arose, led by the wild Cossacks who came riding out of the southwest, burning villages and trampling down fields till they had ruined half of Muscovy. The boyars appealed to the King of Sweden, promising land along the Baltic Sea. Despite Sweden's help, the boyars were defeated by the Cossacks and the Poles. A Polish general then persuaded the boyars to confer with King Sigismund about crowning his son Tsar, and to let the Poles into Moscow to protect them from the Cossacks. So in 1610, the Poles were in the Kremlin; but in 1612 the Cossacks came riding in, and drove out the Poles, while three-fourths of the city was burned to the ground.

A cry then went up from the Troitsa Monastery, a rallying cry to

Russia

all true Russians, all brethren of the Holy Orthodox faith, to rise, to drive out the foreigners, to recapture Russia for the Russians. It was the voice of the Abbot Dionisy, begging them, "For God's sake, lay aside your quarrels and stand together."

First to answer the call was Minin, a master-butcher, who gave one third of his own property and urged others "to sacrifice for the true faith." Prince Pozharski came forward, fighting bravely against Cossacks and Poles. There was talk then of asking King Gustav of Sweden or his brother Karl Filip to be Tsar. It was too late for that.

The boyars wanted no more foreigners in the Kremlin! A circular was sent out summoning representatives of every class of people to come to Moscow and elect as their Tsar a native Russian. A certain nobleman proposed the name of Michael as nearest of kin to the ancient dynasty of Rurik, the people shouted his name, and he was elected.

Michael Romanov was sixteen years old. He had been elected, but where was he? In a monastery on the Volga River, with his mother. Like her husband, she had been obliged to take religious vows by Boris Godunov. She told the delegation of boyars that Michael was too young to be the ruler of Russia. He himself also hesitated to accept. The boyars spent six hours pleading with him, telling him if he refused he would be responsible for the destruction of Moscow. Finally he assented; let them fall on their knees and kiss his hand.

Russia was in a terrible situation. In the north the Swedes held all the Baltic provinces. In the west the Poles held all the western provinces. In the southeast the Cossack leader was making a kingdom on the Volga. Tartar and savage hordes swarmed in from all directions. On his trip toward Moscow, Michael saw charred villages, ruined churches, hundreds of wandering homeless people. At the Troitsa monastery, about fifty miles from Moscow, he had to stop and wait until the Kremlin palace had been re-roofed and repaired enough for him.

All the male population of Moscow went to meet the young Tsar, and in the summer of 1613, he was solemnly crowned.

Five years later, Michael's father, the good Philaret, after nine years' absence, was allowed to return. Tsar Michael went with boyars and crowds of people to escort him into Moscow. Ten days later, Philaret was made a Patriarch of the church, and shared the throne with his son in what was to be a dual monarchy until his death in 1633. So the rule of the Romanov was well begun under the young Tsar Michael and his wise father the Patriarch Philaret.

THE PORTRAICTUER OF CAPTAYNE JOHN SMITH / ADMIRALL OF NEW ENGLAND

Æta:37
Aº 1616

THE NAMING OF NEW ENGLAND

TWO VESSELS, sails filled with wind, were heading west from Plymouth Harbor to that part of the New World still known as northern Virginia. It was early spring of the year 1614. The commander of one of the vessels was Captain Hunt. On the other was Captain John Smith, for the first time in his life in command of an ocean-going vessel. As he paced the deck, stood at the prow, caught the salt breeze in his face, he felt alive again. The past four deadly years spent in England were behind him. All of the troubles and frustrations, all of the misdeeds of his enemies, real and imaginary, all of the misery at not being paid by the London Company, or given credit for what he had done in Jamestown—all these miseries were forgotten, gone like clouds before the wind in the exhilaration of a new adventure. The sun shone, life was good. He was on his way to northern Virginia, to discover what was there. Adventure, discovery—these were the breath of life to John Smith.

One of the passengers who had boarded the ship at Plymouth was going home. He towered head and shoulders above the short blond captain; his bronze skin and straight black hair showed him to be an American Indian. His full name was Tisquantum. He was the friendly Squanto, who years later was to teach the Pilgrims to plant corn. Squanto had spent the past ten years in England. With four others of his tribe, he had been taken to Plymouth by a Captain Weymouth, who had been sent out to discover a northwest passage. Squanto came from that part of the coast near a cape which, as John Smith knew, had been named Cape Cod by Captain Gosnold. Gosnold had been one of the original seven members of the council in Jamestown, and Captain of the *Goodspeed* on the voyage over. Before that he had made a voyage to northern Virginia, financed by Sir Walter Raleigh, and had named Cape Cod, which Squanto said was near the land of the Massachusetts Indians. Squanto had told Sir Ferdinando Gorges that he belonged to a tribe called the Patuxet which lived directly across the bay from Cape Cod.

Sir Ferdinando Gorges was mayor of Plymouth and head of the Plymouth Company, which held the rights to northern Virginia. After talking with Squanto and the other Indians he had been impressed by their dignity, "so far removed," he said, "from rudeness of our common people." He was also most interested in the country from which they came. The Plymouth Company had already tried unsuccessfully to form a colony in Maine. Now they had hired John Smith to make

270

a voyage for them—and also Captain Hunt, who had his greedy eye on Squanto.

This voyage was not one for exploration, or to found a colony. It was a commercial venture. They were to bring back whales, fish, furs, and gold, should any of that desirable article be found.

As soon as they had anchored on an island near the coast of Maine, they started looking for whales. "We saw many," said John Smith, "and spent much time chasing them; but could not kill any." So they gave up whale-hunting.

The fur season was then practically over, so that was out.

Fishing came next. The sailors fished for cod and halibut, but John Smith did not care for fishing. He set out in a boat with eight or nine men, to do what he enjoyed—explore the coast, make a map of it, as he had of Chesapeake Bay, and locate a good place for a permanent settlement. His spirits soared as he went down the coast "from point to point, Ile to Ile and Harbour to Harbour," drawing his map. The paradise of all those parts he said, was Massachusetts. The harbor was wonderful, the wooded shore rose high from the water instead of being low and marshy as at Jamestown, and it was planted here and there with Indian corn. All that was needed in this fine land was people— English people who were willing to work, declared John Smith. Upon his return to Plymouth, he called at once on his "honorable friend," Sir Ferdinando Gorges. He explained to members of the Plymouth Company ideas for a colony, whose support should be based on fishing.

"I engaged to undertake the management of it," he said, and "was assured by them of having the position for life."

He was walking on air as he left the meeting, feeling that they saw that he was singularly perfect for the work. As he himself admitted, "It is not worke for everyone to manage such an affaire as makes a discovery and plants a colony. It requires all the best parts of Art, Judgement, Courage, Honesty, Constancy, Diligence and Industry."

The following June, 1615, John Smith sailed from Plymouth to plant a colony on the shore of what he was beginning to call New

England. He was counting on the help of Squanto, whom he had taken home the previous year. But Squanto was not there. After John Smith had left for home, Captain Hunt had stayed behind and, while loading his ship with corn and furs, had seized, bound, and taken aboard thirty Indians, carried them off to Spain and sold them as slaves in the Malaga slave market. Among them was Squanto.

John Smith did not discover this, because on his second voyage Captain Smith did not reach New England. For six months no one knew where he was. Sir Ferdinando Gorges had about decided he must be dead, when one day in December, John Smith turned up in Plymouth with a wild tale of misadventures to relate. He had been captured by pirates.

French pirates had chased and captured his ship. This had been done by mistake, the French captain told him. They were out to capture only Spanish and Portuguese ships. If Captain Smith would come aboard with them and show his English orders, they would let him go. Smith had done so, and they had seized him and held him while they removed the stores from his ship. Then, when they were ready to let her go, he had not been able to get off the pirate ship in time, and had seen his own ship sail away without him.

Day after day, the pirate ship cruised about, looking for Spanish galleons. "To keep my thoughts from my miserable state," said John Smith, "I busied myself perfecting the map I had made and writing my Description of New England."

Part of the time, whenever the pirates captured an English ship, he was kept locked in the gunroom or the cabin. They captured one going home from Newfoundland with a cargo of fish. A Scottish ship loaded with sugar from the West Indies had just been captured, when there came into view a Spanish galleon, the prize they had been looking for, loaded with treasure for the King of Spain.

The French pirates released John Smith when he accepted their offer to help fight the Spaniards for a share in the gold. This went on all summer. In the fall, as they were nearing the French coast, John

Smith discovered that he had been duped. The French pirates not only did not intend to share the booty with him, they threatened to turn him over to the French government. They knew who he was—the English captain who had burned the French settlement in Canada and carried away the Jesuit priests to Virginia. Let him settle for that!

One dark night, John Smith, taking nothing but his map and manuscript, escaped in a small boat and rowed to an island nearby. A terrific storm came up. The pirate ship was wrecked. Ship, crew, and treasure went to the bottom of the sea. Although he was nearly drowned, our hero made another one of his lucky escapes and reached the port of La Rochelle. With the help of friends, he sailed for Plymouth, to make his report to Sir Ferdinando Gorges and show him his map of New England. From Plymouth he was off to London to find a publisher for his manuscript.

Then, since Prince Charles was heir to the throne, John Smith was eager to meet and consult his Highness about the proper names to put upon the map. Charles, now fifteen, was most intrigued by the map and eager to read the newly printed Description of New England, which Captain Smith had also brought with him.

"New England," said Charles. That was a good name. It should be called New England. And that river running into the big bay, that should be named for him, the River Charles. And Cape Cod should be changed to Cape James. And what was the strange name on that other big cape farther north? Tragabigzanda? Who was that? A Turkish princess who had once rescued Captain Smith? Well, that should be changed, and called Cape Ann, after his mother. He also suggested names for future towns and cities; the one which stayed in the place he marked for it was Plimouth.

The names decided upon, John Smith rolled up his map and took it to a skillful engraver who had just come to England from the Netherlands, and who also engraved the portrait of Captain John Smith, a copy of which appears on the title page of the book and on the map. It was framed in a new title, "Admiral of New England."

IN MEMORY OF SHAKESPEARE

A *Description of New England* by John Smith was published in the year 1616. That year King James brought out a collection entitled *The Works of His Most High and Mighty Prince James,* dedicated to Jesus Christ from "His most humble and obliged servant James I."

Also in 1616, Ben Jonson was made the first poet laureate of England, and published his collected works. All of his best plays, masques, and verses were gathered into a handsome volume of more than a thousand pages. It contained his famous poem *To Celia:*

> Drink to me only with thine eyes
> And I will pledge with mine.
> Or leave a kiss but in the cup
> And I'll not look for wine.

In this same year 1616, Shakespeare died. Jonson had disapproved of Shakespeare's way of writing but he had loved Shakespeare.

"I loved the man," he said, "and do honor his memory on this side of idolatry as much as any. He was indeed honest . . ." The highest praise Ben Jonson could give anyone was to call him honest.

He himself was also honest, but his brutal honesty was very different from the deep, gentle honesty of Shakespeare, just as his blatant self-esteem differed from Shakespeare's humility. And his strictly regulated way of working differed from the freedom of Shakespeare, who created his poems and plays as naturally as a tree bears fruit, giving little thought to preserving them. Possibly the thought occurred to him when he was in London in 1614 and heard of Ben Jonson's plan to publish his collection, for on his return to Stratford, Shakespeare revised those of his plays that needed it. But it was not until seven years after he was gone that they were published in a single volume, by his friends.

In 1610 there had been another epidemic of the plague in London and Shakespeare had given up his lodgings in the city and returned to Stratford to live. There he had written his last and lovely play, *The Tempest.*

Shakespeare died on April 23, 1616. His body was carried from New Place down to the church by the river Avon, where he had been christened in 1564, and there was buried by the altar.

In January, when he was still "in perfect health," he had had a solicitor draw up his will, providing for his two daughters, Susanna and Judith, who was married that spring to the son of an old friend. Shortly after the wedding he became ill, and signed the will. His wife Anne was to have his "second best bed," in addition to her widow's dower. Judith was left her marriage dower. His sister was to have the old home on Henley Street, and the rest of his estate went to Susanna.

To three actors, his life-long friends in the Chamberlain's Company, Richard Burbage, John Hemynge and Henry Condell, he left money to purchase rings. To Hemynge and Condell, Shakespeare entrusted the work of editing his plays, of which there were thirty-six, and publishing them in a single volume. The work was unfamiliar to them. "It would have been well if the Author had lived to have set forth and overseen his own writings," they said in the introduction, but since that was not to be, "we his friends have collected and published them, absolute in their numbers as he conceived them. His mind and hand went together; and what he thought he uttered with that easiness that we have scarce received from him a blot in his papers. . . ."

275

They chose a commercial artist to make the necessary portrait of the author for the frontispiece, and Ben Jonson said the likeness was good. There also had to be poems written in praise of him. Ben Jonson's book had opened with poems in both Latin and English written by nine poets, but Shakespeare was not the poet laureate of England, and his actor friends did not know many poets personally. They did know Jonson, for they had acted in plays which he had written for the King's Men. They approached him as the perfect person to introduce the plays.

"We have collected them," they told him, "without ambition either of self-profit or fame; only to keep the memory of so worthy a friend and fellow alive as was our Shakespeare."

Ben Jonson responded warmly and generously out of his love for Shakespeare, and because, in all honesty, he recognized him as a genius. He said nothing of the "rules" which Shakespeare disregarded. He did mention that Shakespeare had "small Latin and less Greek," but added that only the greatest of the Greek dramatists could equal him and that he far outsoared all those of his own generation.

Jonson wrote eighty lines "To the memory of my beloved, the author Master William Shakespeare, and what he hath left us."

Sweet Swan of Avon! What a sight it were
To see thee in our waters yet appear
    Soul of the age!
The applause! delight! the wonder of our stage.
My Shakespeare, rise. I will not lodge thee by
    Chaucer or Spencer or bid Beaumont lie
A little further to make thee room;
Thou art alive still, while thy book dothe live
And we have wits to read and praise to give,
    Triumph my Britain, thou hast one to show
To whom all scenes of Europe homage owe.
He was not of an age, but for all time.

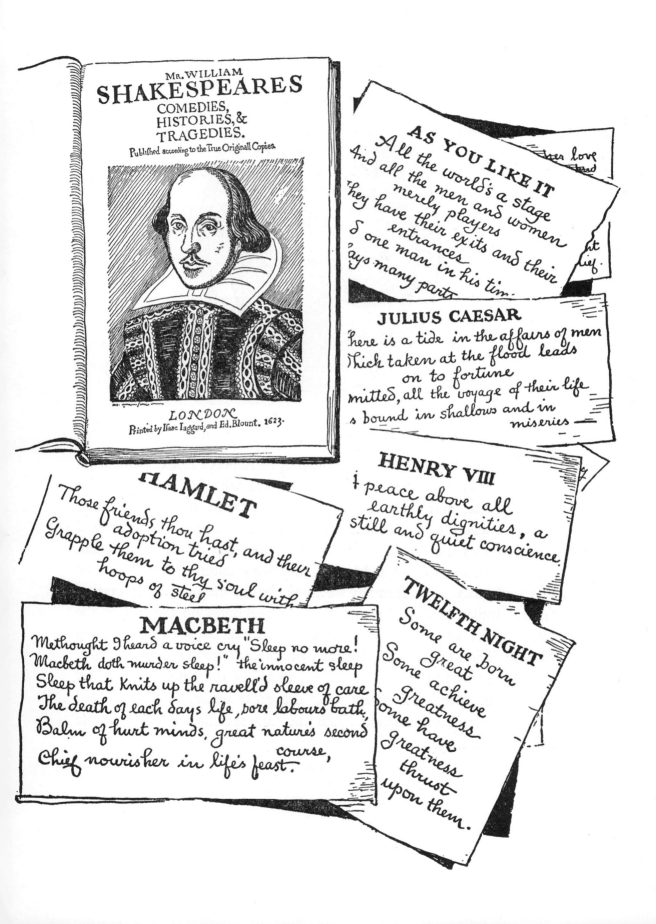

POCAHONTAS IN ENGLAND

THIS IS A PORTRAIT of Pocahontas, or Rebecca Rolfe, painted on the visit to England which she made with her husband, John Rolfe, and their year-old son Thomas, in 1616. It was late spring. Tobacco plants were lush and green in the sunny fields around Jamestown as the travelers rowed out to the ship of Captain Argall, anchored in the river. On May 31 they were entering the harbor of Plymouth, there to be formally welcomed by the mayor and dignitaries. Several Indian girls and men followed Pocahontas up the hill to the castle. Chief among them was a dignified man who carried a long stick, as if it were of utmost value to him. This was Uttamatomakkin, one of the trusted councillors of Powhatan. The old chief had charged him, on the proposed voyage over the great water, to observe and bring back true information about the false-speaking English people and their country.

278

"Seek out John Smith," said Powhatan. "Have him show you the God, the King, the Queen, the Prince, all of which he has said to me in so many words. Is the land what they say? How many people are there? Carry with you a long stick and for every person make a notch."

And so Uttamatomakkin was carrying his stick as he gravely acknowledged the greeting of Sir Ferdinando Gorges, who like everyone else in England was in a flurry of uncertainty as how to receive a royal princess who was also an Indian. Members of the court and of the Virginia Company were most upset by such a confusing situation. Where should she stay? A country house in Brentford, not far from Hampton Court, was decided upon. There the Bishop of London entertained the princess with what was described as "festival state and pomp." Lord and Lady de la Warr presented Pocahontas, accompanied by her royal father's courtier Uttamatomakkin, to King James, Queen Anne and members of the court.

Pocahontas attended the Christmas festivities at Whitehall, and saw a performance of the "Christmas Masque" by Ben Jonson. The Indian princess in a beautiful gown, with her warm-colored skin and laughing dark eyes, was much admired by everyone, though she was not the entire center of attention.

Many cast meaningful glances at a certain handsome young man who had just been created the Earl of Buckingham by King James. The King adored him, and kept his large bulbous eyes focused on Buckingham the entire evening.

Uttamatomakkin observed everything and everybody, but had no idea that he was looking at the King. John Smith had a hard time, when he saw the Indian later, to persuade him that the weak, slovenly man with none of the dignity of an Indian chief was the white man's King.

John Smith had written to Queen Anne, as soon as he heard that Pocahontas was coming, telling her that this was the Indian princess who had saved his life twice, and helped to keep alive the colony at Jamestown. After she arrived, he hesitated to seek her out. After all, this was England, not Virginia. He was only a commoner, and she a princess. When he finally did go to Brentford, she looked at him, he said, and then, "Without any word she turned about and hid her face in her hands." But not long after she began to talk.

"You did promise Powhatan what was yours should be his. You called him father, being in his land a stranger and by the same reason so must I do you."

At this John Smith shook his head. He could not allow it. He would not dare to—not here in England.

"You were not afraid to come into my father's Country and cause fear in him and all his people—except me. And you fear here that I should call you father? I tell you then I will and you shall call me child, and so I will be forever and ever your countryman.

"They did tell us always you were dead, and I knew no other until I came to Plymouth. Yet Powhatan did command Uttamatomakkin to seek you and know the truth, because your Countrymen will lie much."

In March, 1617, the visit was over. Captain Argall had his ship ready to take Mr. and Mrs. John Rolfe and little Thomas, who was now walking, and the rest of the party home to Virginia. Some of the Indian girls preferred to stay in London, and Pocahontas looked back wistfully at the great city as the ship moved down the river, fearing she might never return. She was never to leave England. Before they reached the mouth of the Thames, Pocahontas became so very ill that they had to anchor at Gravesend. In April, in the vestry book of the parish church the parson made this entry, full of mistakes in spelling and names:

Rebecca Wrothe, wyffe of Thomas Wrothe, Gentlemen, a Virginia lady born, here was buried in the chancel.

Little Thomas grew so ill after leaving Gravesend that his father did not dare to take him across the Atlantic. They put in at Plymouth and the small boy was left with a cousin of Sir Walter Raleigh, who was to take him later to his uncle, Henry Rolfe, a member of the Virginia Company, who brought him up in London.

John Rolfe returned alone to Virginia.

THE LAW VS. THE KING?

PARLIAMENT." James I spat out the word as if it left a bad taste in his mouth. "I do not understand how my ancestors allowed such an institution to grow up!"

In the ten years since he had come to England, James had been continually at loggerheads with the House of Commons, who at the very beginning had flung back an answer to his favorite saying: "God makes the King and the King makes the law."

His Majesty had been badly misinformed, the Commons had told him. The King of England had no power to make laws except by consent of Parliament. Nor could he levy taxes. That was the worst of it. He could get no money to spend except by asking Parliament. And every year James was more of a glutton for money as he was for food and drink. Each time he asked Parliament for funds some kind of reform was demanded, so he tried to get money in other ways. He created a new rank of baronet, for anyone who could pay for it, and forced all who had a certain income from land to be knighted and pay for the honor. When the House of Commons protested over something he did, he tore out the page of the official journal on which it was recorded. In 1614, when Parliament refused to supply his wants he dismissed it and ruled for the next seven years without summoning Parliament to express the "will of the people."

The will of the people? Bah! What will had the people but to obey the will of the king? One of the leading members of Parliament strangely enough echoed these sentiments.

This was Sir Francis Bacon, who was now a member of the King's Privy Council, his confidential adviser, and Attorney General.

Parliament, said Bacon, was merely a body to be consulted by the King in an emergency. A statesman was the King's servant. His duty was to carry out the royal will. The King was the supreme power, the center of law and justice.

Squarely opposed to this idea was Sir Edward Coke, who had conducted the trial against Sir Walter Raleigh, and had long been Bacon's rival. Coke was now Lord Chief Justice of England. He held great respect for the Common Law, by which England was ruled.

The Law, not the King, was the supreme power. Justice was not to be decided by royal proclamation, but according to the body of common laws that had developed through the years. A king's word could not make an act a crime, nor interfere with the process of the Law.

In 1616 a case concerning libel against the King came up to be judged. James sent word by Sir Francis Bacon, his willing servant, to the Chief Justice and the other judges to delay the case until he could talk to them about it. The judges all replied that they could not do so—it would be against the law. James was furious and ordered them to appear before him in the Council Chamber, where he violently denounced them for their insolent disobedience. One by one they fell upon their knees promising to obey in the future, should a similar case arise; miserable cowed men, fearing to lose their positions.

The Lord Chief Justice alone dared to remain standing, and to uphold the law. "When the case arises," said Sir Edward Coke, "I shall do that which shall be fitting for a judge to do."

He was dismissed within the year, but as he stepped down from the judges' bench, he went down as a hero in man's struggle for freedom, for without government according to law, there can be no freedom.

RALEIGH'S LAST ADVENTURE

THE MASSIVE OAKEN DOOR in the Tower of London swung
heavily open one March day in 1616. A man stepped out—a
prisoner free for the first time in thirteen years. Sir Walter
Raleigh. He started off toward the river, his first thought being to take
a walk around London and see how the city had changed. From the
bounce in his step, the set of his head, one would not have guessed
that he was sixty-four years old. Nor did he feel it. It was spring! He
was free! And he would soon be off for Guiana—for El Dorado—for
the fabulous gold mine. This time he would find it!

All the years in prison Raleigh had tried in vain to get his release,
until he touched on the King's weak spot, his greed for money. The
possibility that he might get gold from Guiana made James give in,
though he still did not want Raleigh's operations to disturb friendly

relations with Spain. He hedged, played safe. He promised the Spanish ambassador that if Raleigh interfered with Spanish subjects on Spanish territory, he would be handed over for public execution in Spain. He gave Raleigh permission to go, but he did not give him a pardon. He was still a "traitor," according to the trial of 1603.

Friends of Raleigh advised him not to embark on such a risky enterprise, under those conditions. But when had Walter Raleigh feared to take a risk?

"As to Guiana being Spanish territory—that," he declared, "can never be acknowledged for I myself took possession of it for Queen Elizabeth. It was ceded to her by the native chiefs of the country . . ."

Loyal friends helped him raise the necessary funds for a fleet of seven ships, the largest one to be commanded by his son Walter, who came down from Oxford. The crew of 431 men were a wild lot—the "scum of the earth," Raleigh called them. They set out to sea from Plymouth. The crossing to South America was very stormy. Guiana was sighted in November, but by then Raleigh, with many others, was so ill with fever that he was unable to go ashore to search for the gold mine. He appointed another man to lead the party up the Orinoco River, warning him to avoid trouble with the Spaniards.

They failed completely—so completely that the leader of the expedition, after making his sad report, shut himself in his cabin and committed suicide, leaving Raleigh to face the bitter facts alone. They had not found gold. They had had a skirmish with the Spaniards. His son Walter had been killed.

"God knows I never knew before what sorrow meant . . ." he wrote in a heartsick letter to his wife. "What shall become of me now, I know not . . ."

Hopeless as the future appeared, Raleigh's buoyant spirit soon rose again. Would the men go back to Orinoco with him to find the body of his son—or go to Newfoundland—or try to find the long-lost Virginia colony? No one would follow him. He had to return to Plymouth. There Lady Raleigh met him. Together they decided that he should go to France where he had had word from the French court that he would be welcome. Arrangements for his escape were made, but he was betrayed by his own cousin.

A formal letter from Philip III of Spain had expressed the desire that Raleigh should be executed in England.

James consulted Sir Francis Bacon, who advised him that the sentence of 1603, suspended fifteen years, still held good and could be carried out. The condemned man was led before the King's Bench. The new Chief Justice spoke:

"Sir Walter Raleigh is a man to be pitied. He hath been a star at which the world hath gazed. But stars may fall, nay, they must fall when they trouble the sphere wherein they abide."

Still, even in the face of death, Raleigh's spirit did not fail him. He met a friend on the way to the Gate House at Westminster, where he was to spend his last night, and smoked his last pipe of tobacco.

"Come early to the Palace Yard tomorrow morning to get a good place," he called. "For my part, I am sure of one."

Next morning, on the scaffold, when the executioner asked him to kneel facing east, he replied, "What matter which way the head lies, so the heart be right." He refused to be blindfolded, saying, "Think you I fear the shadow of the axe? Strike, man, strike."

His *History of the World,* written during his imprisonment, ends with these words: "O eloquent, just and mighty Death!"

And in his Bible was found this poem:

> "Even such is time, which takes in trust
> Our youth, our joys, our all we have. . . .
> And pays us with but earth and dust
> Who in the dark and silent grave,
> When we have wandered all our ways
> Shuts up the story of our days."

1619

THE HOUSE OF BURGESSES

So TIME had brought to an end the life of Sir Walter Raleigh, who had named the colony of Virginia for Queen Elizabeth. And to that colony which he had never seen, the year after his death brought so many changes that 1619 was to be known as the red-letter year in the history of Virginia.

Jamestown was twelve years old. Had John Smith been able to go back it would have seemed quite unlike the little fort in the wilderness which he had helped to defend against the Indians. Raising of corn and tobacco had taken the place of exploration and searching for gold. Other people besides "gentlemen" who did not wish to work had been going to Virginia, some not too desirable. About Christmas, 1617, King James had issued a proclamation that "the most notorious and lewd persons" in the kingdom should be sent to Virginia, "that they may no more infect the places where they abide in this realme."

The marriage of John Rolfe and Pocahontas had brought a time of peace between the Indians and the settlers, known as the "Pocahontas Peace." Powhatan, the great old chieftain, had died in 1618, but his brother, Opekankano, had sworn that "the sky would fall" before his friendship should cease.

Jamestown was no longer the only settlement. Up and down the James River and across the peninsula, there were eleven settlements; a thousand people. Fields of tobacco and corn were spreading farther into the land that once had been Indian hunting ground.

House of Burgesses

Too many fields—too many white men every year, cutting down the trees—in the eyes of Opekankano. He did not trust the lying white man, in spite of his sworn friendship lasting as the sky.

In London a new governor was chosen by the Virginia Company to replace Lord de la Warr, who had died the same year as Powhatan. His name was George Yeardley. Newly knighted by the King, newly elected governor of Virginia, Sir George Yeardley suddenly saw himself a changed and splendid personage. He spent over $200,000 on a suitable outfit, and went marching about the streets of London followed by fifteen hired servants in fancy livery before his departure for Jamestown. John Smith, then destitute, with no prospect of going anywhere at the time, must surely have seen him.

The London Company had also decided upon a new system for governing the growing colony. There was to be no more communal living—no more depending upon a common store of provisions, no more eating whether one worked or not—no more common ownership of land. Each settler was to own his own land, plant his own corn and tobacco. Those who had come before 1616 were to have one hundred acres—the others, fifty, except indentured servants, whose passage had been paid by an employer for whom they had to work seven years for their freedom.

There had never been more than three women in Jamestown while John Smith was there, and still there were not enough. In 1619, the London Company sent out a shipload of young women, to marry the young planters and establish homes and families, which certainly made it a red-letter year for the newly-wedded couples.

Of all events, however, the one that made 1619 truly remarkable in the history of Virginia and of the United States was the meeting of the House of Burgesses in Jamestown. The first meeting in which people in America came together to help make the laws.

The London Company had become aware of the fact that they were too far away to know all the needs of the colony, that all the power should not be in the hands of one man, the governor. Besides a council to advise him, there should be an assembly of representatives from the settlements, to assist him in making the laws. This would be similar to the House of Commons. Since the settlers were called burgesses, it would be the House of Burgesses. According to plan, Governor Yeardley invited two delegates from each of the eleven settlements to meet with him in Jamestown. This was not actually self-government, because any laws they made could be vetoed by the Governor or by the London Company.

On July 30, 1619, the House of Burgesses met for the first time. Blistering summer sun beat down upon the dusty street as the people gathered and lined up to watch the procession of twenty-two delegates dressed for the occasion rather than the weather, in high ruffs and heavy waistcoats. Led by the Governor in a scarlet cape and gold chain, and members of the council, they filed solemnly into the wooden church, the only building large enough to hold the meeting.

"The most convenient place we could find to sitt in," wrote John Pory, the new Secretary, "was the Quire of the Church, where Sir George Yeardley the Governor, being sett downe in his accustomed place, those of the Council sate nexte him on both hands . . . [and] all the Burgesses took their places in the Quire till a prayer was said by Mr. Buck the Minister." Prayer being ended, they proceeded to give due respect to God's "lieutenant, our gracious and dread sovereign James I."

All the Burgesses were then called in order by name and every man took the oath of Supremacy. They met for five days, opening each day with a prayer used by the Church of England, believing that "men's affairs do little prosper where God's service is neglected."

One of the first laws passed by the House of Burgesses was that nobody was to trade a gun with an Indian and every man must carry his gun to church with him on Sunday. They did not put complete faith in the Indian's oath. Time had not changed conditions as much as that. The white settlers were still living in danger on the edge of the deep unknown wilderness.

SERVANTS AND SLAVES

A DUTCH MAN-OF-WAR was anchored in the river near Jamestown, one hot August day in 1619. The torrid sun beat down upon the water and on the black heads and backs of twenty human beings who were being rowed ashore in small boats to be sold in Jamestown as servants. The first Negroes had been brought to Virginia.

The Dutch man-of-war had been cruising in the West Indies, on the lookout for Spanish ships to capture, when it accidentally met an English man-of-war also looking for Spanish treasure. This ship, the *Treasurer,* had been sent out by Captain Argall, who had been acting as governor of Jamestown for two years before Governor Yeardley arrived. Both ships were freighted with slaves from Africa, most of them to be left in the Bermudas. Negroes had been imported for many years into the Spanish colonies, especially those of the West Indies. They had been brought there when Charles V was Emperor, largely to replace the native Indians, who could not stand the work in the mines and sickened and died by the thousands. A bishop of Haiti who could no longer bear to see them suffer made a journey to Spain, to suggest that each Spanish resident of Haiti be allowed to import twelve Negro slaves to work in the mines. He meant well but later realized that one wrong does not cure another. Charles V took his advice and gave a Flemish favorite of his the right to supply four thousand Negroes a year to Haiti, Cuba, Jamaica, and Puerto Rico. This gentleman sold his rights to some merchants of Genoa. They got the Negroes from the Portuguese, who had originally gotten them from the Arabs or Moors who lived in North Africa.

Fifty years before Columbus discovered the West Indies, a Portuguese officer had captured some Moors, and was told by his King to take them back home. For each Moor he returned, the officer received from the grateful Moors ten Negroes, who were then taken to the port of Malaga and sold in Spain. This looked like a good business, to be continued. So the Portuguese built ships and forts on the west coast of Africa, where the native chiefs helped round up and capture their own people for a nominal sum. The Negroes were taken directly from there to the slave market in Malaga on the southern coast of Spain. From Spain, the descendants of those Negroes were later taken to the Spanish colonies in the New World.

This miserable slave trade had been going on for about one hundred years when the first Englishman got into it—Sir John Hawkins, cousin of Sir Francis Drake. Hawkins' first successful voyage was in 1562. Queen Elizabeth leased a vessel to him, and after two voyages he had made such a reputation in the slave trade that she granted him a coat of arms with a Negro shown in chains on the crest. Sir John Hawkins and Sir Francis Drake were on one of their Spanish treasure-hunting expeditions, to the West Indies, when both these gentlemen-pirates died at sea in 1595—which was seven years after they had helped defeat the Spanish Armada.

The year that the twenty Negroes reached Jamestown, Squanto, who had been sold into slavery, got back to New England. In Spain, where he had been taken five years before to the Malaga slave market, he had been rescued by friars from a monastery. After the good brothers had instructed him in the Christian faith, they let him go free. In time he managed to reach England, where he was employed as the servant of a merchant in London. Squanto went from London to Plymouth and presented himself again to Sir Ferdinando Gorges, who made arrangements for him to go back on one of the Plymouth Company's ships, sailing to Massachusetts.

There, where Squanto had left his people, the bark houses were empty, the cornfields deserted. His whole tribe, he was told, had been wiped out by a dreadful disease brought by one of the white men's ships. Squanto had then gone to live with the chief of a neighboring tribe.

The Dutch man-of-war which had brought the Negroes to Jamestown carried a letter back to England, from the Secretary of the colony, describing to a friend the condition of what he called "our Infant-Commonwealth," saying, "All our riches consist in Tobacco, wherein one man . . . by the means of six servants hath cleared at one crop 1000 pounds sterling." Then he corrects himself. "Our principal wealth (I should have said) consists in servants. But they must be furnished with arms, apparel and bedding, as well as their transportation and expenses."

These were known as "indentured" servants. Poor people in England who could not afford to pay their own way to America would sign an agreement to work for seven years for someone who would pay their passage. There were so many willing and eager to do this that for many years the number of Negro slaves brought to the English colonies in America increased very slowly.

"THEY KNEW THAT THEY WERE PILGRIMS"

ELDER WILLIAM BREWSTER, seated at his desk in his printing establishment in Leyden, unfolded the Map of New England, made by Captain John Smith, and scrutinized it carefully again. He nodded as he located the fortieth parallel. This was verily the place to go. In that northerly part of Virginia they would be free to worship in their own way. There they would be far enough from the colony at Jamestown, where the Church of England was firmly established.

William Bradford and the others in general agreed with him. All who had borrowed and read his copy of John Smith's *Description of New England* thought that the northern part of Virginia sounded like a veritable "promised land." They could make a living by fishing as well as by farming, though farming appealed to many more than fishing. To raise their own vegetables again, milk their own cows, live off land of their own once more, as they had at home in Lincolnshire! Never had they become quite accustomed to city living—to working in mills and warehouses as they had had to do in the cities of Holland.

Some had been tempted by Sir Walter Raleigh's glowing description of Guiana. There, however, they would be in danger, surrounded by Spaniards—and that above all things was something they must avoid. That was one main reason for leaving Holland. The years of peace with Spain which it had been their good fortune to enjoy would soon be coming to an end. Another two years and the twelve-year truce would be over. If war broke out, and the Spanish won, religious liberty would be stamped out again in Holland . . . New England was far away from Spaniards, so that was decided upon.

Two deacons, Robert Cushman and John Carver, were selected to interview members of the Virginia Company in London to see what arrangements could be made. They were well received, but returned with little to report, except that they should draw up a declaration of their religious beliefs to satisfy the Privy Council. The minister, John Robinson, worked with Elder Brewster on this, and when it was done, Mr. Brewster himself went with it to London. Their views on religion were mild enough to be satisfactory, but Elder Brewster suddenly found himself in danger of his life. This was due to a book which he had printed on his press in Leyden. It was one attacking James I for trying to force Scotland to accept the Church of England. A cry went up to bring the publisher to "justice." Brewster was advised by friends not to return to Holland but to hide in England under an assumed name.

By this time Robert Cushman had secured permission for his people to settle in the northern part of Virginia, but the Virginia Company had no money to send out settlers. This was bad news for the people in Leyden. How could they get to America without money?

The prosperous Dutch had an answer. If the Leyden people wanted to settle on Manhattan Island or along the Hudson River, the New Netherlands Company would furnish them free transportation. This was tempting. However, their children would still be speaking the Dutch language and forgetting their English, which was one of their reasons for leaving Holland. Also the Dutch were not strict enough in their way of living, and too luxury-loving. After attending church, they played games on the Sabbath, danced and enjoyed themselves in a worldly manner. The English children of the congregation were being drawn away by this unseemly example. Even so, the Dutch offer might have been accepted, had not a London merchant named Thomas Weston turned up just then in Leyden. He met with Pastor Robinson and William Bradford, who was beginning to assume responsibility.

"Don't meddle with the Dutch," said Weston airily. "Don't depend on the Virginia Company. I and some of my friends will set you forth. You shall not want money nor ships—have no fear. All that is necessary is to draw up articles of agreement, not for myself but for those whom I shall persuade to join in the venture."

The agreement was drawn up, Mr. Weston returned to England. The Leyden people sold their possessions and put their money in a common fund and made preparations to leave. Then came more details of the agreement. And what a shock! The terms were so altered from those agreed upon that William Bradford could scarcely believe his eyes, nor could Pastor Robinson, nor any of the others.

The settlers were to work continually seven days a week for the common good, instead of having two days for their own needs.

They were not to own the lands they improved or the houses they built, until at the end of those seven years, when all would be divided between merchants and settlers. . . . Seven years working off their passage! What did that make them but indentured servants! This was difficult for the people to swallow. Many of their ancestors, for generations, had owned their own land. Many chose not to go under those conditions. The number dwindled. Other volunteers had to be found by Weston and his company, to make up the number, and quickly, for they should be starting in early spring.

William Bradford and Dorothy May went to Amsterdam, to say goodbye to her parents, and leave their little son with them. William also had to see about buying a ship to be used for fishing, when they reached New England. One was found called the *Speedwell,* which could be fitted with a new and larger sail. Meanwhile, a larger ship had been hired in London for the ocean voyage—called by a then common name for ships, the *Mayflower.* They were to meet in Southampton.

"So being ready to departe, they had a day of fasting, their pastor taking as his text:

'And, . . . I proclaimed a fast, that we might humble ourselves before our God, and seeke of him a right way for us and for our children. . . .' "

This is William Bradford's description of their departure:

"And the time being come that they must departe, they were accompanied with most of their brethren out of the citie, unto a towne sundrie miles off called Delftshaven where the ship [Speed-well] lay ready to receive them. So they left that goodly and pleasant citie, which had been their resting place near twelve years; but they knew that they were pilgrimes [heb II] and looked not much on those things, but lifted up their eyes to the heavens . . . and quieted their spirits. When they came to the place they found the ship and all things ready; friends [from Leyden] and also from Amsterdam came to see them shipped and to take their leaves of them. That night was spent with little sleep by the most, but with friendly entertainment and discourse and other real expressions of true Christian love. The next day, the wind being faire, they went aboarde, and their friends with them, where truly doleful was the sight of that sad and mournfull parting, to see what sighs and sobbs and prayers did sound amongst them, what tears gush from every eye, and pithy speeches pierced each harte; that sundry of the Dutch strangers that stood on the key as spectators could not refraine from tears.

"But the tide (which stays for no man) calling them away, their reverend Pastor falling downe on his knees (and they all with him) commended them with most fervent prayers to the Lord and his blessing." Thus "hoisting saile, with a prosperous winde," the *Pilgrims* sailed away.

to God, my countrie, resting
Your's to vse
John Smith.

JOHN SMITH, UNHAPPY ADMIRAL

POOR JOHN SMITH, Admiral of New England without a ship to sail upon! His helmet, cloak, and sword were hanging on the wall. He was impatient to be up and off on some new expedition, eager to make use of the experience he had had, and no one would hire him. Quill in hand, he sat at a desk in London, writing of things he had done and waiting to hear about founding a colony in New England. That was the place he was thinking of now. New England was the new frontier, the ideal spot for a new colony to be supported by fishing. If only the Fishmongers Guild could make up their minds to finance the venture! Waiting to hear from them was sheer agony.

The Plymouth Company had deceived him. They had given him the title, Admiral of New England. They had promised him a position for life, working in the colonies, and now they had refused to employ him. Just because his last voyage had been ill-fated was no reason to think that his next one would be. Yet so it seemed to Ferdinando Gorges and the Plymouth Company.

The agents from Holland—he had seen and talked with them all, Mr. John Carver, Mr. Cushman and the others. He had offered them his services at a reasonable figure, tried to persuade them that he could take them directly to the best spot, save them a "wonderful deal of misery." They could not afford him, they said. They had his maps and books to go by, and that was much cheaper!

He had written a letter to Sir Francis Bacon, but with no result. It had hurt his pride to appeal for patronage, yet he hoped that under the protection of so prominent a man as "The Right Honorable Sir Francis Bacon, now a Baron and Lord High Chancellor of England," he would be able to get backers for a New England colony.

He had written of his experiences in a sixteen-page pamphlet which he called "New England Trials," and had had about three thousand copies printed. One thousand he had distributed among thirty of the chief Trade Guilds, hoping that they might form a joint stock company and hire him. He went in person to the Brown Bakers Hall, inviting the members to invest anything from sixpence to six hundred pounds. He went to the Fishmongers Hall on Thames Street near the Bridge and was now waiting to hear from them.

After his booklet had been exhibited by him at one of their meetings, the Fishmongers decided that it had "come upon them too suddenly" and someone had made the motion that "certain persons should be appointed to meet together and consider the business deliberately as was fitt and necessary."

"The trade of vending fish is very bad already and like to be worse and worse," was one of the discouraging opinions. A more hopeful man thought "it might be wonderful and gayneful, as set forth."

It might be, another allowed, but "if the other companies, the Bakers, Butchers, Cobblers and the like did nothing, then all that they could do would be to no purpose."

Meanwhile Captain Smith waited. And waited! He likened himself to a horse driven round in circles and getting nowhere. "Betwixt the spur of Desire and the bridle of Reason I am neare ridden to death in a ring of Despaire."

Poor John Smith. Admiral of New England! He would never see those rocky shores of New England again, but he refused to believe it.

Part IV

from 1620:

When the Pilgrims landed in New England & John Smith was writing History

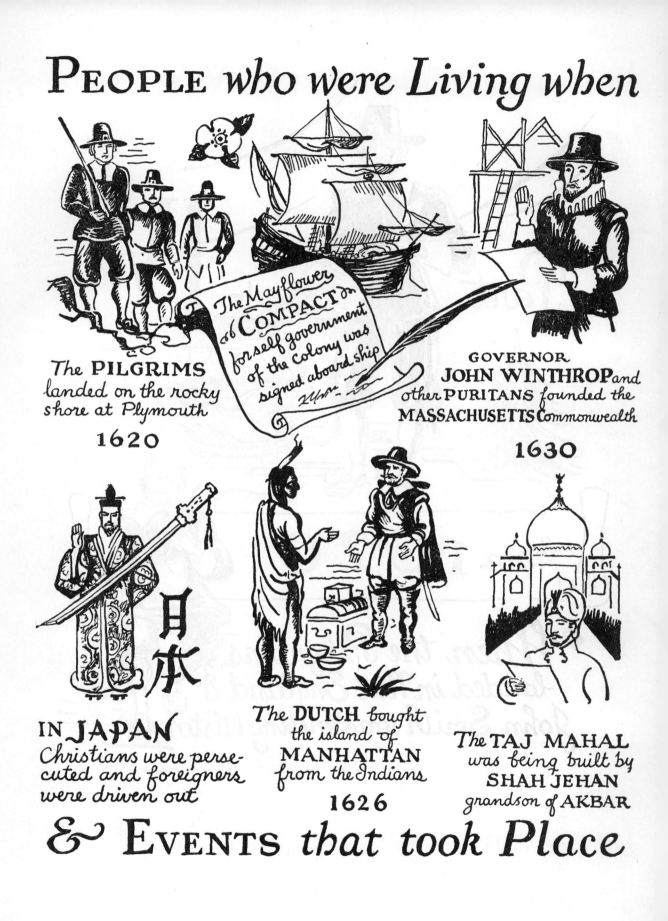

PEOPLE who were Living when

The Mayflower COMPACT on self government of the colony was signed aboard ship

The PILGRIMS landed on the rocky shore at Plymouth
1620

GOVERNOR JOHN WINTHROP and other PURITANS founded the MASSACHUSETTS Commonwealth
1630

IN JAPAN Christians were persecuted and foreigners were driven out

The DUTCH bought the island of MANHATTAN from the Indians
1626

The TAJ MAHAL was being built by SHAH JEHAN grandson of AKBAR

& EVENTS that took Place

JOHN SMITH was a WRITER

The French Princess Henrietta Maria became England's Queen.

CHARLES I became KING of ENGLAND 1625

IN FRANCE

Cardinal RICHELIEU came into power.

PETER PAUL RUBENS was the most productive and diplomatic painter of his day

GUSTAV ADOLPH KING OF SWEDEN died as a hero in battle

DE BELLI PACIS JURE ET

HUGO GROTIUS of HOLLAND wrote a first great book on INTERNATIONAL LAW

Trouble in PRAGUE touched off a WAR to last 30 years.

WILLIAM HARVEY English physician discovered the circulation of the blood.

between the YEARS 1620-1631

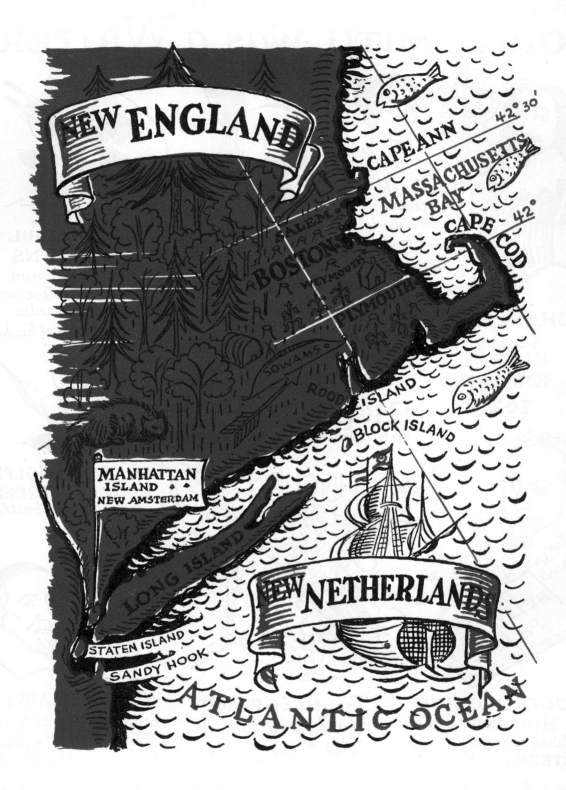

THE MAYFLOWER SAILS

THE SUMMER SUN sparkled on the water. Southampton harbor was full of ships as John Alden came bounding down upon the wharf, a bag of tools in one hand, a roll of baggage under his arm. He was twenty-one years old. He had signed up to go as a carpenter on the ship *Mayflower,* sailing that day for America. According to regulations there had to be a "cooper" on every ship to make new barrels for the voyage back. John Alden, however, had been given the right to stay there in the New World if he liked and take up land. To own land! That was something none of his forebears had ever done. It sounded wonderful. John had no family. He could do what he pleased. He knew he could always earn a living with his tools, and get

303

along with people—that was most folks. He did not know about these—the ones who had come over from Holland. Some said they were rebels, and would be clapped into prison if they set foot in England. They had come in the *Speedwell,* a small boat now anchored near the *Mayflower,* which had come from London.

The *Mayflower* had been in the harbor of Southampton a week before and a week after the *Speedwell* arrived.

The delay had been due, John Alden discovered, to a hullabaloo with Mr. Thomas Weston, who had put up the money for the voyage. The Pilgrims refused to sign an agreement to work for him seven days a week. And so Mr. Weston refused to pay the harbor fee that would allow them to clear the port. To pay this the settlers had to sell about sixty firkins of butter, which took almost all they had brought from Holland for the voyage. That done, the two ships finally sailed, the broad-beamed *Mayflower* followed by the little *Speedwell,* topheavy with sail.

John Alden already knew Captain Jones. Now he had time to look about and take stock of the passengers. There were whole families, men and women, children swarming all over, running up and down the hatches, choosing places on which to put down their sleeping pads. The only one who had a really good place to sleep was the captain, whose cabin was aft, just under the poop deck. There were twenty in the crew—mate, second mate, bosun, quarter-master, steersman, common sailors in bare feet and wound pigtails, and three hired soldiers. The cook baked bread in a circular oven, and doled out food in wooden bowls—mush of meal, peas with salt pork, lumps of dried beef and beer to wash it down.

The first days out most of the passengers were seasick. Soon the *Speedwell* was also ailing and had to be taken into the harbor of Dartmouth for repairs. So the *Mayflower* turned in also and waited. It was the eighteenth of August before they passed Land's End and were actually on the ocean again. Then came a distress signal from the *Speedwell.* The boat was leaking; it could not make the voyage. They turned around again and went back to Plymouth harbor. There the small ship was abandoned. The families aboard were crowded onto the *Mayflower* wherever there was an inch of space. And on September 16, 1620, the *Mayflower* sailed from Plymouth on her memorable voyage.

There were one hundred and two people on board all told, almost evenly divided between "those" from England and "those" from Holland, seventeen men, ten women, thirteen or fourteen children in each group; among them, twenty-four were indentured servants. The people

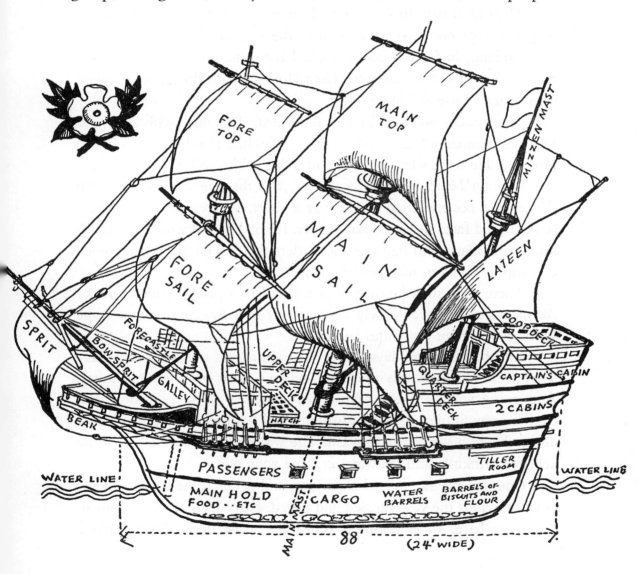

from Holland all knew one another, but John Alden noticed that the families from England were not acquainted with anyone else. Some did not appear sociable—Mr. Mullins, for example. He also kept a sharp watch over his pretty daughter Priscilla, who was not exactly pretty, but sweet-looking and fetching. John Alden noticed her right away. And also young Mrs. Bradford, from Holland, who looked half-sick and unhappy all of the time. William Bradford, her husband, a tall, serious-looking man, seemed to be one of the leaders.

The oldest man in the Holland group was Mr. William Brewster, who had kept out of sight, hidden in the hold of the ship, until they left England, in fear of being arrested for some book he had printed in Holland. His wife had come from Holland with their two youngest sons, named Love and Wrestling.

There were no "gentlemen" on board. The man with the most gracious manner was Edward Winslow, who had also been a printer in Holland. He wore silver buttons and a fine white collar.

Captain Miles Standish, a soldier, was the one with whom John Alden first became friends. He was a short, stocky man with bright red hair, red face, and a red-hot temper. He had served with the English army in Holland and had met the settlers there, though he had joined the ship in London, with his wife Rose.

There they all were, one hundred and two people packed in the *Mayflower* as it plowed slowly westward for sixty-five days, at an average speed of less than two miles an hour.

And for sixty-five days Dorothy Bradford did not see a ship pass. They were alone, in this tiny boat, on this great gray endless water. And going where? Every day the ship smelled worse as people and clothes grew filthier. Priscilla Mullins could hardly bear it down below decks. There was no way to wash. The water in the barrels had to be kept for drinking, and sea-water cracked your skin.

One day the sky turned slate gray and a hurricane struck. In the howling winds the vessel tossed and rolled, every inch of canvas down, the masts bare, water washing across the waist deck. Then came a thundering crack. The great beam had burst! The one that supported the mainmast. Oh, dear God, they prayed, thinking until the storm subsided that the end had come. Fortunately, the people from Holland had brought a great iron screw, and the cracked beam was temporarily fastened together.

In the storm a man had been washed overboard and barely rescued with a boat hook. One day Mrs. Hopkins gave birth to a son on that endless ocean and named him Oceanus. One day Dr. Sam Fuller's servant boy died and was buried at sea. Dorothy Bradford stood too long looking down at the sea, after it had closed over him. She had left her own boy in Holland. . . .

William Bradford, filled with an intense energy, looked forward with eagerness and courage to the first sight of land and the new life that lay ahead. It was a joyful moment when, as he said, "after long beating at sea, they fell in with that land which is called Cape Cod." The long voyage was over! The settlers crowded up the hatchways, scrambled onto the main deck for a first look at the marvelous new world. And what did they see? A curve of sand; a harbor; low sandy hills covered with dry sea grass and knotted trees.

"Let us thank God that we are safely here!" said Elder Brewster, turning his face upward to the One who had led them across the great waters, and whose mercy and goodness he firmly believed would follow them all the days of their lives.

That day was Saturday, November 11.

One more thing had to be done before anyone could leave the ship to go ashore. In his farewell letter Pastor Robinson had told the congregation in Leyden that in the New World they must form themselves into a "body politik." This became even more apparent during the voyage, since among the passengers there were some who bragged about how they were going to do as they pleased, live without laws when they got to the new world. This would be anarchy. Therefore a "compact" for self-government must be drawn up and signed. This they proceeded to do, gathering about a table in the great cabin. There someone, probably Elder Brewster, took a sizable sheet of paper and wrote upon it words which had been deliberated upon. They were read aloud for those who could not read.

Then the men came forward and signed their names—not merely members of the Leyden congregation but also those who had come directly from England, servants and hired men, all who were to form part of the new community. Mr. John Carver, who was elected Governor for the year, signed first. The youngest to sign his name was the twenty-one-year-old carpenter, John Alden.

The Mayflower Compact stands as "the first example in modern times of a government instituted by voluntary agreement, by men of equal rights in a new country."

The original paper was lost but the exact words with their quaint old spelling are in William Bradford's history *Of Plimouth Plantation.*

In the name of God, Amen. We whose names are under-writen, the loyall subjects of our dread soveraigne Lord King James, by the grace of God, of Great Britaine, France, and Ireland King, defender of the faith, etc., haveing undertaken, for the glorie of God, and advancemente of the Christian faith, and honour of our king and countrie, a voyage to plant the first colonie in the Northerne parts of Virginia, doe by these presents solemnly and mutaly in the presence of God and one of another, covenant and combine our selves togeather into a civill body politick, for our better ordering and preservation and furtherance of the ends aforesaid; and by vertue hereof to enacte, constitute, and frame such just and equall lawes, ordinances, acts, constitutions, and offices, from time to time, as shall be thought most meete and convenient for the generall good of the Colonie, unto which we promise all due submission and obedience. In witness wherof we have hereunder subscribed our names at Cap-Codd the 11. of November, in the year of the raigne of our soverainge lord, King James, of England, France, and Ireland the eighteenth, and of Scotland the fiftie fourth. Anº: Dom. 1620

308

And so that was the birthday in America of government of, by and for the people. The seed had been planted in the New World.

THE MAYFLOWER COMPACT had been signed on Saturday. The next day was the Sabbath, a day of rest and prayer. Eager as they were to set foot on land, no one could leave the ship.

Monday the women were taken ashore to wash their clothes, under guard. And sixteen armed men led by Captain Miles Standish went on an exploring trip, on the alert for Indians, but they saw none. On a hill they found Indian graves and nearby the remains of a house, a kettle, and, in a heap of sand, Indian baskets filled with seed corn, which they dug up and carried back to the ship.

Plymouth Harbor was across the bay. They came into it by chance. On another exploring trip they had coasted around the shore from the low sandy hook of Cape Cod, where the *Mayflower* was anchored, to this place where the shore was rocky. They were driven into the harbor in a fierce winter storm, half-frozen and wet to the skin in their open shallop. As it was growing dark, they waded to land in the icy water, built a fire, and spent the night on what in the morning they discovered was an island. It was Saturday night, December 19. Sunday must be spent in rest and prayer. So it was on Monday, December 21, 1620, that the Pilgrims landed at Plymouth, as recorded in William Bradford's notebook.

"On Monday," he said, "they sounded the harbor and found it fit for shipping and marched into the land and found cornfields and little running brooks, a place fit for habitation, at least the best that they could find . . . So they returned to their ship again with this news to the rest of their people."

William Bradford looked for Dorothy "to comforte her hart" with the good news that she would soon have a tidy home here in this new land, but Dorothy was not there. She was somewhere at the bottom of the sea. How or when she had fallen from the ship, no one could say.

From Captain John Smith's description, Elder Brewster, Captain Jones, all who had studied the explorer's Map of New England, recognized this as the harbor he called Plymouth.

The weather was foul, but the first day possible, the men rowed ashore to begin building their village. Some started to cut down trees, some to saw the trees into planks, some to carry pails of clay, some to burn shells for lime.

This was Christmas Day. No man rested. The Pilgrims did not celebrate Christmas, since it was not mentioned in the Bible.

The houses the Pilgrims built were not log cabins. They were made of upright planks and branches stuck together with plaster, which they called "wattle-and-daub." The Common House, about twenty feet square, was the first one they marked out. It was on the north side of the brook, just above the beach, at the foot of what was to be the main street running up the hill. On the top of the hill, they planned to make a platform and mount a cannon. From there, Miles Standish pointed out, they could command all the countryside for miles around. Nineteen cabins were planned, but many days it rained, snowed, and froze so that they could not work.

Seven cabins, only, were completed when the Common House became a hospital, filled with sick and dying, stricken with scurvy, tuberculosis, and pneumonia. In two or three months half of the company were dead. All of the Mullins family died except Priscilla. Six other settlers died in December, eight in January, including Rose, the wife of Miles Standish. Seventeen more in February, and thirteen in March, among them the wife of Edward Winslow. Of the one hundred persons barely fifty remained alive. And of these there were often not more than six or seven well enough to care for the others. Two of these were Elder William Brewster and Captain Miles Standish.

"They spared no pains, night or day," said William Bradford, being among those who were at the point of death, "but with hazard of their own health, fetched them woode, made them fires, drest them meat, made their beds, washed their loathsome clothes, clothed and unclothed them, in a word, did all the homely necessarie offices for them which dainty and queasy stomachs cannot endure to hear named; and all this willingly and cheerfully, without grudging in the least, shewing herein their true love unto their friends and brethren."

On April 5, the little group of fifty people standing on the shore at Plymouth saw the last tip of the *Mayflower's* topsail disappear over the edge of the horizon. While the *Mayflower* was still anchored in Plymouth harbor, a baby boy was born on board ship; the first English child born in New England. He was named Peregrine White. His father soon died, and the young widow Susanna White became not only the first mother in Plymouth but the first bride. The bridegroom was the young widower Edward Winslow. The wedding was a civil ceremony. The congregation stuck firmly to their principles that matters of church and state should be separate. William Bradford tells of it:

"May 2, 1621 was the first marriage in this place, which according

311

to the laudable custom of the Low Countries . . . was performed by the magistrate as being a civill thing upon which many questions about inheritances do depend. That too," he said, "was in accordance with the Bible Scriptures. Nowhere in the gospell did it say that marriage was to be performed by ministers as part of their office."

INDIANS AND THANKSGIVING

ON A WET, WINDY MORNING in March, an Indian with a bow and arrow stalked into Plymouth village—one lone Indian stark naked except for a piece of fringed leather tied about his waist. Edward Winslow and others, at work on some of the unfinished houses, looked up in alarm and went to meet the savage, not knowing what to expect.

"Welcome!" said the Indian to their surprise and relief, and spoke to them in broken English. His name was Samoset, he told them. Edward Winslow smiled, and as the wind was chill, he or someone else found a coat to put about the Indian's naked shoulders. Samoset had learned to speak in white man's words from fishermen who came to his own shore, which was that way, he said, pointing north toward Maine.

"This land," he spread his arms wide, "is Patuxet tribe land." Many Indians had once lived here. Now all Patuxets were dead. All but one, his friend Squanto, who was not here when death came. Squanto could speak more better English than he, Samoset. Someday he would bring Squanto. He left, after having been well fed on biscuit, butter, cheese pudding and a piece of duck, which he liked very well.

At last the mystery was explained. The Pilgrims had long wondered about the Indians who had cleared these cornfields. Not an Indian had they seen since one morning on an exploring trip, soon after they had found and taken the baskets of seed corn. They had been awakened by whoops and yells, after which arrows had come whizzing from behind the trees; but a few musket shots fired by Miles Standish had scared the savages away. Two men working in the woods, who had left their tools for an hour or so, found them gone when they got back. Another day two Indians, standing on top of the hill across the brook, fled when they saw Miles Standish walking toward them. Those were all the Pilgrims had seen until Samoset came. Before long he was back with his friend Squanto. Samoset went back to Maine, but Squanto made himself at home in Plymouth.

Massasoit, the Big Chief, had also come, said Squanto. Massasoit, Chief of the Wampanoags, his brother, and sixty braves were just beyond the hill. He wished someone sent to talk to him. Edward Winslow was naturally chosen as their first ambassador, with Squanto acting as interpreter. Winslow set forth across the brook, carrying a pair of knives and other gifts for Chief Massasoit and a message that their King saluted him with love and their Governor wished to talk peace with him.

After some time, the others watching in the village saw Massasoit, followed by twenty councillors, all very tall but carrying no bows and arrows, walking down the hill toward the brook. Some of them were naked, some wore skins. All had fiercely painted faces. Massasoit's was a "sad red," and he wore about his neck a chain of white bone.

Captain Standish with half a dozen musketeers went to meet the Indians at the brook, while others spread a green rug and placed several cushions in one of the half-built houses. As Massasoit and the Indians approached, Governor Carver approached them, followed by drum and trumpet. The Governor kissed the Chief's hands, the Chief

313

kissed the Governor's and they all sat down on the cushions. The Chief then gravely reached for a small bag hanging from the back of his white bone necklace, took tobacco from it, filled a pipe, drew upon it, passed it to the Governor, who did the same, passing the Peace Pipe on around the circle. He then served his guest strong water and fresh meat, which the Chief shared with his followers.

Then, with Squanto as interpreter, they talked of peace. They made a simple, straightforward promise to keep peace with each other and to help each other in case of unjust attacks. It was made in good faith and kept faithfully for over fifty years.

In July, with Squanto acting as guide, Edward Winslow and one of the other settlers went to pay a visit to their new friend and ally Massasoit, to see how and where the Chief of the Wampanoags lived and how many braves he had. By this time they had learned that the seed corn which they had taken and planted belonged to the Pamet Indians, and that they were the ones who had yelled and howled and shot arrows—trying to scare the white men away. Edward Winslow was to ask Massasoit to tell the Pamets that the regretful Pilgrims wished to pay them in full for the corn.

The forty-mile journey to the Indian village was tiring, after which there were two awful nights spent as guests of Massasoit.

"He laid us," said Edward Winslow, "on the bed with him and his wife, they at one end and we at the other, it being only planks laid a foot from the ground and a thin mat upon them. Two more of his chief men, for want of room, pressed by and upon us. Massasoit would have had us stay with him longer, but we feared we should be light-headed for what with the savages singing themselves to sleep, lice and fleas within doors, and muskeetoes without, we could hardly sleep. So on Friday morning before sun-rising we took our leave and departed, Massasoit being both grieved and ashamed that he could no better entertain us."

The Chief now appointed another member of his Council to be a go-between. Hobomok was his name. He also came to live at Plymouth, like Squanto, who seemed to be as William Bradford said, "a special instrument sent of God for their good."

In the spring, aside from being their guide and interpreter, Squanto taught them how to plant the corn. By July it was standing high and green in the fields. He taught them to catch fish and put them in with the seed corn for fertilizer. Otherwise, in "these old grounds," he said, "it would come to nothing." In every corn hill they put three fish, heads together, tails out, and stood guard over the fields at night to keep the wolves from digging them up.

One warm day in April, Governor John Carver came in very dizzy from the field where he had been planting corn, and died a few days later. William Bradford was then elected Governor. He was thirty-one. Edward Winslow was twenty-six. All the active heads of the colony were young men. As the fall came, and they looked at the twenty acres of Indian corn ready to be shocked and husked, they were pleased they had fared so well and felt that God was to be praised, in a feast of Thanksgiving.

"Our harvest being gotten in," said Edward Winslow, in a letter to a friend in England, "our Governor sent four men out fowling that we might in a more special manner rejoice together after we had gathered the fruit of our labors. These four, in one day, killed as much fowl as served the company almost a week, at which time many of the Indians coming amongst us. And amongst the rest their greatest King, Massasoit, with some ninety men whom, for three days, we entertained and feasted. They went out and killed five deer which they brought to the Plantation and bestowed on our Governor and upon the Captain and others. And although it be not always so plentiful as it was at this time with us, yet by the goodness of God we are far from want. . . ."

That is the original story of the first Thanksgiving celebrated by the Pilgrims. They repeated it the following year and it became a tradition in New England, though it was not until 1864 that a National Day of Thanksgiving was first proclaimed by Abraham Lincoln.

TROUBLE IN BOHEMIA

THE YEAR after the Pilgrims left Holland, two young royal refugees, known as the "Queen of Hearts" and the "Winter King," fled to the Netherlands. Elizabeth, princess of England, and her husband, Frederick V, had been driven out of Germany by the newly elected emperor of the German states, Ferdinand II.

316

It had happened. What the Pilgrims had feared would happen when they left, what Henry IV had feared before he died, what everyone in Europe had feared but hoped could somehow be avoided, had come to pass. War had broken out. Another religious war, and this time to be fought in the German states that made up the Empire, was to continue for the next thirty years.

It started just before the coronation of the new Emperor, Ferdinand II, who was of the German Branch of the Hapsburg family, a cousin of Philip IV of the Spanish Hapsburgs. In this ceremonious portrait, Ferdinand is seen wearing that ancient crown of Charlemagne, the first German to be crowned "Holy Roman Emperor."

For one hundred years, trouble had been brewing in the German states, ever since Martin Luther had first defied the Pope's authority. That actual war had not broken out sooner was due to a treaty known as the Peace of Augsburg, made in 1555, the last year that Charles V was emperor. Then it had been agreed that the Lutheran princes should have equal rights with the Catholic princes, which should be upheld by the emperor. This had been observed by all the four emperors from Charles V to Ferdinand II. Now came a change.

The driving ambition of Ferdinand II, was to re-establish the unity and strength of the Empire. This, as he saw it, meant first of all to stamp out the Protestant religion, which caused the division, and re-establish the single authority of the Roman Catholic Church. In this he was assured of help from his Hapsburg cousin in Spain, who would resume war in the Netherlands just as soon as the twelve-year truce signed with the Stadtholder Maurice, Prince of Orange, had run its course.

In 1618, the year before he became Emperor, Ferdinand II had been elected King of Bohemia. Dishonestly, it was said. That was the fighting word, the spark that set off the explosion. Bohemia whose capital city was Prague, was largely Protestant. The Protestant nobles of Bohemia declared that Ferdinand, being a Catholic, could never have been elected honestly. This led to such a heated argument that one May

317

day in the palace in Prague, Count Thurn and his rebellious followers seized two of the councillors of Ferdinand, dragged them to an open window, and pitched them out headlong into the dry moat, seventy feet below. This outrageous event that started the Thirty Years' War was to be known in history as the "Out-of-the-window-throwing," or "Defenestration," of Prague. After this highly forceful expression, the Bohemian rebels proceeded to choose another king.

Frederick V, Count Palatine, seemed a most logical choice. His own father had formed a Union of German princes to protect Protestants. His grandfather on his mother's side was William of Orange, hero of the Netherlands. His father-in-law was James I, king of Protestant England, who had arranged the marriage of his daughter Elizabeth to strengthen the Protestant cause. They offered Frederick the crown. Foolishly hopeful young Frederick, flattered by the chance to be King of Bohemia, accepted, although he was strongly advised not to do it. He did not or would not face the facts. All spelled ruin after his coronation, when he led the rebel armies against their former king, now the Emperor Ferdinand II.

The Bohemians were not united in any such heroic spirit of self-sacrifice as was needed for the cause. His father's Protestant Union would not support Frederick in Bohemia, because Bohemia was not a German state.

The Lutheran princes would not support Frederick, because he was a Calvinist, which made him almost as repugnant to them as a Catholic. James I had no money to spend on rescuing this son-in-law who had not taken his advice. So what was bound to happen, happened.

On November 8, 1620, exactly one year and one day after young Frederick's coronation, came his crushing defeat by the troops of the Emperor in the battle of White Mountain, and the abrupt end of his reign. The King for a winter, or Winter King, as he was scornfully called, was driven out of Bohemia and also out of his old home, the Palatinate, where Spanish troops were rushing in over the border from the Spanish Netherlands. Frederick's rights as elector were taken from

318

him, and he was outlawed for treason. He was homeless. Travelling from Prague through Berlin, first Elizabeth and then Frederick reached The Hague, thus adding a king and queen to those refugees of all classes, creeds, and conditions who had found a haven in Holland.

Coming in 1620, the royal refugees could not have reached the Netherlands at a more uneasy time. Another year and the twelve-year truce that Maurice, the Stadtholder, had signed with Spain would be over, and Spanish troops would soon be marching toward the border of Holland.

OF KINGS AND BRIDES

ONE MIDSUMMER DAY in 1618, Lady Ebba Brahe was married to a Swedish count, who had been granted a title of nobility by Gustav Adolf, the only title he ever granted. It was a day of triumph for Queen Kristina. She and Karl Filip were the principal guests at the wedding. The young King Gustav was not there. Needing to do something rash on Ebba's wedding day, Gustav went to sea to try out a new warship. He had the idea of sailing across to Rugen and riding in disguise to Berlin to see Maria Eleanora of Brandenburg, with whom his mother hoped to arrange a marriage. He knew himself that it would be good from a political standpoint and would strengthen his position against Denmark. He knew that Frederick V, Count Palatine, was in Berlin pleading his cause against the other suitors, Wladislaus of Poland and Prince Charles of England. However, when the ship anchored at Rugen, he had word from Berlin that the Elector of Brandenburg, whom he needed to see, was not there. So he postponed the visit and returned to Sweden.

The next April he set forth again for Berlin, but did not accomplish very much, for although he saw the Princess Maria Eleanora, who did not disguise her interest in him, her brother the Elector was again away, and her mother did not favor him. So in case the marriage fell through,

Gustav thought he might as well see some other possible choices. On his way to Heidelberg, he was overtaken by a messenger with good news that sent him riding back to Berlin. The day after he arrived he plighted his troth with Maria Eleanora, went home to arrange for her coming to Sweden, and then sent Axel Oxenstierna to bring the bride.

The wedding took place in Stockholm on November 25, 1620. Three days later Maria Eleanora was crowned queen. As part of the celebration a "merry comedy" was performed; one about Olaf, the first Christian king of Sweden, who ruled in 995. It was about one hundred years later, Gustav may have told her, that Rurik, a mighty Viking warrior, had crossed over the Baltic Sea, invaded and conquered all of Russia, and became the first Tsar.

Marriage plans for the new Tsar of Russia, Michael Romanov, were also being considered by his father the Patriarch Philaret in the summer of 1618. Before his father's arrival Michael had been betrothed to a Russian girl, Maria Khlopova, when suddenly she was stricken with a strange malady, pronounced incurable, and with her whole family banished to Siberia. Hopeful of raising the standing of Russia by a foreign alliance, the Patriarch had sent an ambassador to Denmark to ask for the daughter of Christian IV, who fairly snorted and would not even deign to talk about it. Next he sent to Berlin to ask for Katharina, the younger sister of Maria Eleanora, but the very idea of the baptism of a lovely Lutheran princess into the Greek Orthodox Church was simply out of the question. By that time, in Siberia, a hoax had come to light. Maria Khlopova had recovered. A rival family, jealous of the girl's good fortune, had given her poisoned vodka, which had badly injured her digestion. Now that she was cured, she was allowed to return and given a handsome allowance; but to please his mother Michael married another girl named Maria, who lived only a year. Then he finally took as his wife in 1626 the daughter of a small landowner and a commoner, Eudoxia Stryeshnevaya, and she became the matriarch of the imperial Romanov family, which ended in 1918 with the last Tsar of Russia, Nicholas II.

MASSACRES: INDIAN AND WHITE

THE SHOCKING and horrible news that reached London in the spring of 1622 turned John Smith's thoughts back to his first love, Jamestown, Virginia. On March 22, a bloody, frightful Indian massacre had occurred. Three hundred and fifty people in Jamestown and the surrounding settlements had been murdered by the Indians in the space of one hour. Men, women, and children—whole families had been wiped out. It would have been even worse had it not been for Chanco, an Indian boy who had warned the English family with whom he lived. Otherwise the whole weakly defended plantation might have been destroyed, so carefully had the wholesale murder been worked out by Opekankano.

At the name of this treacherous old enemy, John Smith jumped to his feet, rushed to the office of the London Company of Virginia, and offered his services. Let him have one hundred and thirty soldiers, he begged. With even so few as that, he promised to "torment the savages, instruct the settlers in the use of arms, feed as well as defend the colonists and yet discover more unknown land."

The Company turned him down. The expense was too great. The London Company had no money. John Smith walked away, disappointed again—tortured by the thought that, when he saw so clearly what could and should be done, he was unable to go either to Virginia or New England. To John Smith, these colonies took the place of many things that he had never had in life.

"I call them my children," he said, "for they have been my wife, my hawks, my hounds, my cards, my dice and in total my best source of contentment, as close to my heart as my left hand to my right."

The Indian massacre of the whites at Jamestown was followed in 1623 by a white man's massacre of Indians in New England. Though it was a miniature affair compared to the one at Jamestown, and prevented a similar tragedy at Plymouth, the news grieved good Pastor John Robinson when it reached him in Leyden. He wrote to his congregation; "You will say they deserved it. I grant it. But upon what provocations by those *heathenish Christians!*" The "heathenish Christians" the pastor meant were fifty or sixty most objectionable people who had come over in one of Thomas Weston's ships, to form another colony. They had taken everything they could get from the Plymouth settlers, who had made room for them until they founded a place of their own at Weymouth. There they began to abuse and insult and steal from the Massachusetts Indians, until the savages finally plotted to destroy them. Since the Indians naturally thought the Plymouth Colony and the Weymouth Colony were partners, they plotted to make a clean sweep of it and destroy Plymouth also. The plot originated with a Massachusetts Chief called Wituwamat, they were told by their good friend Massasoit.

The first inkling of trouble came one February day in 1622 when an Indian brave strode boldly into the Common House and flung down a bundle of arrows, tied with a snake skin. Squanto and Hobomok both said that the bundle of arrows was a challenge to war. Governor Bradford called a council. All agreed that, weak as they were, they must not try to buy off the Indians with gifts. So they bravely stuffed the snake skin with bullets and returned it, saying:

"If you would rather have war than peace, begin when you will. We have done you no wrong. Neither do we fear you."

That ended the matter. However, the Pilgrims took the warning. They began at once to build a palisade of logs eleven feet high and almost a mile long up the brook around Fort Hill, down the edge of the clearing, completely surrounding the village. And a cannon was mounted on the top of the hill. They felt it had been worth all the back-breaking work when that spring they got news of the massacre at Jamestown.

The miserable group of settlers had been at Weymouth a year, tormenting the Indians, when, shortly after the harvest, they appealed to the Pilgrims to help them trade for corn with the Indians. Governor Bradford went himself, in the shallop, with Squanto as guide and interpreter. They planned to go southward down the coast, but because of the breakers they had to put in to shore at the elbow of Cape Cod. There Squanto "fell sick of an Indean feavor," said Bradford, "and within a few days died, desiring that he, the Governor pray for him, that he might go to the Englishman's God in Heaven, and bequeathed sundry of his things to his English friends as remembrances of his love."

Bradford then turned about and went north to buy corn from the Indians, who complained bitterly about the Weymouth people.

Meanwhile, back at Plymouth word was received that Chief Massasoit, their old friend, was ill and about to die. Edward Winslow and Hobomok set out at once for his house, which they found filled with medicine men making such a "hellish noise" as would have sickened a well man. The old Chief recovered, after taking the medicine Winslow administered, and was filled with gratitude. "Now I see the English are my friends and love me," he said. "And whilst I live, I will never forget this kindness they have showed me."

Massasoit revealed the plot of the Massachusetts Indians against the Weymouth Colony and Plymouth, and sent as his advice to his English friends that they should kill the men of the Massachusetts tribe who had originated the plot.

The Plymouth Colony had about decided to take some kind of action. Governor Bradford called another town meeting. The conclusion was that they must follow the advice of Massasoit, who surely should understand how to deal with his own people.

"We knew no other means," they said, "to deliver our countrymen and preserve ourselves. Though it grieved us to shed the blood of those whose good we ever intended and aimed at as a principle in all our proceedings."

Captain Miles Standish and eight armed men left for Weymouth, to warn the settlers of their danger, and then because it was impossible to deal openly with the treacherous Indians, he was to pretend that he had come to trade. Captain Miles Standish carried off things as smoothly as possible when the Indians came to trade, but something made them suspect that their plot had been discovered. They began then to insult him, sharpening their knives in his face, towering above him, taunting him as being a squat little man.

One day Wituwamat, the Massachusetts Chieftain, and three other braves were together in one room; having about as many of his own men, Miles Standish gave the word to attack. "Then," said Winslow, telling of it later, "the door being fast shut he began himself with one of them and snatching the Indian's own knife from his neck, though with much struggling, killed him therewith. Wituwamat and the other man the rest killed and took the youth to be hanged. But it is incredible how many wounds these two received before they died, not making any fearful noise but catching at their weapons and striving to the last." Then, taking a small posse of men, Standish chased the rest of the Indians into the swamp and thickets.

"For his own part he would not fear to remain there," he told the Weymouth people, "but they were otherwise minded and resolved to leave. And seeing them set sail and clear of the Massachusetts Bay

324

he returned to Plymouth, blessed be God, and brought the head of Wituwamat with him, the head being brought to the Fort and set up."

To set up such a head and leave it where everyone could see it was a customary practice. Both the approaches to London Bridge were lined with such gruesome objects, as a lesson to wrongdoers.

The drastic action brought an end to trouble and fears at Plymouth. Not one of the original Pilgrim Company was killed by an Indian. Except for those first deserted cornfields which belonged to no one, they bought every acre of land, and this was done not "by threats and blows or shaking of sword and sound of trumpets," said Deacon Robert Cushman, "but by friendly usage, love, peace, honest and just actions, and good counsel."

HUGO GROTIUS

THE ROYAL REFUGEES, Frederick and Elizabeth, had been in Holland a year and Spanish troops had begun marching toward the border of his native land, when Hugo Grotius fled as a

325

refugee to France. In 1619, the young lawyer, then thirty-six, had been sentenced to life imprisonment in the fortress-castle of Lowenstein, near Corcum. As soon as possible his heart-broken young wife got permission to be with him, with the understanding that if she ever come out again, she could not return.

Hugo Grotius had studied at Leyden University, completed his studies at fifteen, and brilliantly fulfilled his early promise as a lawyer. Now, sentenced to life imprisonment, his active mind did not allow him to sit down in despair. There was something to be done that he enjoyed—translating the classics from Greek into Latin. Books that he had finished were sent out in a chest, along with linen to be washed in the village, and new books brought in. After a while the guards grew careless and let the chest pass without inspecting it. Madame Grotius noticed this, and one day persuaded her husband to get in himself under the soiled clothes.

"Hold on," said one of the soldiers who soon came to carry the chest out. "What makes this so heavy?"

"Must be an Arminian in it," said the other.

"Arminian *books,*" replied Madame Grotius, more calmly than she felt, for Hugo Grotius was an Arminian. That is why he had been brought to trial and condemned. That is why at the same time the famous old statesman of Holland, Johan van Barneveldt, had lost his head on the scaffold—because he too was an Arminian, one whose religious views differed from those of the old Protestant or Dutch Reform church of Holland.

Maurice, the Stadtholder, had acted quickly without order of the States-General—too quickly, many said—acted like a despot and a tyrant in having Barneveldt and the other Arminian leaders arrested. But Maurice saw it, the Union of the Netherlands was threatened by the Arminians. It was not because of their religious views but because of their political views. They believed in "state's rights." Barneveldt held that the states of the Netherlands were joined together loosely into a confederation, and could secede if they saw fit. Maurice declared that the people of the Netherlands formed one nation indivisible, and that the Union must be preserved. In this he was supported by the Dutch Reformed Church, which stood for one nation and one religion.

Maurice was a remarkable soldier, probably the best in Europe. Johan van Barneveldt was a lawyer and the best statesman in Holland. He had been practically ruler of the Republic, especially during the war years with Spain, when Maurice led the armies. Then the question of the union had not come up. Fear of Spain was enough to unite the people firmly. But after the truce was signed in 1609, when fear no longer held them together, the argument arose, as it did in the United States after 1776, when fear of England was over. It is an argument that cannot help but arise in a Republic. How much authority does the central government have? What rights have the states? Some said Maurice wanted to crush the rights of the states, to make himself king. Others said Barneveldt was being bribed by Spain to divide and thus destroy the Republic.

In religion, the ministers of the Dutch Reform Church, whose members included most of the common people of Holland, held to the strict, intolerant teachings of Calvin. The Arminians followed the liberal teaching of a professor at Leyden University, named Arminius. They were the most educated people of the Netherlands. They held that it was better, when people agreed on "fundamental" principles, to allow for differences in smaller matters of creed, so that all men of good will could live together peaceably.

In 1619, Maurice summoned all Protestant ministers, Arminian and Dutch Reform to a National Assembly, presumably for a religious conference. Actually it was to provide an opportunity for him to destroy the power of the Arminians, whose political views he thought endangered the Union. As they assembled, Maurice acted quickly. Without order of the States-General, he had Barneveldt, Hugo Grotius and other liberal Arminian leaders arrested. He had two hundred Arminian ministers turned away from the meeting. Eighty of them, who rebelled at leaving were transported out of the country.

327

Four days later, at The Hague, seventy-year-old Johan van Barne-veldt was beheaded, and Hugo Grotius began his life sentence. This was the one and only time religion would ever enter politics in Holland. The drastic action preserved the Union of the Dutch Republic. Though most of the Arminians were soon back living peaceably in the Netherlands, Hugo Grotius never returned.

After his escape from the fortress in the laundry chest, Grotius crossed the border disguised as a bricklayer, and made his way to Antwerp. From there he went to Paris, where he was joined by Madame Grotius. Louis XIII granted him a pension, though most of it was never paid, and a nobleman loaned him a chateau in which to live. There he began to work on his famous book of international law.

"I have long had many and grave reasons why I should write a book on this subject," he said, "for I saw throughout the Christian world, men making war for slight reason or no reason at all, and that all respect for *divine* law and *natural* law was lost, just as if men might commit all crimes without restraint."

He divided law into three kinds:

(1) *Divine* law, as revealed directly by God, in the Holy Scriptures
(2) *Natural* law, sense of right and wrong in man's own conscience
(3) *Civil* law, laid down by rulers of a state.

There had been no special need for a book on laws governing nations when all Europe had been one united Christendom. Disputes between various princes and kings had then been settled by the Pope as he interpreted the divine law, or by the Emperor who settled matters by civil law. But when states existed that were subject neither to the Emperor nor the Pope, how then should the disputes be settled between them? What law should prevail? "There must be some code of International Law, based upon the natural law," said Hugo Grotius.

That such natural law existed had been pointed out by great and ancient teachers the world over. The Hebrew psalmist of ancient Israel saw it as the divine law. "I delight to do thy will, O my God. Thy law is written in my heart." Lao-tze, an ancient teacher of China, also called this natural law the Way of Heaven (or Tao). "A man who understands Tao," he said, "thinks of all people as himself. If princes and kings would keep to it all things of themselves would be right."

In other words, if everyone followed the law of God, written in his heart, no other law would be necessary. Unfortunately this is not the case. Many men do not follow what they know is right. They kill and steal and commit all kinds of crimes, so there have to be civil laws to control them. Kings and princes do the same. They seize territory from one another and cause wars to break out. So there have to be international laws to control them. *Concerning laws of War and Peace* was the title of this first of all books on International Law, written by Hugo Grotius.

Several years later Hugo Grotius wrote another small, equally necessary book, called *The Truth of the Christian Religion*. In this he wrote the main beliefs of Christianity, accepted by all Christians, Catholics and Protestants alike. It was widely popular, and was translated into languages for use by missionaries. To be sure, Grotius was attacked by narrow-minded men on both sides, but his greatness was also recognized and appreciated.

After a visit to London, where he was received with great honor at court and the universities, one scholar expressed the "feeling of all who had met him."

"I cannot say how happy I esteem myself in having seen so much of one so truly great as Grotius. A wonderful man!"

Hugo Grotius

A PAINTER GOES TO PARIS

PETER PAUL RUBENS, the most popular painter of his day, made this handsome self-portrait. Shortly after Hugo Grotius had fled to Paris by way of Antwerp, Rubens was also on his way from Antwerp to Paris, but not as a refugee. He had been summoned by the King's mother, Queen Marie, to make wall-sized paintings for her new home, the Luxemburg palace. This was a huge undertaking exactly suited to the Flemish painter's taste. For Rubens the painter was also a diplomat with a keen taste for court life and political intrigue.

At the time of Queen Marie's wedding in Florence, Rubens had been living and painting at the court of her sister's husband, the Duke of Mantua, where Monteverde was then employed as viol player. From Italy, three years later, Rubens had made a special trip to Spain to deliver some Italian paintings to his sovereign, Philip III, to whom he was a most devoted subject. Rubens was even more devoted to Philip III's older sister, the Archduchess Isabella, who made her home in his native city of Antwerp, capital of the Spanish Netherlands.

330

After fifteen years in Italy, Peter Paul Rubens had returned to Antwerp, where he opened a studio. Squeezing out gobs of rich color on his palette, he began painting in the Italian manner. His dramatic, colorful technique differed so from the careful Flemish painting with its subtle shades that his work caused a riotous sensation. Soon he had more commissions than one man could handle. So, being a businessman as well as a painter, Rubens put his pupils to work filling in backgrounds and spaces, and hired assistants until he had fifty men working for him in what was practically a portrait-painting factory.

One of his best pupils was Anthony Van Dyck, a brilliant young painter of twenty-one (over twenty years younger than his teacher). Rubens kept telling Van Dyck that all he needed was a trip to Italy. In fact, as Rubens was soon leaving for Paris, it occurred to him that this was the very time for Van Dyck to make that Italian trip. Madame Rubens, who was her husband's glamorous young model, found Van Dyck's company too fascinating. Just as well, thought Rubens, to have the young charmer far away from Antwerp while he himself was gone.

"Here, my young friend," said Rubens, "is the best horse in my stable. Take it, and go on a trip to Italy."

Peter Paul Rubens, painter and diplomat, then set off for Paris to make the paintings for Queen Marie, who in thirteen years had practically ruined France with her extravagance. She was so hated by her son, Louis XIII, that he had banished her from court for over five years. However, he had now allowed her to return to Paris and live in the Luxemburg, for which Rubens had come to make the paintings. The subject was to be the life of Queen Marie in twenty-four scenes.

Rubens had barely started to work on the sketches when, breezing in to Paris to find a bride for Prince Charles, came the playboy of Europe, the most dashing Englishman of his day, Lord Buckingham. He insisted upon having Rubens paint his portrait. He stirred up court circles with his maneuvers and caused such a juicy scandal by kissing Queen Anne as to almost upset the purpose of his visit.

Buckingham, as everyone knew, was the pampered and dearly beloved favorite of James I. On this amusing, irresponsible favorite of his, whom he called "Steeny," King James had now heaped wealth and titles until he was the richest, most powerful nobleman in England. He was also the foremost member of the Privy Council, so close to the King's ear that he was practically the ruler of the land. This, as might be expected, rendered him far from popular with Parliament and the English people. But Prince Charles, for whom he was now trying to find a bride, adored the gay "Steeny" as much as his father did.

The first choice of a bride for "Baby Charles," as James I still called his grown son, was the Infanta Maria of Spain, younger sister of the new King Philip IV. The Spanish bride would have brought a rich dowry to England. And the dowry was an all-important item to James and the extravagant Buckingham, who were forever out of funds. To cut short the formalities between ambassadors, Buckingham proposed that he and Charles go incognito to Spain, a wildly enchanting idea that never would have occurred to stiffly proper Prince Charles. Disguised as Mr. Smith and Mr. Brown, the two set forth on the romantic but unsuccessful mission. The Infanta Maria did not wish to become Queen of England. The Spanish court would not consider it, unless Charles became a Catholic. So Charles returned to England with no bride. And Buckingham went on to Paris to see what could be arranged for him in France.

Louis XIII's young sister, the princess Henrietta Maria, was then fifteen, eight years younger than Charles. Her dowry would be less than that of the Spanish Infanta, Buckingham was well aware; but whatever it was, it was well worth working for and making certain promises to obtain, such as one regarding Catholics in England, which seemed to be demanded of him. However, the agreement was far from being reached and looked very doubtful to Rubens when he left Paris, taking his half-finished paintings to be completed by his pupils in Antwerp.

By the time he returned with his paintings ready to be hung, there had been a great change in France. French affairs had been placed in the capable hands of Cardinal Richelieu, whom Louis XIII had then made his chief Councillor. All had been swiftly and deftly arranged for the French-English alliance.

The wedding took place on May 11, 1625, outside of Notre Dame Cathedral, with the Duke of Guise representing his cousin Charles, the absent bridegroom. A week later the elated Buckingham had come to Paris to escort the pretty French bride and her attendants to England, trusting that the dowry, which was then most desperately needed, would speedily be paid.

Cardinal Richelieu, the Frenchman chiefly responsible for the wedding, was well satisfied that the alliance with England would be of benefit to France. It would offset the strong influence of Spain caused by the Spanish marriages which Queen Marie had foolishly arranged for Louis XIII with Anne, and for his sister Elizabeth with Anne's brother, now King Philip IV.

ENTER CARDINAL RICHELIEU

THIS IS CARDINAL RICHELIEU, an ambitious man of great power and ability who had very few friends, many enemies, and who almost single-handed built France up into the powerful nation she was to become under the next king, Louis XIV, who was born just four years before Richelieu died.

In his later years, when Cardinal Richelieu had become fabulously rich and powerful, living in lonely grandeur in a palace near the Louvre, he rebuilt the old family chateau where he had spent his childhood. The chateau Richelieu was a typical castle built in the middle ages as a fort as well as a residence, with eight round pointed towers and a deep moat. As a boy, Richelieu had always been ashamed that the nearby chateau belonging to the family of Montpensier was so far more splendid than theirs. So when he was able at last to do so, he bought it, tore it down, and used the stones to rebuild the chateau Richelieu into a birthplace worthy of being pointed out as his.

Strictly speaking, the castle Richelieu was not his birthplace. In 1585, when he was born, his parents were residing in Paris temporarily, and he was christened there Armand Jehan du Plessis de Richelieu. His father died when young Armand was five. At the age of nine he was sent to Paris to the College of Navarre, where he studied Latin and Greek. His ambition was to be a soldier like his ancestors, so he next entered an academy where he was drilled in fencing, riding, the use of arms, and all things needed by a courtier and a soldier. Armand was a delicate, sickly lad, but his mind was keen, and strong and flexi-

ble as one of the rapiers with which he learned to fence. And just about as cold.

It was money matters that led his mother to turn the would-be soldier from the army into a career in the Church. As was the custom, his father had been rewarded for some service to the King by being allowed to appoint a bishop and manage the lands of the diocese. For years Madam Richelieu had used the bishop's income to feed and educate the family, letting the cathedral and buildings fall into wrack and ruin. Finally she was forced by the authorities to appoint a bishop. To keep the income in the family, she appointed her eldest son Alphines, who was then twelve. When he became of age, he honestly protested that he was not fitted to be a bishop, and became a monk. His ambitious, younger brother Armand had no such scruples. Seeing in the Church a better chance for advancement than in the army, he entered the University of the Sorbonne in Paris to study theology, and in 1606 was nominated as Bishop of Luçon by Henry IV. He was only twenty-one, four years too young to be a bishop without special dispensation by the Pope. So Armand set off for Rome to see Pope Paul V and get the dispensation. Then he went to his parish to live, "the poorest, dirtiest most disagreeable in all of France," he wrote. He craved elegance and was on the lookout for promotion, writing very humble letters to anyone in power who might further his desires.

After the death of Henry IV, he wrote to Queen Marie, praising her and protesting his loyalty "to the most wise and virtuous princess sent by God for the needs of France." In 1614, when the Estates-General was summoned by the Queen, the young Bishop of Luçon was one of the delegates, representing the clergy. Young Bishop Richelieu spoke to the Assembly for one hour, emphasizing how important a member of the clergy was in the government of the State.

Many hearing him spoke a good word for him, but found their friendship forgotten later when they could no longer be of use. Soon Richelieu received appointment as one of the king's secretaries of state. As the king was then only fifteen, and the Queen Mother was in power, Richelieu attached himself to her and her favorite minister, who was an Italian adventurer—a worthless creature. It was then that the Spanish marriages arranged by the Queen for her two children had taken place. Richelieu very shrewdly did not disclose that he was any less friendly toward Spain than the Queen and her minister.

Louis XIII was young, ignorant, badly educated—but just the same, he told himself, he was king, and he was tired of being pushed aside by his mother's Italian adviser. One day he gave orders to the captain of the guard that the Italian should be murdered. It was done in April, 1617. His body was hung up by the heels on the Pont-Neuf. When the guard reported to the King that the bloody service had been performed,

Louis XIII shouted, "Thanks to you! *Now* I am King!" jumped up on a billiard table and began issuing orders.

Queen Marie, who had never earned any love from her son by showing any love for him, was ordered by him to retire to Blois and take no more part in the affairs of state. Riding with her, in what looked like a funeral procession leaving the Louvre, was the Bishop Richelieu, lucky to have been merely banished instead of being imprisoned with others in the Bastille. The Queen's power had then ended forever. Her misrule was over.

Five years later, the King allowed his mother to come back to Paris and live in the Luxemburg Palace. Bishop Richelieu came with her—pleased to have reconciled them. That year he was honored by the new Pope Gregory XV, and became Cardinal Richelieu.

Two years later, in 1624, summoned by Louis XIII, Cardinal Richelieu became the chief minister of the state, and actually the ruler of France for the remaining eighteen years of his life. His many enemies never succeeded in destroying Louis XIII's loyalty to the brilliant Cardinal, mainly because that astute gentleman never failed to ask his sovereign's royal but worthless opinion, and never assumed that he was anything but the loyal servant of his master the King.

Years later he described the miserable condition in which he had found France, when he was called into power:

"When your Majesty called me to your Councils, I can truly say that the Huguenots divided the State with you; the nobles conducted themselves as if they were not subjects, and the governors of provinces as if they were independent sovereigns. Foreign alliances were despised, private interests preferred to public, and the dignity of your Majesty so debased it could hardly be recognized. I promised your Majesty to use all my industry and power to ruin the Huguenot party, lower the pride of the nobles, lead all subjects to their duty, and restore the country's name among foreign nations."

Richelieu's first step in fulfilling the promise had been to arrange the marriage of Henrietta Maria and Charles I.

337

BROKEN PROMISES

CHARLES STUART and Henrietta Maria were King and Queen of England at their marriage. James I had died two months before. Buckingham had begun pouring advice into the ears of his new King, long before he went to Paris to bring back the pretty Queen. Charles met her at Canterbury, where she arrived in a green traveling costume with a feathery hat perched on her brown curls. As Henrietta glanced up at this strange English-speaking Protestant King was was now her husband, her lord and master, she saw a very serious, proper young man with huge dark eyes and a delicate manner, most solicitous. Obviously he was very happy to see their escort, Lord Buckingham, that most gay gentleman, who had arranged her marriage.

He it was who had also made the important promise that King Charles would not enforce any old English laws punishing Catholics, nor make them support the Church of England. Otherwise Richelieu and her brother the King would never have allowed her to come.

What Henrietta did not know was that Charles had made a contrary promise to the English Parliament, since otherwise they would not have accepted a French Catholic queen. Nor did she know that Charles himself did not feel bound to keep his promises. He had been forced into the French one. As for the one to Parliament, that was absurd.

338

What right had people to demand any promise of a king, who took his right to rule over them directly from God?

Whatever Charles's opinion might be, however, he was faced with some demand whenever he asked Parliament for money, which he was obliged to do five days after the Queen arrived.

The House of Commons suspected that some promise had been made to France regarding the Catholics in England, and at Buckingham's suggestion. So they repeated their demands and also politely asked Charles to dismiss Buckingham from the Privy Council.

Dismiss Buckingham! What an insolent demand! Charles's answer to that was to dismiss Parliament; which only increased their suspicions, stirred up their anger, and left Charles with no money.

Buckingham saw that something had to be done to pacify the angry Commons. Disregard the promise to France, he told Charles, forget about it. As for the money, he would send a fleet out to seize Spanish treasure ships, while he himself took the crown jewels to Holland to pawn them. That should suffice until the dowry came from France.

Now the French who came to England with the Queen naturally began to talk. Henrietta Maria began to look and listen. She reminded Charles so often about his promise that for answer he dismissed all her chattering French attendants and shipped them home to France.

Meanwhile the dowry still had not been paid, neither of Buckingham's wild financial plans worked out, and Charles was forced into calling on Parliament again. Again they demanded that the King dismiss Buckingham, if he wanted them to vote him any money.

"That's no way to bargain with a King!" cried Charles. Clenching his small white fists, he dismissed Parliament again.

Buckingham now saw that something drastic had to be done to remedy his own unpopularity. He came up with a crazy scheme to offset the promise he had made regarding the Catholics in England by helping the Protestants in France. The Huguenots were being beseiged in their city of La Rochelle by the Cardinal and the King. He, Admiral Buckingham, would sail to their rescue, and return a hero!

LA ROCHELLE AND THE HUGUENOTS

THE SEAPORT of La Rochelle, on the coast of France, was the stronghold of the Huguenots. Cardinal Richelieu's next step toward making France a strong and united nation was to crush the power of the French Protestant party. This was not because of their religion, but because of their independent defiant attitude toward the authority of the King. They acted like a "state within a state." They refused to open the gates of La Rochelle to any royal officer.

Cardinal Richelieu therefore raised an army, took command of it himself, and with bishops and friars serving under him, besieged the Huguenots at La Rochelle in the name of the King.

In June, 1627, Lord Buckingham, in command of a large English fleet, sailed into the harbor of La Rochelle. On an island in the harbor was a fort occupied by the royal French troops, which Buckingham fired upon and blockaded. Surrounded, cut off from food, the royal defenders of the fort were just about to surrender one stormy night in September when, under cover of the storm, Cardinal-General Richelieu managed to get provisions out to them in small boats from the mainland, and the force was able to hold out. Buckingham, exhausted, sent a call to England for ships and reinforcements, but none came. The duke returned home completely defeated for the time being.

Richelieu proceeded without delay to have a massive dike of stones built across the harbor of La Rochelle, so that no ships could ever again enter to fire on the fort. Blockading the city by land, he settled down for a long siege to starve out the Huguenots.

Meanwhile, back in England, King Charles as usual was being starved for money. After dismissing Parliament he had tried on his own to get what he needed by levying taxes, but was so unsuccessful that he was forced to summon Parliament again. It was then March, 1628. The House of Commons now prepared a written promise or statement for His Majesty to sign, calling it a *Petition of Right*.

1. No taxes should be levied by the King without consent
of Parliament
2. No one should be imprisoned for refusing to pay such
illegal taxes.

This was nothing new. It merely repeated provisions in the Magna Carta which the nobles had forced King John to sign four hundred years before. But when they asked Charles I to sign the Petition, he refused.

"And yet the wording was very mild and respectful," said one member of the House of Commons, "no more than a worm trodden on would say if he could speak." No one would have considered addressing a King in any other way.

"The Duke of Buckingham advised him not to sign," said another member, eager to lay no blame upon the king. Other equally loyal subjects were quick to agree that Buckingham was to blame. Sir Edward

Coke was sure of it. "The Duke of Bucks is the cause of all our miseries," he positively declared.

King Charles finally signed his name to the Petition.

By then it was too late to save Buckingham and still get the money. The House of Commons demanded that Buckingham be dismissed. The King refused again, and again dismissed Parliament.

Now the people on the street were beginning to talk about what was going on. Pasted up all over London were posters for them to read:

Who rules the kingdom? The KING!

Who rules the King? The DUKE!

Who rules the Duke? The DEVIL!

"Get rid of him," cried the people. "Get rid of Buckingham."

At Portsmouth, in August, Buckingham was murdered. He had gone there to see about assembling another fleet to be sent to La Rochelle. A disgruntled soldier who had served under him and had not received a commission watched Buckingham go into a tavern for breakfast, waited beside the door until he came out, and stabbed him to death.

Late in 1628, after a long siege, the city of La Rochelle surrendered to the Cardinal-General Richelieu. On All Saints' Day, the Cardinal met the King at the gates carrying the keys. A long procession of monks marched through the streets singing *Te Deum*.

In another year the power of the Huguenots as a separate organization within the kingdom of France ceased to exist. So far as their religion was concerned, they were, according to the Edict of Nantes, on an equal footing with all other loyal subjects of the King. And Richelieu treated them as such. For this he was blamed by the narrowminded of his own faith and scornfully referred to as the "Huguenots' Cardinal."

But Cardinal Richelieu was far too intelligent to be bigoted. "I have no enemies," he said, "but those who are enemies of France."

And now, having subdued the enemies within France's own borders, the great statesman was able to turn his attention to the outside enemies—the German Emperor and the King of Spain, who threatened to close the Hapsburg ring around France and strangle her to death.

NEW FRANCE AGAIN

THE LONG-POSTPONED and final payment of Henrietta Maria's dowry is tied up with the story of New France. In midsummer of 1628, while war between the French and English at La Rochelle was still going on, four French ships, with two hundred settlers aboard bound for Quebec, were captured by the English. The English captain also captured the French supply ship, for which Champlain had been waiting anxiously since early spring, not knowing why it was delayed. Indeed, he knew little of what had been happening in France, since he had been in Canada for over two years.

The past winter at Quebec had been a hard one. The food supply had run dangerously low, even before the supply ship was due. There were fifty-five men, women, and children to be fed. There were the company officials living in the Habitation, Champlain and others in the fort on top of the rock, and men who tended the cattle at Cap Tourmente down the river. Old Captain Pontgravé, seventy-five, was also at Quebec, having come on the annual fur trade. Father Joseph too, eager as ever, was there with others of his order, and likewise Jesuit fathers, soon to be given by Cardinal Richelieu the sole right to convert the Indians. There were also three Indian girls, dear little girls. The good Champlain had taught them to pray and made designs for them to embroider, but they too had to be fed, and food was running low.

At last in July, when only a few barrels of biscuits and dried peas remained, two cowherds and an Indian appeared who had paddled up

343

from Tadoussac, where they said that six ships had arrived! Six, why six? The next day another cowherd from Cap Tourmente came in a small boat, saying that the six ships were English, not French. The commander had destroyed his cattle, captured his boat, and then told him to deliver this letter. He drew forth a paper and handed it to Champlain, who unfolded and read it.

In very courteous words the writer explained that he had orders from King Charles of Great Britain to take possession of Canada—that he hoped the fort would be surrendered with courtesy—that if so, Champlain might rest assured of good treatment, on the writer's faith and hope of Paradise. It was signed David Kirke.

Champlain wrote his reply in the same courtly style, saying that he had no doubt about the commission from the English King, but that if they should surrender the fort while they still had corn and beans left, they would not be worth the name of men in the presence of their King and would also merit punishment in the sight of God. Honor demanded that they fight to the death.

A few days passed. Then came a small boat, manned by eleven French sailors. They said that the French and English were at war, and that four French ships, with two hundred settlers aboard, had been attacked off the Gaspé Peninsula and captured by an English general named Kirke. Champlain nodded. As the sailors continued, he also learned at least part of what had been happening in France.

Cardinal Richelieu had become disgusted with the record of the fur-trading companies who had not kept their part of the bargain in taking out settlers. Only eighteen colonists in the last eleven years. It was true that French people in general did not want to leave their beautiful country. But it was obvious that the old system did not work. A new company should be formed and means found to attract settlers.

To offer titles of nobility might be the answer. Surely there were many wealthy bourgeois merchants who would snap at the opportunity to be made noblemen, if buying a membership in the new company and founding a settlement was all that was necessary.

344

The new company formed by Cardinal Richelieu was called the Hundred Associates, with each member paying a membership fee of nine hundred livres, and with twelve titles of nobility to be distributed. The Company was to control the fur trade forever, and in return must take two hundred settlers to New France each year, but no Protestants and no foreigners. The first two hundred had thus failed to reach their destination.

The eleven French sailors, added to the fifty-five already there, made sixty-six to be fed on the peas and beans and biscuits while they lasted, and then somehow or other kept from being starved into surrendering the fort before help came. All fall and winter Champlain carefully doled out the food. Peas, eels, and finally acorns mixed with bran, straw, and whatever roots could be eaten, somehow kept them alive until the following summer. Then two other Kirkes arrived, Commanders Louis and Thomas. They asked that, in pursuance of their brother's letter to him, Champlain place the fort and Habitation in their hands.

On July 20, 1629, the English commanders formally occupied Quebec, and raised above the fort the flag of the English. They showed much deference to Champlain, admiring his courage, but they could not lessen his agony as he saw the French flag come down, then the red and blue cross of England flying over his Quebec.

"May the good God return Quebec to the French," he prayed. If so he would come back and build a church to Our Lady. It was a vow. He would build and dedicate a chapel to Our Lady of the Recovery.

In October, Champlain crossed the ocean for the first time on an English ship. They landed at Plymouth. And there it was learned that France and England were no longer at war. Peace had been declared in April. Quebec had been taken over in July. So it had been captured after the war was over! The capture therefore was illegal.

Alive with hope again, Champlain went at once to London, to see the French ambassador, who went at once to see King Charles and returned with encouraging words which Champlain seized upon and set off for Paris. There he saw Cardinal Richelieu. He saw the King. He talked to all the company members. "I made them listen," he said, "and hear all about my voyages and what they should do for the well-being of New France."

But a war was raging in Europe. France itself was in danger. The enemy was on the very doorstep. Much as Cardinal Richelieu was concerned about losing Canada, the safety of France was paramount. However, scarcely had Champlain time to be disheartened when a solution presented itself.

Charles I, as usual, was in need of money. And he was especially in need of money at this time because his uncle, Christian IV of Denmark, was about to enter the war on the side of the Protestant princes of Germany. Charles had agreed to furnish thirty thousand pounds a year.

Charles I and Henrietta Maria had now been married four years and her dowry had not yet been paid. If France would pay the four hundred thousand crowns, England would return Canada to France. The bargain was signed, the dowry paid, and Canada handed back.

Champlain made his twelfth and last voyage in 1632, and was to spend the last three years of his life in almost complete happiness, there in the new land he loved. Where the Cathedral of Quebec stands today, he built his votive chapel, to Nôtre Dame de la Recouvrance. There, every Sunday, he heard cheerful bells ring and Jesuit fathers sing the mass.

Sad bells rang on Christmas day of 1635, but he did not hear them. As the evergreens hang heavy with snow and the ground was white, Samuel de Champlain's life came to an end. It had been a good life. To those who had known his loving kindness he would always be spoken of as Monsieur de Champlain of happy memory—*Monsieur de Champlain d'heureuse memoire.*

ON THE WAY TO CHINA

CHAMPLAIN'S FOURTH BOOK was published in 1632—his *Voyages,* giving the whole story of the French in Canada from the earliest visit. Included was the most modern map of New France. On the map, near Montreal, were to be seen La Chine Rapids—"Chinese Rapids" in the St. Lawrence River! The hope of finding a northwest seaway through to China had not yet been given up. Two years later, Jean Nicolet, an explorer and friend of Champlain, went to make peace between the Hurons and other Indians near the Great Lakes. Just in case he might reach the Orient, he took with him a robe of China damask, embroidered richly in brilliant birds and flowers, in which to appear at the court of the Chinese Emperor. This was also to be the dream of the Jesuits for years to come as they made their way through the Canadian forests—the dream of reaching China.

While the Jesuit missionaries and explorers from Europe were pushing west through the wooded wilderness of the New World hoping to reach China, explorers and missionaries from Russia were travelling eastward toward China over the wide plains of Asia.

Michael Romanov was scarcely proclaimed Tsar when a great migration to the east began. Before that, in the "Time of Troubles," exiles, prisoners, impoverished and homeless people of all kinds had escaped into the wild wasteland of swamps and forest—as well as Cossacks and soldiers, hunters for furs, and wanderers known as "waders."

In Europe, Russia was narrow and cramped. The western border was only 175 miles from Moscow. But the eastern border was seventeen hundred miles away, across the northern part of Asia. This part, known

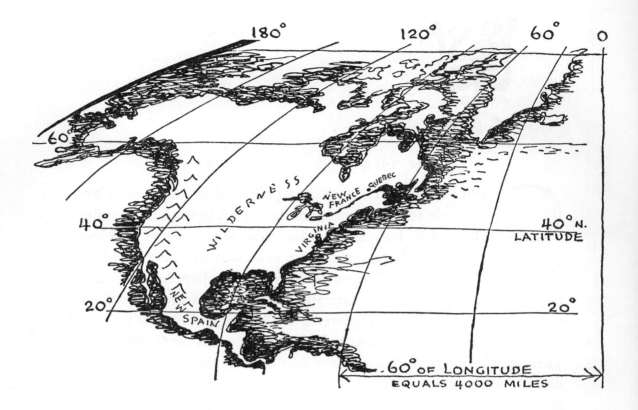

as Siberia, had been added to Russia in the days of Ivan the Terrible, by a wild Cossack named Irmak. Heading a band of runaway slaves and prisoners of war, adding to them troops with a promise of plunder, he had crossed the Ural Mountains, attacked a Tartar Khan, captured his land, and seized his possessions. Then, rather than be caught and hanged as a deserter and a rebel, Irmak presented this land of Sibir or Siberia to the Tsar. To this he added thousands of sable, ermine, white fox and bear skins, hundreds of sacks of gold and silver, heaps of emeralds, diamonds, and rubies. Ivan the Terrible rewarded Irmak with gunpowder and an ermine cloak, after which the Cossack got drunk and was found later that day lying wrapped in his ermine on one of the streets of Moscow.

From this time on, all kinds of people whom the Tsar wanted to get rid of were sent off to Siberia, some to be held there for a certain

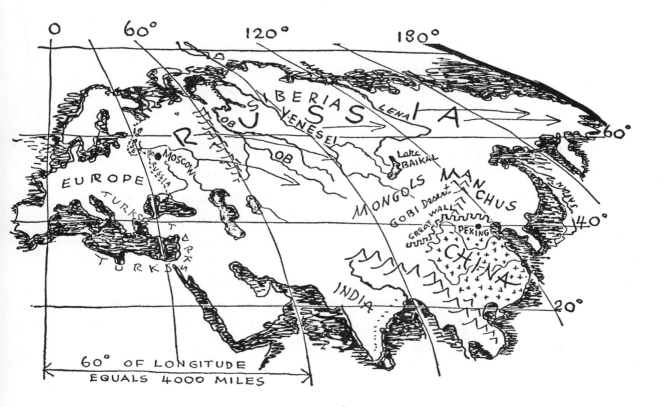

period of time, some to stay for life. Whole communities grew up of Poles, Tartars, Russians, and all kinds of people mixed together, from prisoners to priests.

From Siberia, explorers pressed on toward a great unknown river called the Ob. In 1611, Isaac Massa, a Dutch merchant who went with the company of Russian explorers, kept a wonderful record of the trip, which began by tracing the Ob to its headwaters thirteen hundred miles to the south. There they found huts of people, called the Tungusi, who told them that beyond the Ob was another larger river, with high mountains on the east where volcanoes cast out fiery brimstone. This river was the Yenisei.

Eager to see it, the explorers got permission from the Russian governor at Tobolsk, who also furnished soldiers. About seven hundred men set out and travelled through the land of the Tungusi, till they reached the great river. Beyond, said the Tungusi again, was another river larger than the Yenisei. With the Tungusi to guide them, the explorers set out for that next great river, which was the Lena. It was early spring when they reached it, said Isaac Massa, but they did not venture to cross, hearing what they understood to be the sound of bells. When wind came from across the river it often brought a noise of people and horses. Ships with square sails passed upon the river with a din of guns. Their hearts rejoiced at the sight of the beautiful country . . . "But," added Isaac Massa, "the Muskovites are crude people, caring only for profit." They did not cross the river, to his obvious disappointment.

However, he collected all accounts he could hear about the lands to the east, and got one map of the Arctic sea coast where the English and Dutch, seeking a northeast passage, had failed to find it. If they had been able to get through, Isaac Massa felt sure that they would have reached America. "It is very possible," he said, "that America is connected with China by an isthmus like the one which joins Africa to Asia at the Red Sea."

Isaac Massa's description of what the explorers had seen roused much interest at the Kremlin when it was received.

In December, 1619, an imperial order went out from "The Lord Tsar and Grand Duke Michael of all Russia," to the Imperial governor at Tobolsk, saying, "We have learned from Cossacks and fur traders, who have been on the Yenisei River that the land is Tung land, and that beyond is another great river. Now when you have this order and the Tungus people come in to the new *ostrog* [fort] give them to eat, make gifts to them and persuade them to go with the Russian Cossacks to discover that great river so that we may learn for certain if it be really a river or an arm of the sea."

Ivan Petlin, a Siberian Cossack living at Tomsk on the river Ob, also received imperial orders from "The Lord Tsar Michael of all Russia." He was told to seek tidings of the Chinese Emperor, and other kingdoms that lay beyond the uncrossed river. Chief of these rulers of whom the Tsar wanted tidings must have been the Great Khan of the

Mongols. The title of Great Khan had been a symbol of might and power since the days of Marco Polo, when the great Genghis Khan had swept westward out of Asia and conquered an empire that included Russia. The imperial order also said that the explorers were "to seek a lake called Baikal, where it was said rare rubies and emeralds were to be found suitable for his Majesty's treasure."

Ivan Petlin also sent back an interesting account of his journey. Pressing on where the others had left off, Petlin and a comrade made their way into and through the borderland of the Mongols, risking their lives among the nomads, until they came at last to Lake Baikal. They found no jewels, only silver that came out of China. Journeying still farther brought them, said Petlin, to a Great Wall "made of stone fifteen fathoms [90 feet] high . . . along the side of which they traveled ten days. They saw small towns and villages outside, but no people on the wall at all. They came to a gate," he said, "where lie great cannon and three thousand men stand watch. Men of the Great Khan journey to this gate with horses to sell but are not permitted to come within the wall except a very few at a time."

The soldiers asked Ivan Petlin why he had come. He replied, "To find the empire of China and other kingdoms," and was allowed to enter. As he journeyed through the cities of China he memorized the route to mark it out later on a map. He saw many strange things, among them gigantic painted statues in the Buddhist temples that frightened him. At last he reached Peking, "the white city where the Chinese Tsar dwells among beautiful and wonderful things." If he had had gifts to offer, Ivan Petlin believed he might have seen the Chinese Tsar.

After Petlin's return, the invasion of Asia by the Russians took on almost the fury of a gold rush. Hunters, traders, Cossacks, government inspectors went swarming into the east seeking furs, jewels and treasure. The peasant farmers plodded after them at a slower pace, remaining on the fertile steppes of the Volga and the Ob, where wheat could easily be grown. But priests and monks of the Greek Orthodox Church followed close upon the heels of the explorers, leaving a trail of monasteries and small wooden churches with their onion-shape towers in the scattered settlements.

Elisha Buza, a Russian explorer of Tartar stock, traced the Lena River to its mouth in the Arctic Sea, passing through the land of the Mongols. There the Mongol tribesmen could be seen roaming the grassy plains with their herds of cattle, hunting with falcons which soared and whirled through the wide windy spaces of the sky. Minstrels could be heard chanting of ancient days. They sang of the Great Genghis Khan. Somewhere south of the Mountain of Power lay his grave, they said, where on the first day of every spring his white horse rose again from the spirit world.

The present "Great Khan" of the Mongols, the Russians learned after loading him with gifts, had no power, only the title. The Dalai Lama in Tibet was his overlord. He had never heard of the White Tsar of Russia. When the Russians asked him to take an oath as the servant of the Tsar, he replied, "It has never been the custom of the Khan himself to take an oath." He was willing (for the sake of trade) to put his blood kin, clan and horde under the high hand of the Tsar, only as a subject, not as a servant.

Also he would not pay tribute, but he would send gifts to the White Tsar at Moscow by a Buddhist lama as ambassador. The gifts were three hundred sable skins and also *Chai,* dark leaves that came from China to be soaked in water for a beverage. This the Russians did not like at first, until they discovered it was very good after drinking too much vodka. Then tea became popular.

The Great Khan sent a list of gifts he expected in return, saying, "For the Khan there should be things of gold and silver and shining beadwork, strings of coral, precious stones of different colors, a good coat of iron chain mail with a sword and a firearm with six barrels; a gold brocade; the gift of a horse of Turkish breed, also a bell, a drum with horns for service in the temple, a clock that strikes, along with a monk from Jerusalem to teach Christian prayers; an interpreter knowing Russian and Mongolian speech and writing; a doctor with medicines, a silversmith, a gunsmith and a skilled leather tanner." The Russians did their best, but when they came to his encampment in the pastures north of Baikal, the Great Khan thought they did not deliver the presents fast enough, so he and his horde folded their tents and disappeared in the night. Then, to speed matters up, the Mongol riders came galloping in upon the Russians, stole the presents and rode away with them to the Khan.

The Mongols were now being pushed west and south toward the Gobi Desert by a tribe called Manchus, living northeast of the Great Wall. These Manchus were soon to invade China, overthrow the Ming Emperor, and establish China's last dynasty of Emperors.

Two thousand miles to the southwest, another descendant of the great Genghis Khan was bringing the Moghul or Mongol power to a peak in northern India. This was Shah Jehan, the grandson of Akbar, son of Prince Salim, for whom Akbar had built Fathpur Sikri as a thank-offering for his birth. Salim, who had taken the name Jehangur (Conqueror of the World), was as unlike his father Akbar as a son could be, so vicious and degenerate that the cruelties he delighted in are too horrible to tell. To religion, he was as indifferent as he was to government. All he wanted was enough alcohol to be continually drunk. His son Jehan (King of the World) tried to seize the throne, unsuccessfully. In 1627, when his father died, Shah Jehan rushed to Agra, proclaimed himself Emperor, murdered all his brothers so that they would not rebel against him. Then, to make the Moslem religion secure, he began a persecution of Christians and wholesale destruction of Hindu shrines and temples. With his peace of mind thus well established, the ruthless young ruler turned to architecture and adorned India with some of the most extravagantly magnificent buildings ever seen, the Pearl Mosque at Agra, the great Mosque at Delhi, the royal palace with the fabulous peacock throne made entirely of gold and silver and precious jewels, diamonds, emeralds, rubies and pearls. In 1632, he began to build for his favorite wife, the beautiful white marble mausoleum, the Taj Mahal, one mile east of Agra.

353

INSIDE THE GREAT WALL

FATHER MATTEO RICCI, the wise Jesuit missionary who had been welcomed by the Ming Emperor Shen Tsung, died in Peking in 1610. Six years later a Tartar chieftain, northeast of the Great Wall, calling himself the Emperor of Manchu, boldly began seizing territory to the east, west, and south and three years later defeated in battle 100,000 troops of the Ming Emperor, Hsi Tsung. Soon all of northeastern China was under the rule of the Manchu. The Ming Emperor was about to abandon Peking when the invaders were driven off by cannons designed by the Portuguese. Hsi Tsung was so impressed that he sent to the Portuguese headquarters at Macao, summoned a western scientist to the imperial court, and made him high official in charge of designing firearms. Also, on the advice of a Chinese Christian, the Emperor invited a German scientist to assist with the yearly calendar.

The Chinese Imperial Board of Mathematicians at Peking had made their usual error in miscalculating an eclipse of the sun. In 1622 the German scientist, a Jesuit by the name of Adam Schall, came to Peking, but was driven away by political enemies. However, a mistake was made again in 1629, while the European calendar was accurate. The Imperial Board of Rites then authorized Adam Schall, assisted by three colleagues and some Chinese students, to compile an almanac. The work took five years, and seemed to be highly satisfactory and well received

354

when presented to the Emperor wrapped in yellow silk. However, before the Ming Emperor could declare the calendar in force, the Manchu invader had marched into Peking and Ming dynasty had ended.

The first Manchu Emperor, who called himself the Emperor of Ch'ing, or Purity, published the almanac and made Father Adam Schall Governor of the Peking Observatory. But with the second Manchu Emperor reaction set in. One Chinese writer declared that the calendar made by the Christian was a sham full of errors, and wrote an essay "Against All Infidels."

Christianity nevertheless continued to grow in China. In 1624, there were three Jesuit fathers and a brother in Peking, and nineteen new priests arrived to take care of the six mission centers in the provinces. One said happily, "The wintry season of tempests and persecutions has passed. Spring is bringing flowers worthy of the Paradise of God."

A very real reason why Christianity flourished in the year 1625 was that an old long-buried tablet came to light which proved Christianity to be a teaching brought to China a thousand years before, and therefore ancient and worthy of respect. A workman, digging near the old capital of Ch'ang An, had hit upon the stone tablet with his spade. A local Chinese scholar looked at it, notified the Jesuit scholars at Peking. They were overjoyed to see it, for it told of the introduction of Christianity by missionaries from Syria in the year 635. The inscription read:

"In the time of the accomplished emperor, illustrious founder of the dynasty of Sung, among the enlightened and holy men who arrived was a most virtuous one from the country of Syria. Observing the azure clouds he bore the true sacred books; beholding the direction of the winds, he braved the difficulties and dangers. In the year 635, he arrived at Ch'ang An."

The inscription then went on to tell of his favorable reception by the Emperor, the honors bestowed upon him, and then, most heart-warming of all, of the friendly welcome given him by the Buddhist priest-official.

The much older religion of Buddhism had reached China by the Year I, which on the Christian calendar marks the birth of Jesus. The birth of Gautama, the Buddha, "The Enlightened One," had occurred five hundred years before in India, where he had been born a prince. As a boy his father had kept all knowledge of evil from him, so that Gautama was grown before he saw misery or suffering. Then, giving up his kingdom, he set out to seek a way of living that would free people of their misery and give them true happiness. And when he found it, it was so simple that his pupils found it hard to believe, and harder still to follow. His way did not consist of elaborate rites and sacrifices. The only sacrifice one had to make was that of selfishness. "He who gives up the thought of self makes his heart pure; joy, peace, and bliss will dwell within him, the peace of Nirvana, which is life everlasting."

One pupil said, "I have faith in thy teaching, I understand there is no self. But how shall I find the way?"

And the Buddha said, "By practice only. Practice the truth that thy brother is the same as thou."

For more than two hundred years the teachings of Buddha had been handed down by word of mouth until Asoka, an Indian king, had them written down, after which they were carried east and west by missionaries. By five hundred A.D. although Buddhism had been dying out in India, it had become firmly established in China and was entering Japan. However, in all those centuries it had grown far away from Buddha's simple teaching. It had become a religion divided into many sects, loaded with elaborate rituals and prayers and man-made formulas. Yet in the heart of it still remained to be found the teaching of Buddha, just as the teaching of Jesus lies in the heart of the various forms of the Christian religion.

NAGASAKI

TOKIO

JAPAN'S CLOSING DOOR

OUTSIDE OF TOKYO in Japan, the stone lantern had been standing but two years above the grave of Anjin Sama, Mr. Pilot, English friend and counsellor of the Shogun Iyeyasu, when, in 1622, an intense persecution of all Christians began that would close the door of Japan against them for two hundred years.

Some suspicion that Europeans might endanger his government had been held by Iyeyasu himself before he died. He also realized his mistake in thinking European trade with Japan depended upon the Catholic missionaries, whose teachings tended to divide rather than unite Japan. One religion for Japan was sufficient. Buddhism was varied

357

enough to supply the needs of all kinds and conditions of people from the most ignorant, who worshipped stone idols, to those who sought the truth by Zen, or the meditation through which Buddha himself had become "Enlightened." In between were Sects of Lotus, Spirit, Pure Land, True Word and many others. What need had Japan for more sects or for another religion brought in by Europeans?

The next Shogun of the Tokugawa family was further aroused against the Christian religion because of the abuse which each Christian nation heaped upon the others. The Spanish and Portuguese railed against the Dutch and English, the English against the Spanish and Portuguese, aided by the Dutch, who, however, seemed far more concerned about trading. There were then about 300,000 Christians in the country, including native believers, Jesuit priests, and Franciscan monks, also unfriendly toward one another. The hatred came out of their religion, a disrupting evil that should not be allowed to spread further in Japan. Like a cancer, it had to be rooted out. The anti-Christian feeling reached a climax in the years 1622–1624. The Japanese used the same methods that the Spanish had used in getting rid of the Jews. Those who were willing to forsake their faith were spared. All others were driven out, persecuted, and eventually killed.

Under the next Shogun, Iyemitsu, European traders were also driven from Japan. In 1623, the first year of his reign, the English voluntarily closed their unprofitable trading post on the island of Kyushu. The next year all Spaniards were driven from Japan and all trade with the Philippine Islands ended. By 1636, Japanese were forbidden to leave the country. Those who had gone abroad were not allowed to return. The next year there was one last desperate uprising of the native Christians—thirty-seven thousand Japanese on the Island of Amakusa, who defended themselves for almost three months against the emperor's troops. When they could hold out no longer they were slaughtered to the last man. The Portuguese were expelled next, being suspected of having helped in the uprising. The Dutch had also helped, but even so, the Dutch traders were allowed to remain. Their trading post was moved, however, to a small island in Nagasaki Harbor, where conditions were made as inconvenient and humiliating for them as possible.

The door of Japan had closed. It was not to be opened again until 1858. No longer influenced by her great neighbor China, to whom she had so far been indebted for her art, language, and civilization—no longer distracted by European ideas, Japan developed in those two hundred years a way of life, a culture, and an art that was distinctly her own. The most perfect expression of that unity of feeling that pervaded all life was depicted in the Ukiyoye School of "Pictures of the Passing World," showing the simple people and everyday life of Japan. This art was shocking at first to the proud Samurai, who considered it a theme unworthy of painting when they saw it begun by the painter Matabei. His work, however, inspired a Tokyo designer of kimono patterns to cut similar scenes on wood blocks from which they could be printed, and so about thirty years after the door was closed Moronobu began the making of the beautiful Japanese prints, which were first carried to Europe by the Dutch.

One of the last thoughts to come from China before the door was closed was the philosophy of Confucius, taught by a Japanese student whose name was Hayashi Razan. Iyeyasu had known him, but it was his son Iyemitsu who made it fashionable for the Samurai to attend Razan's lectures in 1630. His school in administration and the teaching of Confucius was to develop into the University of Tokyo.

Christianity, Razan told them, was full of myths and fancies. Buddhism was a drawing away from life that would weaken the Japanese nation.

"Your priests tell you," he said, "that the world is full of sin, withdraw from it, seek your own salvation. By these enchanting words they cause people to forget their duties toward others."

"The way of the wise man is not separated from everyday life," added one of his scholars. "It is selfishness to seek happiness in the future world. Think not that God is something distant, but seek for him in your hearts; for the heart is the abode of God."

359

IN AND OUT FOR CHRISTIAN IV

BACK IN EUROPE, the disgraceful war between Protestants and Catholics was still going on in Germany—the second, or Danish, part. This was led by Christian IV of Denmark who in 1625, buckling on a sword about his colossal stomach, set out to battle against the Emperor Ferdinand and the forces of the Catholic League, after having first made a treaty with the rulers of Holland and England.

Shortly after the treaty had been signed, James I and Prince Maurice had both died, leaving Charles I and Prince Frederick Henry to continue the alliance with Christian IV. Holland was fighting for her life against Spain. England wanted to recover the Palatinate for Prince Frederick and Princess Elizabeth, who were refugees in Holland.

360

Christian IV was merely greedy for some good German land along the Weser river bordering Denmark, and thought this was the time and way to get it. Christian IV, who as a boy had been such a boring nuisance to Tycho Brahe, and later drove the famous old astronomer out of Denmark, was far from the stuff of which heroes are made. He went to war with no lofty purpose of aiding fellow-Protestants in the German states.

The Emperor Ferdinand viewed the Danish king's entrance into the battle with little concern, being well satisfied thus far with the progress of the war and the success of his commanders, General Count Tilly and the brilliant generalissimo Prince Wallenstein. They could handle the new enemy from Denmark. As for England and Holland, even though Frederick Henry was just as able a soldier and a far better statesman than his father, the Spanish forces were gaining ground in Holland, while England had been more hindrance than help to her ally.

A so-called "Protestant hero" had been hired to lead the English forces. This was a German count by the name of Mansfeld, a soldier of fortune. After shopping around from court to court in Europe for employment, he had arrived in England and been given money by the King to raise an English army. He had then set out for the Palatinate, going by way of Holland. The Dutch town of Breda was being besieged by the Spanish when Mansfeld and his English troops landed in Flushing, but, acting on orders, he did not go to the relief of the starving defenders of the Dutch town, who finally had to surrender. Also, since Charles I sent no money to supply and feed the English army, the hungry soldiers were allowed to plunder the countryside for miles around, and then disbanded, having accomplished nothing.

Mansfeld, meanwhile, had gone blithely on into Germany and raised another army of German soldiers, with the promise of booty and plunder, using the same methods that Wallenstein had been using to increase the Imperial army. Mansfeld and his new army were soon being pursued by Wallenstein, acting on orders from the Emperor. Wallenstein would have preferred to march against Christian IV, in order to be on hand when Denmark was defeated and the land divided up. But Tilly and the forces of the League had orders to take care of the army of Christian IV, while Philip of Spain was to send a fleet of Spanish ships against those of Denmark, and for that receive a port on the Baltic Sea. By the summer of 1627, all was over and done as far as Christian IV was concerned. Instead of gaining more land, he had lost all he had, and sat cramped up on a small island in the Baltic Sea, while the forces of Tilly went marching up through Denmark. By that time Wallenstein the invincible was also there, having defeated Mansfeld and chased him into Hungary, where he died. As a reward for his services, the mighty generalissimo had received from the Emperor the fine German state of Mecklenburg. This roused the wrath of all the German princes, Catholic as well as Protestant. To have German land handed over to the overbearing Wallenstein, already calling himself "Duke of Mecklenburg," was going too far. They demanded that the Emperor make peace with Christian IV and give him back his Denmark.

Christian, frantically eager to get off the tiny island and back into his comfortable kingdom, ready to make peace on almost any terms, did so without consulting his allies, promising to stay out of German affairs from then on. Heaving a sigh of relief, he went back to his heavy feasting and hunting.

Cardinal Richelieu was utterly disgusted with him. "That wretched Prince," he exclaimed, "has betrayed his allies and wriggled out of the war untouched."

The French Cardinal was growing continually more alarmed for the safety of France as the victories and power of the Emperor increased. Before throwing the French forces against the Emperor, however, Richelieu preferred to stand by and see if the Protestant nations could not finish the fight themselves, while he aided them secretly with money and advice. Now that Denmark had crawled out of danger, Richelieu was looking toward Sweden, and saw in the young King Gustav Adolf the next leader of the Protestant cause, "the new rising sun."

JOHN WINTHROP OF GROTON MANOR

ABOUT DUSK on a November evening in 1628, a solemn middle-aged man entered his gloomy lodgings, among those of other lawyers in the Inner Temple, wishing he were almost anywhere but in this sinful, foul-smelling city of London. Most of all he wanted to be home at Groton Manor. His slim face with its pointed beard was pale and drawn. His shoulders drooped from exhaustion after a day of plodding about the filthy, foggy streets. His hair hung lank and limp as he removed his hat, slipped out of his cloak, and stood a few moments by the spark of an open fire. He then lit a candle and sat down to write his wife a letter, dating it November, 1628, addressing it to his dear sweet Margaret.

As he wrote the name, John Winthrop's thoughts carried him away to Groton Manor. He could see Margaret opening his letter by the window where his mother and grandmother used to sit. Winthrops had lived at Groton Manor since 1544, when his grandfather, Adam Winthrop, a cloth merchant of London, had purchased the land directly from the King. It had belonged to a monastery, which, with other lands of the Church, was then being broken up and distributed by Henry VIII.

Life at Groton Manor had seemed so secure, so comfortable to John Winthrop when he was a boy, so eternally set in its gracious pattern. It was like a small world in itself, ruled over by his father. There was the great house with its chimneys, the huge half-timbered barn with its thatched roof, plenty of servants to care for everything, inside and out. There were horses and cattle, woods to hunt in, broad meadows and rolling hills, fields of grain and ponds filled with fish. There were tenant farmers in the small houses to plow the fields and harvest the grain. Sometimes, as a little boy, John went with his father to collect the rents, and saw the inside of the cozy cottages.

There was no talk then of poverty, of hard times and low prices. Those were happy days. Now times were so bad that, all about Suffolk County, weavers were out of work, and it was no longer possible to live off the grain and produce raised on the land of Groton Manor.

John Winthrop had been born the year of the Armada, 1588, which made him just forty as he sat there in the gloomy London room looking back on a happier past. He remembered when he was seven, going to school to the vicar of the nearby church to prepare for the university which would be Cambridge, where his father had gone. John had entered at fifteen, stayed two years, and then stopped school to be married. His enterprising father had arranged for his marriage to a young woman whose dowry would add a considerable tract of land to that of Groton. Ten months later, John's son John, Jr., had been born, then Henry, Forth, and Mary—four children had been born to him in the ten years before their mother died. Those had been ten happy years spent in managing his estate, doing the work for which God had intended him. To do this better he had studied law, for, as lord of the manor, it was his duty to hold court every three weeks and settle disputes among his tenants. The children needed a mother, he needed a wife, so six months after his wife's death he had married again, but the second Mrs. Winthrop had lived only a year.

So Margaret was John Winthrop's third wife. They had been married ten years and had three small boys: Stephen, eight; Adam, seven; and Dean, four. All of them were at home in Groton, while their father was here in London working for the government to support the growing family. John Winthrop was in need of the government job, but he was ashamed of the work he had to do. It gave him no peace of mind. He was attorney for His Majesty's Court of Wards. This was an ancient institution, which he felt had grown so corrupt and caused so much misery that it should not exist. The "Wards" were wards of the King. If the owner of land such as Groton Manor, who had received it directly from the King, should die leaving a son not yet of age, that boy would become a "Ward of the King." His land would be managed by the court, and given back when the boy was twenty-one and able to manage the estate himself. Usually by that time so much had been taken from it for the King's use that it was almost worthless. The forests had been cut down, the farmland depleted, the buildings allowed to fall into ruin. It was robbery under the name of justice. Much as he needed the income, John Winthrop was ashamed to be connected with such a business. And this was but one example of the evils, wickedness, and rottenness of this country of England.

Puritans, such as he was, had long felt that their only hope of correcting some of the evils lay in Parliament. But Charles I blocked every effort they made at reform. Some dreadful punishment was sure to fall on this wicked land, under the wrath of God. John Winthrop verily believed that the Lord would destroy this wicked city of London as he had destroyed Sodom and Gomorrah of old—and that the good would perish with the bad.

And what could he do? What should he do? Desert the country just to save himself, and leave the rest to perish? That did not seem right. What should he advise his sons to do?

Puritan merchants had that very year organized the New England Company and been granted a charter to settle near the Charles River in Massachusetts. They had sent over Captain John Endecott, a veteran from the Dutch wars, with a shipload of Puritans to form a colony. They had gone this past summer. John, Jr. had proposed going with the group. His father had not discouraged him, but suggested that he should not yet commit himself permanently to living in the New World. John Jr. had gone instead on a trip to Constantinople. Henry, the wild one, had taken off for Barbados.

Salem was the name of the place in Massachusetts where Captain Endecott had settled. Half of the people, it was reported, had died soon after landing. Fortunately the nearby settlement of Separatists at Plymouth had a good physician and surgeon, and Captain Endecott had appealed to the governor, William Bradford, who had sent Dr. Samuel Fuller to help them. This, John Winthrop had to admit, was a friendly thing he had not expected of Separatists. He did not feel at all in sympathy with those people who had separated from the Church of England, any more than he did with monks or recluses of any kind who withdrew from the world to save their own souls and keep from being contaminated by their fellow men. It also seemed to him to be denying life, shirking responsibilities as a member of society. How could he, head of Groton Manor, responsible as he was for the welfare of his tenants, pick up and leave England? If he took them with him, what of the estate that had been handed down to him? That land and property would have to be sacrificed, for times were hard and the price of land was low. The thought of property brought back to his mind the case of the poor widow and her young son which he had recently handled, and whose estate had been practically stolen by the Crown. This was a lamentable business in which he was engaged. It gave him no peace, no content of mind. The candle spluttered, and a drop of hot wax fell on the sheet of paper. He dipped his quill again and finished the letter. Then he removed his clothes, put on his nightshirt and cap, and, since the servant had neglected to put in the warming pan, climbed into a very cold bed and tossed all night. He had barely dozed off when morning light fell through a crack in the bed-hangings. Then the clock also told him it was time to rise and begin another distasteful day's work.

How long would he, John Winthrop, be able to endure it?

366

t'Fort nieuw Amsterdam op de Manhatans

NEIGHBORS: NEW AMSTERDAM
AND PLYMOUTH

THIS IS THE FIRST DRAWING ever made of the great city of New York, the little village of New Amsterdam, founded by the Dutch, who in 1626 had purchased the island of MANAHATTIN from the Indians for twenty-four dollars. The purchase of what is the most valuable piece of real estate in the world today seemed no more important then to a member of the States-General in Holland, than the cargo of furs which the ship had brought into the harbor of Amsterdam. These are his words:

"Here arrived yesterday the ship which sailed from New Netherland out of the Hudson River on September 23. They report that our people have bought the island of Manhattan from the wild men for the value of sixty guilders [$24]. The cargo of the aforesaid ship is 7,246 beaver skins, 178½ otter skins, 48 mink skins, 36 wildcat skins."

Peter Minuit, acting for the Dutch West India Company, was the man who struck the bargain with the Indian chief. Peter Minuit originally came from Wesel, a German town just across the Rhine from Holland. Toward the end of 1624 he had been appointed Director-General of the Dutch Trading Company to reside on Manhattan Island and build it up from a mere fur-trading post into a settlement.

The fur-trading post had been set up two years after Henry Hudson discovered the island, by a man named Adrian Blok, sent out by the Amsterdam merchants. In the spring of 1613, his newly built fort had been destroyed by Captain Argall from the English colony of Virginia, who had also destroyed the French settlement at Port Royal. In November, Adrian Blok's ship, anchored in the Hudson River, caught fire and burned. He and his crew wintered on the island and that spring, in a new ship, built with the help of the Indians, Adrian Blok explored Long Island Sound and went as far up the coast as Cape Cod. He gave Dutch names to Block Island, Rhode Island (from the Dutch word for "red"), and Staten Island (from the Staaten, or States-General of Holland). As a result of Blok's explorations, the Amsterdam merchants formed the New Netherland Company. They built another fur-trading post up the Hudson River at Albany, calling it first Fort Nassau and

368

then Fort Orange, in honor of their
ruler. There in 1617, while the French
were making a treaty with the Algonquins in Canada, the Dutch made a
treaty with the five Indian nations,
known as the Iroquois, with whom
trading was carried on largely by means of the Indian money called
wampum.

The New Netherland Company did better at fur-trading than establishing a colony. It was difficult to persuade the native people of Holland
to leave home, where they were comfortable and happy, to settle in
the wilderness. However, it was thought by the Directors that some of
the refugees in Holland might go there if their passage was paid. The
proposal had been made to the English Pastor John Robinson and his
congregation in Leyden, but they had decided to go instead to New
England, where they founded the colony of Plymouth.

Huguenot refugees from France were approached next, and also
other French-speaking people called Walloons, who had fled into Holland from the Spanish Netherlands. They agreed to go, and in 1624
they formed a large part of the thirty families who were the first permanent settlers on Manhattan Island. Two years later, when Peter Minuit
came to be their Director-General, he found about two hundred colonists
living around the trading post. By 1628, when the first minister, Reverend Jonas Michaelius, arrived, he found the colonists making a windmill
to saw lumber, and building a fort "of good quarry stone," and calling
the settlement New Amsterdam.

They had also gotten in touch with their neighbors in Plymouth.
Peter Minuit's secretary and right-hand man, Isaak de Rasiers, had

369

sent a letter to Governor William Bradford in both Dutch and French, addressing it to "the noble worshipful wise prudent Lords, the Governor and Council residing in New Plymouth. Our very dear friends," the letter read, "The Director and Council of New Netherland often wished for an opportunity to congratulate you and your prosperous and praiseworthy undertakings there. And the more in that we also have made a good beginning to pitch the foundation of a colonie here. If it so falls out that any goods that come to our hands from our native country may be serviceable unto you, we shall (trade) either for beaver or any other wares you should be pleased to deal for . . . If you please to sell us any beaver, or otter or such like commodities for ready money, let us understand thereof by this bearer in waiting . . .

"In the meantime, we pray the Lord to take you, our honoured good friends and neighbors into his holy protection.

ISAAK DE RASIERS, *Secretaris.*
From the Manhattans, in the fort Amsterdam
March 9, 1627.

Ten days later, the bearer had reached Plymouth and delivered his letter. Governor Bradford had read it, and in his house on Maine Street, was composing an equally friendly letter to be sent back to his neighbors in New Amsterdam. Amsterdam—the very name brought back a flood of memories of those "years of freedom and good content for which," he said in his letter, "we and our children after us are bound to be thankful to your Nation and shall never forget."

It was now over seven years since he and Dorothy had sold their house in Leyden and come as Pilgrims to the new world. Their small son John, whom they had left with his grandparents in Amsterdam, was now in his teens, and was coming to live in Plymouth with his father and stepmother. Mrs. Alice Southworth, whose first husband had been a silk weaver in London, had come to Plymouth in the summer of 1623 and very soon become Mrs. Bradford. Little William was three years old and baby Mercy, newborn, was probably asleep in her wooden cradle by the open fire as her father finished and signed his cordial letter.

Not long after the letter had been sent Governor Bradford was entertaining a New Amsterdam delegation. Isaak de Rasiers made a formal entrance with trumpeters and attendants, and stayed for a visit of several days. The Dutch brought sugar, linen, and other commodities to trade, but most important, they brought wampum, which the Plymouth people had never seen. Hesitating at first, they were persuaded by the Dutch visitors to take about fifty pounds' worth and try it out, and it was not long before the Plymouth people had almost a monopoly on fur-trading with the Massachusetts Indians.

After his return to New Amsterdam, de Rasiers, who had impressed Bradford as a man of "fair and genteel behavior," gave his impression of the Plymouth Colony, which, he said, had then about fifty families. "Their farms are not so good as ours because they are more stony. The Indian tribes in their neighborhood are better conducted than ours because the English give them the example of a better life, and from the very first, gained their respect."

Two years later, in 1629, the Dutch West India Company, still struggling to get Dutch farmers to settle America, held out what they thought would be an inducement. They issued what was called a Charter of Privileges and Exemptions. This provided that anywhere in New Netherlands except Manhattan Island, any member of the Company might take his choice of a tract of unoccupied land, if he would promise to plant a colony of fifty people on it within four years. The land could extend sixteen miles along the seacoast, or eight miles along one bank of a navigable river, like the Hudson or Delaware, and extend as far back as could be arranged with the Indians. Any private farmer might rent land from the founder of the colony, who was to be known as the Patroon. Members of the company naturally hastened to sign up for the best locations—Staten Island, both sides of Delaware Bay and the Hudson River. It was all very fine for the Patroon. But why would farmers who owned their own land in the Netherlands want to come over and live like a serf under a Patroon? They were contented at home.

371

VELÁZQUEZ

THE GREAT SPANIARD, Velázquez, painted a portrait of King
Philip IV of Spain in 1623, the first of forty portraits of his king
painted by Velázquez. As soon as he saw it, Philip IV declared
it was the first *real* portrait of him that had ever been made. All those
previously painted he had removed from the walls and announced that
from then on no one should paint his royal portrait but Velázquez.

Philip IV was a lover of art, and fancied himself a poet and a
painter, but he was weak and worthless as a king, and even less interested in government, if possible, than his father Philip III. All the
tedious work of running a nation he left to his minister Olivares. And
why not? Why, just because his grandfather Philip II had worked day

and night, should he be obliged to bore himself to death with politics?

His aunt, the Archduchess Isabella, still as interested in affairs of state as she had been at fifteen, was now the ruler of the Spanish Netherlands. In 1628, when the war was not going too well for Holland, she thought Charles I might be about ready to desert his ally and make a friendly alliance with Spain. She called upon Peter Paul Rubens to go to Madrid and sound out her nephew Philip IV on the subject. Rubens packed up his paints and betook himself to Spain as a diplomat.

Velázquez was appointed to escort the famous Rubens around and show him all the art treasures to be seen in Spain—in Madrid, in the Escorial, in the older cities of Toledo and Seville.

Seville was where Velázquez had lived before he sought his fortune at the court. He had then painted the everyday scenes of Spanish life. After his first portrait of Philip IV, young Velázquez had been hailed as the leading painter of Spain. Older artists sneered, but a competition was then announced by Philip IV for a painting of "The Expulsion of the Moors from Spain." Velázquez won the prize, and from then on was recognized as the leading painter at the Spanish court.

It was the following year that Rubens arrived as an ambassador and was entertained by the king as a diplomat, not as a painter. The favorite painter at the court sat at table with the dwarfs, clowns and other players who amused the King. Velázquez did not mind. If such was the way of the world, so be it. His strong face, with its deep-set, honest eyes and firm, generous mouth, showed no lines of envy or discontent. He had his work, his painting, his family. He was at peace with life.

Velázquez, whose full name was Diego Rodriguez de Silva y Velázquez, had been born in 1599, which made him the same age as Rubens' former pupil Van Dyck. Rubens also began to tell the young Velázquez that he needed a trip to Italy to see and study the great Italian masters of the Renaissance. The next year, 1629, Philip IV gave Velázquez permission to go, making him a present of four hundred ducats, to which Olivares added two hundred.

Rubens went to England that year as representative of Philip IV, honored by a new title: Secretary of the King's Privy Council for the Netherlands. Rubens was expected to exact a promise from Charles I not to take any action against Spain until a treaty could be agreed upon. As promises meant nothing to Charles, that cannot have caused Rubens any trouble or marred in any way the pleasure of this first trip to England. In 1630, the painter was knighted by King Charles I.

He was also given a commission to decorate the ceiling of the Banquet Hall at Whitehall, for which he designed an allegory entitled "The Blessings of Peace." In November, Charles I quietly deserted the Netherlands and made peace with Spain.

Christmas, 1630, old Ben Jonson, poor, sick, proud, and furious at being ignored for five years, was asked for one last time to write the Christmas masque for the King and Queen, to be given as usual in the now newly decorated Banquet Hall. Another poet who went to consult the cantankerous old playwright said of him:

> "His whole discourse
> Was how mankind grew daily worse and worse
> How God was disregarded, how men went
> Down even to Hell, and never did repent."

A week after Christmas, Charles I signed a secret treaty with Philip IV to go to war against the Netherlands, and after defeating the Dutch to carve up their territory and divide it between them.

VELÁZQUEZ SEES ROME

THE VILLA MEDICI stood on a high hill northeast and just outside of the city walls of Rome. Velázquez lived there for a while during his visit to Italy. He made paintings of the beautiful gardens surrounding the villa, and often stopped to enjoy the marvelous view from the hill overlooking the city. Across the Tiber River, beyond the far walls, he could see the magnificent dome of St. Peter's Cathedral. At high noon it was clear and bright against the deep blue of the

374

SISTINE CHAPEL

VATICAN

sky, at evening dark gray with the sunset behind it and the west streaked with fiery clouds. In early morning the rising sun's first rays touched the gold cross on the top. Ever firm and beautiful it stood there as the sun rose and set. How little could one realize that the great cathedral and the earth were moving while the sun stood still!

Next to the cathedral, the long, lower building of the Vatican could also be seen, the palace of the Pope. Velázquez spent many hours in the Vatican studying and copying the paintings of Raphael and those of Michelangelo on the ceiling of the Sistine Chapel. This small chapel, between the Cathedral and the Vatican, was where the Cardinals met when it was necessary to elect a new Pope.

The present Pope was Urban VIII. In 1626, it had been his pleasure to dedicate the great cathedral of St. Peter's, which at last after 175 years of building had been completed.

GALILEO'S FINAL VISIT TO ROME

THE VILLA MEDICI belonged to the Grand Dukes of Florence.
Cosimo II had always arranged for Galileo to stay there on his
visits to Rome. He was there in 1611 when he brought his telescope and, to their delight and amazement, had shown the members
of the Papal Court the four newly discovered moons of Jupiter, which
he called the Medicean stars.

He was there five years later in 1616 when he had been condemned as a heretic for teaching the great truth of which the discovery of those moons had convinced him.

And again, on a bleak February day in 1633, Galileo in his seventieth year arrived at the Villa Medici. He was very frail from a long illness and exhausted by his winter journey from Florence. A damp, chill wind blew through the dark evergreens on the Pincian Hill, as, walking slowly, head bent, half-supported by two attendants, the old scientist passed on into the palace. There he was to be held for two months, awaiting a second trial by the Inquisition.

This had been most unexpected. Commissioners had quite suddenly arrived in Florence and, in spite of his illness, had insisted that Galileo come with them to Rome. The young Grand Duke Fernando II had not offered a word of objection to the priests. Galileo did not blame him. He would not have dared to because of his grandmother, the Grand Duchess, a dominating woman, whose question had resulted in Galileo's first appearance before the Inquisition. She was now a religious fanatic, dressed in a heavy black veil of mourning for her son Cosimo II.

Fernando II was a good boy, though not very brave by nature. Only ten years old when his father died, and far too young to rule, he had been and still was under the domination of his grandmother.

It had been a great sadness to Galileo to see Cosimo II, his devoted pupil, die so young. He was only thirty-three. But even in 1616 when Galileo returned from Rome, the Grand Duke had been a confirmed invalid as a result of a lingering fever. When he died in 1621, he left eight little children, the eldest being Fernando II, who inherited the title.

All of them, one after another, had become the pupils of their father's old tutor. Galileo had taught them all. During those years he lived very quietly in his villa on the Arcetri Hill, near the more luxurious villa of the royal family. Also during those years, he had written a book on comets which was published in 1623 and dedicated to Pope Urban VIII. Even though a few words had been quietly slipped in regarding

Copernicus, the book had been acclaimed by churchmen as well as scientists, and the next year Galileo spent two happy months in Rome, during which Pope Urban granted him six audiences. He also wrote a letter to the Grand Duke in Florence, praising the great astronomer not only for his learning but for his piety. Galileo was so elated that he actually dared to believe that the Holy Father might use his influence to set aside the old decree. In this he was disappointed. Many friends, however, felt sure that the decree would never be strictly enforced. A Dominican monk wrote that Pope Urban had expressed his disapproval of it. And one of the Cardinals reported that Pope Urban had said that to declare that the earth moved could not be condemned as heresy; it was only rash.

Little wonder then that Galileo had returned to Florence expecting that the book which he was then writing would be well received and might bring him more renown. Its title was:

Dialogodei due massimisistemi delmondo
Dialogue of the two great systems of the world

In it three characters take part in the dialogues:

Salviati, who gives the views of Galileo himself.
Sagredo, who is a very intelligent listener.
Simplicio, who is well-meaning, but stupid.

It was a brilliant book, and after its publication in January, 1632, it was greeted with praise and applause by scholars all over Europe.

Anyone who read the book, however, could see that it violated the edict pronounced against the author. Some thought Galileo intended Simplicio, the stupid one, to represent Pope Urban, and quickly brought this unhappy notion to the Pope's attention.

Six months later the sale of the book was prohibited, and a year later Galileo was in the Villa Medici waiting to be tried. On June 21, he appeared before the Court of the Inquisition, held in a Dominican monastery. He was accused of holding the Copernican theory in defiance

378

of the decree against him. Galileo declared that never since his condemnation in 1616 had he held the Copernican theory.

On June 22, in the church of Santa Maria sopra Minerva, built on a ruined temple to the Roman goddess of wisdom, Galileo fell to his knees, denied what he knew to be true, and received his sentence. He was to recite the seven penitential psalms once a week for three years. He was to be imprisoned when, where and if the tribunal so desired. The sentence was signed by seven Cardinals, but it did not receive the customary signature of the Pope. Nor was the imprisonment strictly enforced.

After one week spent at the Villa Medici, Galileo was allowed to depart from Rome in the custody of an archbishop, and a few months later he reached Florence, where he was to live in seclusion for the remaining eight years of his life, the last five in total blindness.

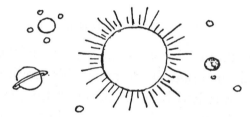

To continue our story, we must turn back to the year 1629, when Galileo had not yet finished writing his book and the Thirty Years' War was about to enter the next period, in which Sweden was to take the lead.

Fernando II was nineteen, his next younger brothers eighteen and seventeen. The Emperor of Germany, Ferdinand II, was their uncle —their mother's brother. The two younger Medici boys were eager to take part in the great war, and their mother eager to see her brother. So they started for Vienna. The mother died on the way, but after her funeral in Florence, the two young Medici princes started out again with money, armies, and two regiments supplied by Tuscany, to serve under their uncle's famous general Wallenstein, and learn the art of war.

379

GUSTAV ADOLF

FROM HIS PALACE in Vienna in the year 1629, the Emperor Ferdinand looked out upon the future of his empire with utter satisfaction. The war had been in progress for ten years and so far victory had been his. He would now cripple the Protestant German princes and put them under his absolute control, by issuing the final Edict:

Every Protestant prince must return all property in his domain which had ever belonged to the Catholic Church.

The power of the Holy Roman Empire thus established, linked with that of Spain, would be incontestable. Of that fact the Emperor was well aware, as was also Cardinal Richelieu, who saw that such a powerful empire would endanger the very existence of France. Gustav Adolf must now be moved onto the chessboard of Europe to block the Emperor. Richelieu secretly opened negotiations with the young Swedish King, promising to furnish money if he would invade Germany.

Gustav Adolf saw Sweden also endangered if the Emperor controlled all German ports and lands along the Baltic Sea. He needed no persuasion. But the Swedish ministers and councillors raised many objections that Gustav Adolf had to answer.

"You say," he replied to the nobles, "that we haven't money to pay for the troops for more than four months. I grant that. But once we are on German land, God and the hour will teach us how to strengthen our position." To Oxenstierna, who pleaded with him not to risk his life in person, he reacted as any knight of old, ready to hazard his life on a cause he held to be worthy.

To his council, who feared that if Sweden entered, the war could not be kept away from the Swedish border, Gustav pointed out that the border of Sweden was already in danger—that to protect it was the reason they must enter the war.

"Denmark is used up," he said. "The Catholic armies are on the Baltic, they will soon plant a foot on the shores of Sweden. The danger is great. It is no time to ask whether the cost will be more than we can bear. The fight will be for parents, for wife and child, for house and home, for Fatherland and Faith." His apparent sincerity convinced all who heard him. The nobles voted heavy taxes for three years, the merchants rose to support the troops. The entire council, even those who most opposed him, rallied behind the young King as he prepared for war.

The Emperor Ferdinand was merely amused when told that young Gustav Adolf was preparing to meet the seasoned troops of his old victorious generals Wallenstein and Tilly. It struck him as ludicrous when his ambassador, returning from Sweden, reported that Gustav Adolf would not talk of peace until all the land in the German states had been put back as it had been before the war. "So we have a new little enemy, have we?" scoffed the Emperor.

Wallenstein was also scornful of the young Swede. "That snow-and-ice king will soon melt if he sets foot in Europe."

Wallenstein was now the most thoroughly hated man in Germany.

All the princes, Catholic as well as Protestant, despised him for the way he had allowed his troops to plunder and lay waste the country. Everywhere German towns lay in ruins. Thousands of German families were homeless. Cardinal Richelieu was aware of this fact, and shrewdly suggested to the Electors that now was the opportune time to demand that Wallenstein be removed. They had been requested by the Emperor to name his son "King of the Romans," a title which practically assured his later election as Emperor. Following Richelieu's coaching, the electors made their demand. The Emperor, caught in this position and convinced that Tilly could finish the war alone, dismissed Wallenstein.

On May 19, 1630, Gustav Adolf assembled the Estates of Sweden for his farewell address. Those who were there were never to forget the solemn occasion, for it seemed to everyone that it was truly a farewell. The King appeared before them holding his three-year-old daughter Kristina in his arms; entrusting her to their protection. He spoke again of his reasons and of his hopes.

"God is my witness," he said, "that I do not fight from any lust for war, but because the Emperor has insulted my ambassadors, oppressed my friends and persecuted my religion . . . The down-trodden States of Germany cry to us for help, and God willing we will give it to them."

The Swedish army which Gustav led was not large, but the soldiers were the best drilled in the world. However, the first victory went to Tilly, who captured the great city of Magdeburg and destroyed it, boasting of having left no one stone upon another, a complete destruction. It was his last boast! On September 17, 1631, at Breitenfeld, Gustav Adolf won a tremendous victory and immediately was hailed as the greatest general in Europe. All Protestant German princes rallied behind their new leader; his army swelled by thousands. By spring he had crossed the Rhine, and all southern Germany was at his mercy. He had driven the Duke of Bavaria from Munich, and the Emperor Ferdinand, who had been thinking so lately of having all Germany under his power, now feared losing even his own land of Austria. He cried aloud for Wallenstein, who replied that he was done with earthly ambition, but was at last persuaded to resume his command—but alone. "Not even if God himself wished to divide it with me," he said, would he endure it.

In November, 1632, the armies of Wallenstein and Gustav met at Lützen almost in sight of the former battleground of Breitenfeld. Because of the gout, Wallenstein was carried on a litter to a point where he could command the movement of his men.

Gustav Adolf appeared before his troops, without armor, as his custom was, riding a white charger, and without having eaten. He prayed, and prayers were read at the head of each regiment. The soldiers sang Luther's hymn, "A Mighty Fortress is our God." Then the king addressed them as his dear countrymen and friends: "There, my friends, you have the enemy before you. Not on a mountain top. Not behind entrenchments, but on the open plain. He cannot escape us. Fight then, my countrymen, for your country, your King and your God!" Waving his sword over his head he rode onto the foggy field. About eleven o'clock the sun and winds lifted the mist. From then on, the battle raged for nine hours. Darkness had set in by the time victory was finally won by the soldiers of Sweden. And without their king. Gustav Adolf was dead. As he had plunged recklessly ahead on the charge that was to turn the tide of battle, he was shot and fell to the ground. His white charger, streaming with blood, went plunging riderless and wild among the lines.

The news of the King's death did not reach Stockholm until a month after he was gone. A letter from Axel Oxenstierna, telling how the King's "unwonted impetuosity" had caused his death, brought forth a "cry of woe" from young and old, rich and poor, priests and laymen, nobles and peasants, who believed, as Oxenstierna said:

"In all the world there is not his equal, nor has there been for centuries, and I doubt whether the future will produce his peer. This is acknowledged not by us alone but by all nations whether friend or foe. Truly we call him Gustav the wise and great."

And some one perhaps might imagine the young warrior's spirit, crossing the bridge of Valhalla to join the souls of his ancient ancestors.

PLANS FOR MASSACHUSETTS

O N THE AFTERNOON of March 2, 1629, St. Stephen's Chapel in Westminster was the scene of a stormy session in the House of Commons. As the members were filing in to be seated on the long rows of benches lining the walls, they could be heard mumbling about illegal taxes, forced loans, and other forms of injustice not to be endured. Charles I had completely disregarded the Petition of Right which he had signed the year before. It was an outrage. The air was charged with excitement as the Speaker took his seat, glanced down at the clerks before him ready with their quills and paper. Then, casting a suspicious glance in the direction of Sir John Eliot, leader of the Puritans, he cleared his throat and called the meeting to order. One excited member after another denounced the tyranny of the King. Then Sir John Eliot rose with a paper in his hand. As soon as all eyes were upon him, he proceeded to read a resolution which expressed their ideas.

"Let it be agreed that whoever shall levy or pay taxes not voted by Parliament—whoever attempts to make any changes in religion is an enemy to the Kingdom."

Sir John then asked that his resolution be put to a vote, but the

Speaker of the House had previous royal orders. He announced the meeting adjourned. The King's friends started to leave. The other members sat tight, refusing to move until the vote had been taken. As the Speaker rose from his chair, several Puritans sprang forward, pushed him back in his seat, and held him there until the "remonstrance" as they called it, was voted upon and passed.

Next day Sir John Eliot and nine other leaders were seized by order of the King and imprisoned in the Tower. All Puritans were in a fearful state of anxiety, and many were desperately sure that there was no longer any place for them in England. Some spoke of leaving for Salem to join the colony under Captain Endecott.

Sir Richard Saltonstall and a group of associates calling themselves the Massachusetts Bay Company had planned to form another colony. On March 4, 1629, exactly two days after the stormy session in the House of Commons, a Royal Charter was signed by King Charles, giving them the right to found their colony on Massachusetts Bay.

John Winthrop was in Groton at this time, but very shortly, back in London, he heard the shocking news of what had happened to the Puritan leaders in Parliament. The situation grew continually worse. Sir Thomas Wentworth, once a defender of the people's rights, had gone over completely to the King and proposed to stop at nothing until Parliament was crushed and the power of the King was absolute. Bishop Laud of London declared that the voice of Parliament was "a noise that he hoped would never again be heard in the land," and set out to make the King's word absolute in religion as well as politics. Thoroughly disheartened, John Winthrop, having either lost or given up his job with the court, returned to Groton to talk to Margaret about the uncertain future.

Every day he heard of more people planning to leave England. And why not he? Was it not utter folly to sit still and wait for God in his wrath to destroy this sinful nation?

Yet, in going, would he not be deserting his fellow men, acting like a Separatist? God grant that that should never be said of him!

Surely, though, it would be far better for his young children to be away from this wicked land, and his older sons, too. The arguments pro and con became so distracting that he finally listed them in separate columns and weighed them carefully. At last, after much deliberation, he accepted an invitation of Sir Richard Saltonstall and other members of the Massachusetts Bay Company to attend a meeting at Tattersall Castle in Lincolnshire. Plans for the proposed colony were to be discussed. He found them most promising, surprisingly so because of a happy accident—an omission in the charter. Like Jamestown, Massachusetts was to be governed by members of a council. But there was no mention made of *where* the meetings of the council were to be held. It had been assumed, no doubt, that the meeting place would be London, but it had not been stated. And what a wonderful opening that oversight gave the members of the company!

The Council for the Massachusetts Bay Colony, they declared, should live and hold their meetings in the colony itself! There in Massachusetts, far from London and any interference by the King, they would be able to set up a self-governing Commonwealth, made up of the best and most carefully chosen people, like themselves. Such a possibility of perfection was irresistible to John Winthrop. And as he later told Margaret, when some of the chief leaders assured him that the welfare of the plantation depended upon his going, it would have been impossible for him not to join in this wonderful undertaking.

So on August 26, 1629, John Winthrop of Groton Manor signed an agreement with eleven other Puritans meeting at Cambridge, to be ready by the following March to embark for Massachusetts.

JOHN SMITH IS NOT INVITED

CAPTAIN JOHN SMITH was filled with disappointment again. The Massachusetts Bay Company had refused his services.

One August morning in that year 1629, he was walking through St. Paul's Churchyard on his way from the printers. He felt uncertain whether or not to call again upon Sir Richard Saltonstall or one of the other London merchants who were members of the company.

"Much conference have I had with many of them," he said to himself. Yet he had been unable to convince them that they needed anything more of him than his Map and Description of New England.

In March, when he first heard that the Charter had been granted, he had at least been busy. Now he was at loose ends. The final chapters of his book, *True Travels,* had been finished, and the manuscript delivered to the printers. So as he walked slowly across the courtyard, his thoughts were particularly concerned with New England and these men who were going to establish a colony there. All were men of wealth and property, well educated but inexperienced in such an undertaking. He could give them much help if they would let him.

He knew even more of the company members from Lincolnshire than of those in London. One of his old acquaintances was Thomas Dudley, who had been at Tattersall Castle as steward to the Earl of Lincoln for many years. Lady Arbella, daughter of His Lordship, was also going to Massachusetts with her wealthy but untitled husband, Isaac Johnson.

Hearing of the meeting to be held in Tattersall Castle, a rush of memories must have carried John Smith back thirty years to the days when he had been taking fencing lessons in the tiltyard, listening to tall tales of valor in the guardroom and looking forward to great adventures of his own. Those adventures were now behind him, all recorded in the books which he had written. He was fifty years old. Still he felt himself quite vigorous enough to take an active part in the Massachusetts adventure.

The Puritans were to sail without him as the Pilgrims had done. The next year would find John Smith living at Essex as house guest of a young nobleman and his charming family on their country estate called Danbury Place. Soon he was writing another book, a small one filled with advice regarding the forming and governing of a colony in the new world. He called it *Advertisements for Unexperienced Planters of New England or Anywhere.*

One thing he recommended was that every settler should own his own land. Common ownership of land had not succeeded well in Virginia. He also recommended that all men should be allowed "as much freedom as may be, and to temper correction with mercy."

He wrote a few sentences and then sat gazing out of the window at the tall, waving trees that reminded him of Virginia. After all, this, too, was a pleasant place to be living, here in Essex. It was in the country and yet not too far from London, about thirty miles. On clear days one could see the city in the distance, beyond many shining curves of the Thames . . .

GOVERNOR WINTHROP

THE LAST MONTHS preceding his departure for the New World were busy ones for John Winthrop. Not only was he preparing to sell and leave Groton Manor, but at a meeting in October he was elected by the Massachusetts Bay Company to be Governor of the new colony.

That meant that he had to see to procuring ships for the voyage and enlisting passengers. By spring he had eleven vessels and seven hundred persons ready to depart, horses, cattle, and all things necessary for a thriving settlement. They were to depart—but not to separate. They were not Separatists, they insisted, like those people of Plymouth. They were leaving England, but not separating, either from England or the Church of England!

As the parting drew near it was difficult for John Winthrop to say goodbye to his dear Margaret, who was not to leave until after the new baby had been born. Henry's wife was also waiting for the birth of a child, though Henry was to go. Forth was about to be married, so he and his bride would also come later. John, Jr., was finishing up all the family business and would keep sending supplies to the colony for the first year. Mary, little Dean, and two-year-old Samuel were to stay and come later with their mother. Stephen and Adam were thrilled to be going with their father on the *Arbella*. That, he had told them, was the name of their ship. On the last day John Winthrop and Margaret made a pact to meet each other in thought every Monday and Friday between five and six o'clock. Then he kissed her tenderly again and again, bidding her goodbye.

"Raise up thy thoughts," he said to her at last, "and be merry in the Lord."

Determined to do the same, John Winthrop then left Groton Manor, where he had lived all of his forty-one years, and set out to make a new home for himself and his family in the New World.

On Easter Monday, March 29, the ships sailed from Southampton. The Reverend John Cotton, a brilliant young Puritan minister from Boston in Lincolnshire, came to the harbor to bid goodbye to those who were leaving and pray that God would bless their undertaking. John Winthrop also prayed that he might be worthy of the trust placed in him, and as leader of the colony do nothing to merit the wrath of the Lord and bring his punishment upon them.

About ten o'clock in the morning, the first four of the eleven ships weighed anchor and set sail—the *Arbella*, the *Talbot*, the *Ambrose* and the *Jewel*. That night, on board the *Arbella* about ten miles from Southampton, John Winthrop open a new notebook, and made the first entry in a journal he was to keep faithfully from then to the day of his death nineteen years later. The first days at sea were fairly uneventful, but Friday was filled with alarm and wild activity. Early in the morning the sailor on the top mast reported that they were being followed by eight ships.

"Supposing they might be Spaniards," wrote Winthrop, "our captain caused the gunroom and gun deck to be cleared, all the hammocks were taken down, our ordnance loaded and our powder-chests and fireworks made ready, and our landmen quartered among the seamen, and twenty-five of them appointed for muskets. Out of every ship were thrown such bed matters as were subject to take fire. The Lady Arbella and the other women and children were removed into the lower deck.

It was much to see how cheerful all the company appeared; not a woman or child that showed fear, though all did apprehend the danger. About one o'clock the fleet seemed to be within a league of us; therefore our captain, because he would show he was not afraid of them, tacked about and stood to meet them, and when they came near we perceived them to be our friends—English and French ships bound for Canada and Newfoundland . . . and so (God be praised) our fear and danger was turned into mirth and merriment."

That was the most exciting day of the long, monotonous voyage. April and May passed, with little to mark the days except changes in the wind and weather. They were headed for Salem, and by the end of May the anticipation of seeing what must now be a flourishing settlement increased, and speculation as to how soon they might be in sight of land. On June 6, John Winthrop wrote that the captain, thinking that they might be nearing Cape Cod, had soundings taken and found ground at eighty fathoms.

On Tuesday, June 8, he says, "there came a smell off shore like the smell of a garden. There came a wild pigeon into our ship and another small land bird." That was truly encouraging.

On Friday, June 11, they were in sight of Cape Ann all day. And then on Saturday they were in Salem. "About four in the morning we were near our port," John Winthrop wrote in his journal. "We shot off two pieces of ordnance and sent our skiff . . . to fetch Mr. Endecott, who came to us about two of the clock. We . . . the assistants, and some other gentlemen, and some of the women and our captain returned with him to Salem, where we supped with good venison pasty and good beer, and at night returned to our ship. In the meantime, most of our people went on shore upon the land of Cape Ann, and gathered a store of fine strawberries."

Though he does not say so, Salem was a bitter disappointment. Nothing but a straggling collection of huts where they had expected to find a flourishing settlement. Only a few acres cleared, instead of rich fields of the Indian corn they had heard so much about.

Many were so heartsick they were ready to turn about and go back home on the next ship. Many did. But no such weak thought entered the mind of Governor John Winthrop.

"I am not discouraged," he wrote Margaret, "nor do I see cause to regret or despair."

This was a wonderful country. There was no reason why they should not find a suitable location on Massachusetts Bay and build up a substantial community.

The place Governor Winthrop and his council decided upon after exploring the coast line appeared to them to be an excellent location. It commanded an entrance to the bay and was easily defended from attack by land. It was called Charles-town. The Governor was filled with enthusiasm. He promptly engaged the captain of a ship, the *Lyon,* then anchored in Salem harbor, to return to England and bring back supplies to be furnished by John, Jr.

Next he began to gather in corn for the winter from the Indians and was most pleased and impressed with their grave dignity, inviting one sachem who came dressed in European clothes to sit at the dinner table, where, as he wrote in his diary, the chief "behaved himself as soberly as an Englishman"—which, had the Indian known it, was the highest of praise.

One large, deserted frame house had been found on the site of Charlestown that was usable. Carpenters and servants were set to work at once felling trees, sawing boards and building new houses. Everything seemed to John Winthrop to be going well, and he thanked God for his blessing, when suddenly a mysterious and fatal illness struck the community. It spread so rapidly that soon many people were dying every day. What possible sin had he committed, John Winthrop asked himself, to merit this punishment? He searched his soul for the reason. Unable to find an answer, he appealed to Captain Endecott at Salem, in a letter describing their miserable plight at Charlestown and asking what in his opinion could be done to pacify the wrath of the Lord.

PILGRIMS AND PURITANS

Two visitors from Plymouth happened to be in Salem with Captain Endecott when he received Governor Winthrop's letter appealing for help and advice—Dr. Samuel Fuller and Edward Winslow. After talking over the problem of the Charlestown people they concluded that "the sixth day of that week should be set apart to humble themselves before God, beseeching the Lord to withdraw his hand of correction from them and also direct them in his ways." Edward Winslow wrote this in a letter to Governor Bradford, adding that "they do earnestly entreat that the church at Plimoth should set apparte the same day for the same ends."

Dr. Samuel Fuller also wrote to Governor Bradford, from Charlestown, where the good doctor had gone at once to help care for the sick in the badly stricken community. He wrote that there were many at Charlestown eager to see the people of Plymouth, "some out of love; others to see whether we be so evil as they have heard. We have the name of love and holiness. The Lord make us answerable that it be more than a name or else it will do us no good." Dr. Fuller stayed on until he felt he could do no more, having used up all of his drugs and materials.

Fortunately, Governor Winthrop managed to escape the illness and, despite all the misery and anxiety, kept up his courage and went ahead with the necessary business of organizing the colony. He and several others had already formed a church before Dr. Fuller left. Since they, the members of the Congregation, formed it and chose their own minister, it was naturally a Congregational Church, like that of the people at Plymouth.

On Monday, August 23, Governor Winthrop summoned his assistants and held his first council meeting. One important thing they did was to set the wages of workmen, so that all would be equally and fairly paid. Carpenters, joiners, bricklayers, sawyers, and thatchers were to get two shillings a day, which was considerably more than they had been getting in England.

By that time, however, few were well enough to do a day's work. So many had died, so many continued to become ill, that the council was convinced the location of Charlestown must have been a poor choice. Possibly the water was not pure. They decided to move.

The new location they chose was near the mouth of the Charles River, where they found a spring of excellent water. Three small mountains or large hills rose from the shore of the bay. There they built a dock and started a new town, which they named Boston, after the home town in Lincolnshire. Now Governor Winthrop was truly optimistic. "I have never had more content of mind," he wrote Margaret.

As soon as possible, on an early day in October, the Governor called a general meeting of the colonists, which was the first New England Town Meeting ever to be held in Boston. All members of the Congregation were invited to attend, that is, all the so-called "freemen." There were 116 present in the meeting house. The following plans for governing the colony were read aloud and assented to "by general vote of the people and the erection of hands."

1. The freemen should have the power to elect the Assistants.
2. The Assistants should have the power to elect the Governor.
3. The Assistants should make the laws and choose officers to enforce them.

So the Commonwealth of Massachusetts was formed by and of the same congregation that formed the church, but not *all* of the congregation. Only freemen—no servants. To allow everyone to vote, ignorant people who could not even read or write, would have seemed utter folly to Governor John Winthrop.

"God Almighty in his most holy wisdom," he said, "hath so disposed of mankind, that some must be rich, some poor, some high in power and dignity, others in subjection." Those in power, however, he believed carried responsibility. The best and smaller part of the community must care for the larger, more ignorant part. They also had the responsibility of preventing any one member from committing a sin against God that would endanger the whole. Therefore it was decided that the Governing Council of the Commonwealth must and did have the right and power to:

1. Punish every sin committed in Massachusetts.
2. Force everyone to attend church on the Sabbath.
3. Teach children to read so that they might read the Bible, especially the Ten Commandments.
4. Investigate the morals of every person before allowing him to join the congregation.

Now came November. Winter set in, a severe New England winter, unlike anything ever known in England. Over one hundred people died. Many others were just hanging on to life until the ship came and they could leave this miserable frozen wilderness. But not Governor Winthrop. He liked it so well here that all he wanted now, he declared, was to have the rest of his family with him. The Reverend Willson, the

395

minister, also liked it, and was going home to England to bring back his wife as soon as the ship came in.

Early in February, the good ship *Lyon* sailed into Boston harbor, bringing two hundred tons of supplies which John, Jr., had purchased, and about twenty new settlers. Among them was a charming young minister, with his wife and two small children, who introduced himself as Roger Williams. He was a graduate of Cambridge.

The arrival of the young minister just as their own was leaving seemed most timely to the council. They felt that if on further examination the young man proved to be as godly as he was charming they might well have him officiate in the church during the Reverend Willson's absence. In due time, they issued the invitation. To their amazement, Mr. Roger Williams flatly refused.

"I durst not officiate to an unseparated people," he announced, "as upon examination and conference I find you to be."

But their church, Governor Winthrop pointed out to him, was a Congregational Church, like that of the people of Plymouth, who had been Separatists in England.

They had indeed, agreed Roger Williams. But not the Boston people. They had not been Separatists. They had belonged to the Established Church, which admitted all manner of sinners into its membership along with the good. Unless the members of the Boston congregation would make public declaration of their repentance for having had communion with the Church of England while there, he could not accept the ministry. His conscience would not permit it.

There was another point also on which Mr. Roger Williams expressed disapproval of the Massachusetts Commonwealth. No government, he said, should be given the power to punish a man for sin. Nor should any government have the right to force a man to attend church on the Sabbath, or dictate to him on any religious matter. That was up to a man's own conscience.

The young man was very positive, and his views were in sharp contrast to the discipline Governor Winthrop felt necessary to keep a community in proper order. Therefore, when Roger Williams, disillusioned with Boston, departed and went on to Salem, the Governor sent what was practically an order to Captain Endecott not to accept the radical young thinker as their minister. So he went on to Plymouth.

The Plymouth colony was friendly. Elder Brewster, Governor Bradford, and the others welcomed Roger Williams and made a place for him as assistant to the minister. The Plymouth colony, he saw at once, was very different from the Puritan community at Boston. The people who had come to Plymouth had been accustomed to a plainer, simpler way of life. They had been poor when they came ten years ago, and they were still lacking in worldly goods, and the congregation was still small. The amount they were able to drop into the collection box each Sabbath in the meeting house was very meager, a mere pittance compared to that collected by the Boston congregation. Out of that the minister had to be paid, which left very little for the assistant. Roger Williams spent his first summer in the new world hoeing corn and fishing in the town brook to eke out a living.

That summer of 1631 saw Boston thriving and growing. There was now a beacon light on the middle hill to be seen from the harbor. More ships were sailing in every month, bringing God-fearing people able to pass the moral test required to join the church and vote in the Commonwealth. Plantations had spread all around the bay and up the rivers.

Governor Winthrop had chosen six hundred acres of land on the Mystic River, where he could once again live comfortably as lord of a manor. His servants were clearing out stumps and stones, cultivating the cleared fields, using the stones for fences and also building a roomy stone house to be ready for Margaret. He was eager to have her see it. At last, one day in November, Margaret was there!

The *Lyon* came sailing into Boston Harbor and anchored off the long center island. A small boat was let down, and in it John, Jr., was rowed ashore. The Governor took the boat back to the ship and soon had Margaret, God bless her, in his arms, had kissed Mary, and lifted up Samuel to see how heavy he was. And Dean, where was Dean, he asked. Left home to finish his school year, they told him. And the baby, Anne, whom he had never seen? Died at sea, he learned, a week after they had sailed. But here were John Eliot, a minister and his wife, and sixty other new persons all in good health, waiting to meet him. Meanwhile on shore the word had spread among the plantations, and people were making preparations to greet the Governor's Lady.

Early next day, Governor Winthrop and his family went ashore with the captain in the small ship's boat. Guns were fired from the ship as they left, and volleys of shot were fired by the companies of soldiers lined up on Dock Square where they landed. What a welcome it was! Most of the people from the plantations around the bay were there. For several days they brought or sent great store of provisions: "fat hogs, kids, venison, poultry, geese, partridges etc., so as the like joy and manifestation of love had never been seen in New England. It was a marvel, at so few hour's notice!"

That is what the Governor wrote in his journal. He also recorded that on November 11, "We kept a day of thanksgiving at Boston," and that on November 17, "The Governor of Plymouth came to Boston and lodged in the ship." And so they met, exactly ten years after the first Thanksgiving in Plymouth—these two capable early Governors of Massachusetts.

The Plymouth leader appeared to Governor Winthrop to be a "very discreet and grave man."

Governor Bradford was pleased and amazed to see what a great and prosperous community the honorable gentleman from Groton and his assistants had established here on Massachusetts Bay. Here, ten years ago, they who had come on the *Mayflower* had seen only wilderness. How wonderful it was, he thought, for Plymouth to have had even a small part in this great undertaking.

"Thus," he wrote in his *History,* "out of small beginnings greater things have been produced by His hand that made all things out of nothing and gives being to all things that are. Let the glorious name of Jehovah have all the praise."

THE BELL TOLLS

AND SO in the New World, by 1631, two English colonies had firmly taken root: Virginia and Massachusetts, the two oldest of the original thirteen colonies that were later to form the United States of America.

And Captain John Smith had helped to give them a foothold in the wilderness. It was the part of his life he liked best to remember.

Twenty-four years had now passed since the *Sarah Constant,* the *Goodspeed,* and the *Discovery* had anchored on the James River in the spring of 1607. There John Smith had helped to build the three-cornered fort, and later as Governor of Jamestown he had kept the feeble Virginia settlement alive.

He had been Admiral of New England in 1616, having made the

map which the Pilgrims used four years later in founding the colony at Plymouth.

The Puritans meeting at Tattersall Castle had read his *History of New England* and while choosing the location on Massachusetts Bay and the Charles River, names which he had placed upon the map.

It is little wonder that as long as he lived, although allowed no further part in their development, the brave little Captain should have always thought of the colonies in America as his children.

In the summer of 1631 John Smith's life, which began in 1580, was drawing to a close. Although he came to the end of it poor in money, he was rich in friends. He spent his last days in the home of Sir Samuel Saltonstall in Newgate, just outside the city wall on the west of London, where he would hear the bells of St. Sepulchre's Church, the "bells of old Bailey."

An essay written by Sir Samuel's son described their guest as a "Captain who is the Atlas of the Commonwealth, who knows that virtue consists in action and that the way to honor lies through piles of danger. Fortune may overthrow him but never conquer him, for in the midst of adversity his manly patience gives him the victory. He needs no tomb for his fame is a living monument."

As the bells of St. Sepulchre's were tolling, John Smith's helmet and armour were hung on the south side of the choir where his body was laid. On the wall above him a tablet was placed bearing these words:

> Here lies one conquer'd that hath conquered Kings
> Subdu'd large territories and done things
> Which to the World impossible would seeme,
> But that the truth is held in more esteeme.

And so as the bells stop their ringing and the heart always set on brave adventure is still, we have come to the end of our story. The long, marvelous, never-ending history of the world continues, but it is no longer the World of Captain John Smith.

INDEX OF PEOPLE

Adams, Will, English pilot: visits Japan, 102–106; grave of, 357

Akbar, Emperor of India: the man, 95; letter from Queen Elizabeth, 96; son Salim born, 97; studies religions, 98–99; death, 100

Alden, John, sails on Mayflower, 303–308; signs Mayflower Compact, 308

Alden, Priscilla, wife of John: on board Mayflower as Priscilla Mullins, 306

Alva, Duke of, Spanish general: in France, 17; in Holland, 19, 20

Anne, Princess of Denmark: marries James VI of Scotland, 117–118; becomes Queen of England, 151–153; in Christmas masque, 155; and Ben Jonson, 158; pleads for Raleigh's life, 161; daughter's wedding; 260–262

Argall, Samuel, English captain: burns French and Dutch settlements, 257; tricks Pocahontas, 258; takes her to England, 278; in slave trade, 290; governor of Virginia, 290

Bacon, Sir Francis, English lawyer: writes on education, etc., 162–165; member of Privy Council, 282; advises against Raleigh, 285; letter from John Smith, 298

Barneveldt, Johan van Olden, statesman of Holland: under Maurice, 327; beheaded, 328

Block, Adrian, Dutch fur trader: establishes trading post on Manhattan Island and explores coast, 368

Bothwell, husband of Mary Stuart, 25

Bradford, William, governor of Plymouth: as a boy, joins Separatists, 173–176; goes to Holland, 235–236; in Leyden, 240; married, 242; leaves Holland as Pilgrim, 293–296; on Mayflower, 306–308; his copy of Compact, 308; at Plymouth, 310; elected governor, 315; replies to Indian threat, 322; at Squanto's death, 323; helps Salem colony,

366; entertains Dutch from Manhattan, 370; visits Boston, 398

Brahe, Tycho, Danish astronomer, 116–119

Brewster, William, Pilgrim leader: young man goes to Holland, 42; leaves London for Scrooby village, 48; postmaster and Separatist, 173; goes to Holland to live, 235; leaves Holland, 293–296; on Mayflower, 306–308

Buckingham, Earl of, favorite of James I, 279; painted by Rubens, 331; in Paris, seeking bride for Charles I, 332–333; denounced by Parliament, 339; attacks French at La Rochelle, 340; murdered, 342

Burbage, Richard, actor: friend of Shakespeare, 75, 76; collects his work, 275

Burghley, Lord, English Secretary of Treasury: opinions, 7, 10; meets Raleigh, 33; and Mary Stuart, 43

Carver, John, Pilgrim: leaves Holland, 294–296; governor elect of Plymouth, 308; confers with Massasoit, 313–314; death, 315

Cecil, Lord, son of Lord Burghley: Prime Minister to James, 159; against Raleigh, 160–161; discovers Gunpowder Plot, 172

Cervantes, Miguel, Spanish author: *Don Quixote,* 43

Champlain, Samuel de, French founder of Canada: reports on Mexico, 177–181; visits Canada, 187–191; with Henry IV, 191; helps make first French settlement, 196–198; on Lake Champlain, 223–228; founds Quebec, 224; takes missionaries to Canada, 254–257; surrenders Quebec, 343–345; sees Richelieu, 346; death, 346

Charles I, son of James I, 152; ten years old, 249; heir to throne, 260; names places in New England, 273; marriage to Henrietta Maria, 333; King, 338; trouble with Parliament, 338–342; loss of Buckingham, 342;

returns Canada for Queen's dowry, 346; receives Rubens, 374; treaty with Philip IV, 374

Charles V, German emperor, 13–14; and William of Orange, 18; and slave trade, 291

Christian IV, young prince of Denmark, 117; and Tycho Brahe, 119; war against Sweden, 264–265; in Thirty Years' War, 360–362

Clavius, Monk; makes new calendar, 115

Coke, Sir Edward, English jurist: condemns Raleigh, 160–162; defends law against the King, 282

Dale, Thomas, governor of Virginia, 259

Dare, Virginia, first white child born in Virginia, 54

Darnley, Lord, father of James I, 24, 25

Davison, William, council member under Queen Elizabeth, 42, 43; and Mary Stuart, 47–48

Dimitri, Ivanovitch, son of Ivan the Terrible, 146–147

Donne, John, poet, 262

Drake, Sir Francis, homecoming, 5–7; hero, 10; knighted, 11; rescues Roanoke settlers, 37; and Armada, 56; death of, 291–292

Eliot, Sir John, Puritan leader: in House of Commons, 384

Elizabeth I, Queen of England: hears of Drake, 8–11; and French prince, 21–22; and Mary of Scots, 23–25; and Raleigh, 32; Virginia named for, 35; and Holland, 41–43; and Armada, 56–60; *Faerie Queen*, 69–70; letter to Henry IV, 79; writes Akbar, 96; death, 150

Elizabeth, Princess: daughter of James I, 151; sees *A Midsummer Night's Dream*, 155; marriage, 260–262; descendants, 262; refugee to Netherlands, 316–318

Endecott, John, Captain: founds Salem, Massachusetts, 365; help from Plymouth, 366; letter from Governor Winthrop, 393

Essex, Lord, favorite of Queen Elizabeth, 56; helps Henry of Navarre, 78

Fawkes, Guy, plots to blow up Parliament, 170

Feodor, Tsar of Russia, son of Ivan the Terrible: death, 147

Ferdinand II, German emperor, 316; continues Thirty Years' War, 361–362; his nephews, 379; war against Gustav Adolf, 380–382

Francis, French prince: and Queen Elizabeth, 21–22; dead, 41

Frobisher, Martin, 33

Frederick, Count Palatine: letter from Gustav Adolf, 123; marriage, 260; driven out of Germany, 316; King of Bohemia, 318; Holland, 319

Frederick Henry, Prince of Orange: allied with England and Denmark, 360

Fuller, Samuel, doctor on Mayflower, 307; helps Salem colony, 366; helps Massachusetts colony, 393–394

Galilei, Galileo, astronomer and physicist: professor in Padua, 126; early life, 128–130; perfects telescope, 243–246; mathematician to Cosimo II, 246; in Rome with churchmen, 250–253; summoned to Rome again, 376–379

Galilei, Vincenzo, musician, father of Galileo: pioneer in opera, 135

Georges, Fernando, mayor of Plymouth, 270–271; welcomes Pocahontas, 279; sends Squanto back to America, 292

Gilbert, Humphrey, explorer, 33, 34

Godunov, Boris, Tsar of Russia, 144–149

Granganimeo, Indian chief, 35

Greco, El, painter in Spain, 82–84

Gregory XIII, Pope, established new calendar, 115

Grenville, Sir Richard, admiral: to Virginia, 36–37

Grotius, Hugo, jurist: in Holland, 325; writes on international law, 329; writes on Christianity, 329

Guise, Henry, Duke of, cousin of Mary of Scots, 25; head of French Catholic party, 28–31; war of the Three Henrys, 61; death of, 63

Gustav Adolf, prince of Sweden, 120–123; favored by James I, 260; King of Sweden, 263; war with Christian IV, 265; marriage, 319; in Thirty Years' War, 380; death, 383

Hapsburg family, 317

Harvey, William, physician in school, 130; circulation of the blood, 301

Hawkins, John, sea captain: against Armada, 56; in slave trade, 291; death, 291–292

Henrietta Maria, French royal princess: baby, 249; marries Charles I, 333; questions Charles I, 339; her dowry and Canada, 343–346

Henry II, King of France, and William of Orange, 17

Henry III, King of France, 27–31; war of Three Henrys, 61; death, 64

Henry IV, King of France: as King of Navarre, 28–31; war of three Henrys, 61–64; battles for throne, 77; crowned, 80; Edict of Nantes, 81; marries Maria d'Medici, 131–133; receives Champlain, 177; death, 247–249

Henry VIII, King of England, declared head of Church of England, 29

Hobomok, Indian friend of Pilgrims, 314–315

Howard, Lord, admiral, 56

Hsi Tsung, last Ming emperor of China, 354

Hudson, Henry, explorer: engaged by Dutch, 219; on Hudson River, 220–222; death, 228

Irmak, Russian explorer: and Siberia, 348

Isabella, daughter of Philip II, 15; Archduchess in Antwerp, 330; sends Rubens to Spain, 373

Ivan IV, the Terrible, Tsar of Russia: letter to Queen Elizabeth, 33; opinions of, 145

Iyemitsu, Shogun of Japan: persecutes Christians, drives out foreigners, 358
Iyeyasu, Tokugawa Shogun, 104–106

James I, King of England: born, 25; King of Scotland (James VI), 49–51; writes Queen Elizabeth, 51; visits Tycho Brahe, 117; marries Anne of Denmark, 117–118; King of England, 151–153; has Bible re-translated, 166–169; sees Guy Fawkes, 172; writes about tobacco, 234; daughter's wedding, 260–262; publishes works, 274; and Buckingham, 279; and Parliament, 281; defied by Coke, 282; proclamation on Virginia, 286; death, 338
James V, King of Scotland, father of Mary, 24
James VI, King of Scotland, see James I
Jehan, Shah, grandson of Akbar, 353; builds Taj Mahal, 353
Jonson, Ben, poet, playwright, 156–158; publishes works—his poem, 274; tribute to Shakespeare, 276; old man, 374

Kepler, Johann, scientist: meets Tycho Brahe, 119; letter from Galileo, 127; letter to and from Galileo, 246
Knox, John, Scottish preacher: at coronation of James VI, 50

Lane, Ralph, governor of Roanoke, 36–38
Leicester, Robert, Earl of, favorite of Queen Elizabeth, 8–11; and French prince, 22; to Holland, 42–43
Louis XIII, King of France, son of Henry IV, 133; made King, 247; marries, 249; and Hugo Grotius, 328; and Cardinal Richelieu, 333; assumes power, 336–337
Luther, Martin, reformer: on trial, 13

Manteo, American Indian: to England, 35; and Governor White, 53; made Lord Roanoke, 54
Marlowe, Christopher, poet, 72
Mary, Queen of Scots: prisoner, 23–25; fate in question, 43; condemned and beheaded, 44–48
Massasoit, Indian chief: friend of Pilgrims, 313–315; reveals plot of Indians, 324
Matabei, Japanese painter, 359
Maurice, Prince of Orange: Stadtholder of Holland, 317–326; and Hugo Grotius, 326–327
Medici, Catherine d', Queen Mother of France, 27–31; War of Three Henrys, 62, 63
Medici, Cosimo II d', son of Fernando, 130; pupil of Galileo, 245; sees telescope, 244; Grand Duke, 245; employs Galileo, 251; death, 377
Medici, Fernando I d', Grand Duke of Florence, 129
Medici, Fernando II d', son of Cosimo II, 377–379
Medici, Maria d', Queen of France: weds Henry IV, 131–133; letter to Galileo, 245; dismisses States General, 249; painted by Rubens, 330

Minuit, Peter, Dutch official: purchases Manhattan Island, 368; his secretary, 370
Moronobu, first print maker of Japan, 359
Monteverde, Claudio, composer: writes opera, 135

Newport, Christopher, captain of Virginia fleet, 195; at Jamestown, 206–208; with Powhatan, 215–216; crowns Powhatan, 229–230

Oñate, Juan, founder of New Mexico, 182–186
Opekankano, Indian chief, brother of Powhatan, 210–211; swears friendship to English, 286; and massacre, 321
Oxenstierna, Axel, chamberlain to Sweden's king, 123; letter on Gustav Adolf, 383

Parma, Duke of Spain, general, 57–60
Philip II, King of Spain, 8–9; at Escorial, 12–15; and Holland, 17–20; death of William of Orange, 41; builds Armada, 55–60; and El Greco, 82; death, 84
Philip III, son of Philip II, 15, 84; letter about Raleigh, 285; and Rubens, 330
Philip IV, succeeds Philip III as king, 332; visited by Charles I, 333; painted by Velásquez, 372; treaty with Charles I, 374
Pocahontas, daughter of Powhatan, 204–205; saves John Smith's life, 213; tricked by Argall, 258; marries John Rolfe, 259; visits England, 278; death, 280
Powhatan, Indian chief, 203–205; meets John Smith, 212–216; crowned by Newport, 229; and Argall, 258; questions about England, 279; death, 286

Raleigh, Sir Walter, courtier: with French prince, 22; promotes Virginia, 32–36; smokes tobacco, 38; sends another colony, 52; and poet Spenser, 69–70; seeks El Dorado, 88–90; imprisoned by James I, 161; in Tower, 192; visited by Queen Anne, 194; trip to El Dorado, 283; beheaded, 285
Rasiers, Isaak de, secretary to Peter Minuit: writes Bradford and visits Plymouth, 369–371
Richelieu, Cardinal, French statesman: empowered by Louis XIII, 333; early life, 334–337; besieges Huguenots at La Rochelle, 339–348; plans for Canada, 345; meets Champlain, 346; comments on Christian IV and Gustav Adolf, 362
Ricci, Matteo, Jesuit missionary: in China, 107–115
Robinson, John, Pilgrim pastor in Holland, 239–242; bids Pilgrims farewell, 296; letter to Plymouth, 322
Rolfe, John, colonist: shipwrecked in Bermuda, 233; in Jamestown, 234; marries Pocahontas, 259; visits England, 278
Romanov, Michael, Tsar of Russia, 265–268; marries, 320; and exploration of Asia, 347–353
Rubens, Peter Paul, painter: in Antwerp, 330;

in Paris, 331; in Spain, 373; in England, 374

Rudolf, German Emperor: welcomes Tycho Brahe, 119

Saltonstall, Sir Richard, Puritan colonist: helps form Massachusetts Bay Company, 385
Saltonstall, Samuel, writes about John Smith, 400
Samoset, Indian: visits Pilgrims, 312, 313
Shakespeare, William, playwright: young poet, 71–73; early life, 74–76; Globe theatre, 153–155; plays for James I, 155; and Ben Jonson, 156; death, 274; tribute by Ben Jonson, 276; title page portrait and quotations, 277
Shen Tsung, Emperor of China: receives Matteo Ricci, 107–112
Sidonia, Medina, Spanish nobleman: commands Armada, 57–60
Smith, John, English colonist in America: birth, parents, *viii–x;* walks, 11; six years old, 39; in Italy, 124–125; fights Turks, 136–139; slave in Constantinople, 140–142; home to England, 192; off to Virginia, 195; at Jamestown, 206–209; captured by Indians, 210; saved by Pocahontas, 213; explores Chesapeake Bay, draws map of Virginia, 217–218; President of Jamestown, 229; to New England, 269–271; captured by pirates, 272; with Charles I, 273; map of New England published, 274; visited by Pocahontas, 280; interviews Pilgrim leaders, and fishmongers, 296–298; writes Francis Bacon, 298; Virginia Company refuses services, 321; appeals to Massachusetts Company, 387; writing history, 388; death, 399
Spenser, Edmund, poet: his *Faerie Queen,* 69; and Raleigh, 69–70
Squanto, India n of New England, 270; taken into slavery, 272; sent back to America by Fernando Georges, 292; at home with the Pilgrims, 313; death, 323
Sigismund II, king of Poland, 121; and Russia, 266
Standish, Miles, colonist: on Mayflower, 306;

exploring, 309–311; meets Massasoit, 313; takes part in Massacre, 324
Schall, Adam, Jesuit missionary in China, 355
Sully, Duke of, French statesman: friend of Henry IV, 79–81; about marriage of king, 132; disapproves of New France, 181, 191; dismissed, 249

Tirado, Jacob, Portuguese Jew, 237
Tulsi, Das, poet of India: his *Ramayana,* 101

Uri, Moses, German Jew in Holland, 237

Van Dyck, Anthony, Flemish painter: pupil of Rubens, 331
Velásquez, Diego, Spanish painter: portraits of Philip IV, 372; visits Rome, 374–375

Warr de la, Lord, governor of Virginia, 231; arrives, 233; death of, 288
White, Peregrine, born on Mayflower, 311
White, John, colonist: painter, governor at Roanoke, 52–54; seeks for lost colony, 65–66
William, Prince of Orange, Stadtholder of Holland: young man, 17–20; assassinated, 41
Williams, Roger, clergyman: arrives in Massachusetts, 396; to Salem and Plymouth, 397
Wingfield, Maria, president of Jamestown, 206–209
Winslow, Edward, colonist: on Mayflower, 306; remarried, 311–312; ambassador to Indians, 312–315; visit to Massasoit, 323; describes massacre, 324; writes to Bradford, 393
Winthrop, John, first governor of Massachusetts: Lord of Groton Manor, and family, 363–366; joins Massachusetts Bay Company, 386; sea voyage and arrival, 390–392; settled at Charlestown, 393; moved to Boston, 394–397; and Roger Williams, 396; welcomes Governor Bradford, 398

Yeardley, Sir George, governor of Virginia, 288; assembles Houses of Burgesses, 289

INDEX OF PLACES, EVENTS, AND GENERAL TOPICS

America, North: map, 202; claimed or settled
- by Dutch: Hudson River, 219; Manhattan Island, 367
- by English: Drake's "New Albion", 6; Newfoundland, 34; Virginia, 35; Jamestown, 206; New England, 307; Cape Cod, Plymouth, 309

- by French: Cartier, 181; Huguenots in Florida, 182; Port Royal, 197; Quebec, 224
- by Spanish: Mexico, 179; Santa Fe, 182; St. Augustine, Florida, 182
America, South: map, 177; El Dorado, 88; Guiana claimed for England, 283

Amsterdam: Jews in, 235; Puritans in, 235; harbor, 236–237
Armada, defeat of, 55–60
Arminians, 326–329
Asia, maps, 94, 349

Bermuda, 233
Bible: chart of translations, 168; Martin Luther and, 13; King James Version of, 166, 167, 168, 169; Protestant reading of, 173, 241; and science, 251
Blood, circulation of, 130, 301
Bohemia, 317
Buddhism, 356
Burgesses, House of, 286–289

Calendar, Chinese, 114, 354; Gregorian, 115
Canada: map, 187; John Cabot, 33; Cartier claims, 181; Champlain and fur trade, 187–191; and Port Royal, 196–198; Quebec, 223–228; French missionaries in, 254–257; captured by English, 343–346; returned to French, 346
Catholic Church, see Roman Catholic
Catholic League, 31, 61, 64, 77
China: map, 94, 349; search for northeast or northwest passage to, 33; (Ming) Shen Tsung, 107; missionaries to, 107, 354; overland journey from Russia to, 347–353; Hsi Tsung, 354; (Manchu) Ch'ing, 355
Christian Religion: division of, 13, 29; wars resulting in France, 27–31; in German states, 317, 360, 380; introduced into China, 355; *The Truth of the Christian Religion* by Hugo Grotius, 329
Church of England: formed, 29; Bacon writes on, 164; conference, 166; word "Episcopal," 167; forced attendance, 171, 173, 338; and Puritans, 396
Confucius, teaching of, 112; in Japan, 359
Congregational Church: in England, 173; in New England, 396
Copernicus: theory of, ix, 127; forbidden, 250–253; Galileo and, 378

Denmark: map, 121; king Frederick II and his Observatory, 116; Tycho Brahe, astronomer, 116; Princess Anne and James I, 117; Christian IV, 117; war against Sweden, 264; Thirty Years' War, 360

Education, old form of, 128, 164
England: map, 4; Queen Elizabeth I, 5; died, 150; war with Spain, 55; James I, 150; died, 338; Gunpowder Plot, 170; Charles I, 338 on; Parliament, 341, 384; Tudors and Stuarts, family tree, 26; see Separatists, Puritans, 173, 239, 389, 396
Estates-General: National Assembly in France, 249; Richelieu, member of, 336

France: map, 61; Henry II, 17, 29; Catherine d' Medici, 25, 28; Henry III, 25, 64; wars of religion, 30; war of Three Henrys, 61; Henry IV, 80, 247; Edict of Nantes, 81; Grand Design, 248; Louis XIII, 248 on; Estates-General, 249, 336; Cardinal Richelieu, 333 on
Franciscans, in Canada, 254–257

German Empire, states of: map, 316; emperors: Charles V, 13; Rudolf II, 119; Ferdinand II, 316; Thirty Years' War, 316, 360, 380
Greek Orthodox Church, 145, 320
Greek Philosophers: Euclid, 111, 129; Ptolemy, 113, 127; Aristotle, 128, 129; Hippocrates, 128; Galen, 128; Archimedes, 129

Holland: map, 241; leader of Netherlands against Spain, 16–20; under William of Orange, 20–41; Hague, capital of, 41; refuge of persecuted, 176, 235–241, 316; under Maurice, 317, 326; Arminians, 326–328; Frederick Henry, 360, 361
Huguenots: French Protestant, 28; and Henry IV, 79, 81; in Florida, 182; in Holland, 235; in La Rochelle, 339–342
Hungary, war in, 124–125, 136

India: map, 94; Emperors: Akbar, 95–101, Salim, 97; Shah Jehan and the Taj Mahal, 97; *Rig Veda*, 100; *Ramayana*, 101
Indians, American, map of tribes, 202
Islam, see Moslems
Italy: map, 124; sights in, 125, 374; **see** Galileo, and Medici Family

Jains, 100
Jamestown: early days, 206–218, 229–234, 286, 290, 321–324
Japan: map, 102; first Tokagawa shogun, 104; English visitors welcome, 104; Tokyo founded, 105; hostile to Christians and foreigners, 357
Jesuits: in India, 98; in Japan, 102; in China, 109; in Canada, 257–347
Jesus, and Golden Rule, 112
Jews, of Spain and Portugal, refugees in Holland, 236–238

Laotze, teaching of, 329
Law: in England, 169, 281; Grand Design of Henry IV, 248; defended by Coke, 282; International, Hugo Grotius, 328–329; in Massachusetts, 395
London, map, 74–75

Manchus, 353, 355
Manhattan Island, maps, 219, 367; claimed, 367
Massachusetts: map, 302; Charter, and Bay Company, 385; see New England
Mayflower: ship sails, 303; plan of, 305; anchored Cape Cod, 307; at Plymouth, 310
Mexico: map, 177; Champlain's visit, 178; New Mexico expedition, 182
Mongols, 96, 97, 352, 353
Moscow: 145–149; Red Square and Kremlin, 265–268; on map, 349
Moslems, 96, 98

Netherlands: Declaration of Independence from Spain, 14–20; Spanish Netherlands, 330; see Holland
New Amsterdam, founding of, 367–371
New England: map, 302; naming of, 269–273; Pilgrims, 293–296; and John Smith, 297–298; Mayflower sails, 303; landing of Pilgrims, 309–311; Indians and Thanksgiving, 311–315; massacres, 321–324; neighbors, 364; plans for Massachusetts, 384 (see Puritans); John Smith's book on, 388; voyage of and settlement, Puritans, 389–398; see America, North
New Spain, map, 177
Norway, 117, 118, 121, 264

Opera, first performed, 134

Panama, idea for canal, 181
Paris: Catherine d'Medici in, 28, 29; Henry of Navarre enters, 80–81; visitors to, 330–333; Richelieu in, 334–337
Parliament: under James, 281; and Gunpowder Plot, 170–172; under Charles, 341
Parsees, 99
Pendulum, principles discovered, 126–128
Pilgrims, see Separatists
Pirates, 272
Planets: movement of, 119; discovery of four, 244
Plymouth, landing at, 309
Poland, 121, 266
Popes: Clement VII, 29; Leo X, 29; Gregory XIII, 115; Paul V, 336; Urban VIII, 375, 377
Portugal: missions in India, 98; traders in far East, 102; missions in China, 109; Jews from, 236
Potato, 35, 69
Presbyterian Church: in Scotland, John Knox, 50, 167
Protestants, beginning of, 13; in France, 28
Puritans, 73, 152, 160, 166, 169, 365, 384; see John Winthrop, Massachusetts, New England

Quebec, founding of, 224

Roanoke Island, map, 35, 52; lost colony, 65
Roman Catholic Church: unity of, 13, 29; in Holland, 18, 19; in England, 170, 338; in German states, 317; and Galileo, 250, 376–379
Rome, Holy Year, 124; Calendar room, 115; St. Peters, 374–375
Russia: map, 349; English arrive in, 33; Tsars: Ivan IV, 33, 145; Feodor, 147; Boris Godunov, 144–149; Dimitri, 146; Michael Romanov, 265; explorers in Asia, 347–353; Siberia added, 348

Santa Fe, founding of, 182–186
Scotland: map, 4; rulers of: Mary, 23; James V, 24; James VI, 25, 49; Stuart family and Tudors, 26; Union with England, 164
Separatists: in England, 173; in Holland, 239–241, 294; in Plymouth, 310; and John Winthrop, 366, 389, 396
Servants, indentured, 292
Slavery, Indian, 272; Negro, 292
Spain: map, 12; rulers of: Philip II, 8, 12, dies 84; Charles V, 13; Philip III, 15, 84; Philip IV, 332; Armada of, 55
Sweden: map, 120; rulers: Charles IX, 120–123; Gustav Adolf, 263; war against Denmark, 265; Thirty Years' War, 380

Tartars, 141, 348
Telescope, 242
Thames River, 193
Thanksgiving: celebrated by Pilgrims, 315; by Puritans, 398
Theatres, 73, 75; Globe, 153
Tobacco, 36–38, 234
Tokyo, founding of, 105
Turkey, 124, 136

Universe, chart of Ptolemy, 113

Venice, Republic of, 130; and telescope, 243
Violin, first made, 135
Virginia: Raleigh and, 32–36; second expedition, 36–38; Roanoke, 52–54; lost colony, 65–66; three ships to, 192–195; Indians in, 203–205; Jamestown, 206–211; Pocahontas, 212–216; further exploration, John Smith, 217–218; John Smith President, 229–231; starvation time, 232–233; tobacco, 234; Pocahontas married, 258; in England, 278–280; House of Burgesses, 286–289; servants and slaves, 290–292; massacres, 321

World, maps, ix, 349